Ashley Mallett's cricket ambition was to take 100 Test wickets, a feat he achieved in his 23rd Test, and one shared with Shane Warne, Glenn McGrath and Graham McKenzie. During Ian Chappell's reign as Test captain, Ashley became Australia's front-line spinner of the 1970s. He is regarded as Australia's best-ever off-spin bowler. In his role as head coach of Spin Australia, an international spin bowling coaching program, Ashley has worked with all the top-flight spin bowlers in Australia, England, South Africa, New Zealand and Sri Lanka over the past twenty years. Some of the spinners he has worked with include Australia's Shane Warne, Tim May and Stuart MacGill; New Zealand's Daniel Vettori, England's Monty Panesar and Sri Lanka's Ajantha Mendis. While establishing a spin bowling academy in Colombo for the Sri Lanka Cricket Board, Ashley discovered the amazing talent of Mendis, whose finger-flick leg-breaks and googlies have taken the world of cricket into a new era of spin.

This is his 27th book.

Also by Ashley Mallett

Non-fiction

Rowdy
Spin Out
100 Cricket Tips
Bradman's Band
Eleven: The Greatest Eleven of the 20th Century
Chappelli Speaks Out
The Black Lords of Summer
The Bradman of Spin
One of a Kind: The Doug Walters Story
Nugget: Man of the Century
Scarlet: Clarrie Grimmett—Test Cricketer

Children's

Don Bradman
Doug Walters
Geoff Lawson
Kim Hughes
Rodney Marsh
The Chappell Brothers
Dennis Lillee
Allan Border
John Kosmina
Mark Williams
Wayne Johnston
Robert Flower
Tim Watson
Evonne Cawley

THOMMO
SPEAKS OUT

The authorised biography of Jeff Thomson

ASHLEY MALLETT

ALLEN&UNWIN

First published in Australia in 2009

Allen & Unwin
83 Alexander Street
Crows Nest NSW 2065
Australia
Phone: (61 2) 8425 0100
Fax: (61 2) 9906 2218
Email: info@allenandunwin.com
Web: www.allenandunwin.com

Cataloguing-in-Publication details are available
from the National Library of Australia
www.librariesaustralia.nla.gov.au

ISBN 978 1 74175 435 3

Internal design by Lisa White
Typeset in 11 pt Minion by Midland Typesetters, Australia
Printed and bound in Australia by Griffin Press

10 9 8 7 6 5 4 3 2 1

CONTENTS

1 IN THE FAST LANE

Did you see that painting on my wall at home . . . of me hitting Fletcher
in the head . . . You won't see too much cricket shit in my joint, but there it
is—a painting of Fletcher getting hit on the head . . .

Jeff Thomson was the fastest bowler to draw breath. Batsmen who faced
Thommo on the Test stage marvelled at his frenetic pace and were
eternally grateful that they managed to survive the experience.

There was a disarming quality to Thommo's approach to the
wicket for he jogged in, taking casual-looking short steps; his blonde
hair bobbed and there was no hint of the explosive energy to come
until he reached his delivery stride. His right foot moved behind
his left, similar to Neil Hawke of an earlier period; his left arm shot
instinctively towards the heavens; and, like a discus thrower in Ancient
Greece, his delivery exuded the most exquisite natural power and
grace. Thommo's back foot was pointing backwards, his heel pointing
somewhere in the vicinity of cover as he assumed an almost perfect
side-on delivery, and he held the ball only inches from the ground
before he began that extraordinary sweep of his arm to propel the ball
towards the batsman.

As a nine-year-old kid I saw Frank Tyson in full flight. Talk to the oldies like Test great Neil Harvey and he will tell you that Tyson and the West Indian Wesley Hall were as fast as they get. I am certain that Tyson and Hall were mighty fast, but Thommo was simply on a higher plane—a Stealth fighter compared with a Sabre jet. When you're a kid all Test cricketers are veritable gods from Olympus. Fast bowlers are of hurricane pace to young eyes.

Today's fast bowlers, such as Brett Lee, Shaun Tait and Shohab Aktah, consistently reach 150 kilometres per hour or better and hit 160 kph at times. Thommo was clocked at 160 kph, but that was a couple of seasons down the track from two serious shoulder operations and wear and tear at the Test bowling crease. At full tilt in the 1974–75 Ashes series, Thommo was operating at a consistent speed more like 170 kph. It was during that series that Thommo was at his zenith.

I played in Thommo's first Test match, against Pakistan at the Melbourne Cricket Ground in 1972–73, when he took 0/110 and was less than impressive on that flat Melbourne wicket, but we later learned that he played that game with a broken bone in his foot. After Thommo's first Test match failure he was axed from the New South Wales side and he took some months to get himself back into top gear. Even after his broken foot had mended, Thommo was left out of the New South Wales side, but he bounced back with a vengeance, proving both his fitness and his ability to bowl faster than anyone.

By January 1974, Thommo was ready. Cricket writer Phil Wilkins watched Thommo bowl in a club match and was astounded by what he saw:

There is another speedster in Australia [other than Dennis Lillee] who has batsmen running for cover when he takes the new ball— but he cannot even gain a place in the NSW Sheffield Shield team.

He is Bankstown-Canterbury's Jeff Thomson, who opened the bowling for Australia in the second Test against Pakistan with Lillee last summer with Max Walker first change.

Thomson is 23, superbly built for fast bowling with a temperament to match and unless [Dave] Colley livens himself, Thomson will be back in the State side so fast that Queensland will think they have been hit by a stray cyclone on February 8.[1]

Phil Wilkins was right. Thommo did return to the NSW side for the game against Queensland in February 1974, and they did indeed face a veritable tornado. Thommo stormed through 20.5 overs of the most explosive pace the Queenslanders had ever seen, taking 7/85, including the prized wicket of Greg Chappell, who instantly envisaged Thommo playing for Qld from that game onwards. Qld wicket-keeper John McLean said Greg didn't mince words:

I'd rather have that bloke Thomson on my side than have to face him twice a year. We've got to get him to Brisbane.[2]

Ironically Thomson's fiery bowling for NSW prevented Qld from winning its first-ever Sheffield Shield. Greg Chappell was relatively new to the Qld captaincy and he saw in Jeff Thomson genuine firepower to help both the northern state and to become Dennis Lillee's regular new-ball partner for Australia. And back in that club match of January 1974, the 'bullets' were starting to fly.

'Thomson's bowling was the fastest I have encountered since Frank Typhoon Tyson played in a game in Peterborough in Northamptonshire', former England all-rounder Barry Knight said this week.

'I have never seen stumps flying so far out of the ground. Thommo just went berserk. He yorked four batsmen and hit three in the head. Greg Bush was taken to hospital with a blood clot behind the eye and Robert Jeffrey was knocked on to his stumps. It was 6–9 when I went in and it was not much better when I went out. We were 7–14.'

The 'bullets' were flying at Bankstown Oval and were no doubt caused by the presence of former Test all-rounder David Colley, in the Mosman side against Bankstown. Colley is one of three bowlers—the others being Steve Bernard and Gary Gilmour—who are in the NSW team, keeping Thomson on the outer.

Interestingly, Knight said that Thomson's slinging action was a benefit for it was more difficult for batsmen to pick up the ball leaving the hand, 'rather like Charlie Griffith, who shielded the ball until the last instant. The point is Thomson does not have Griffith's hooked elbow. He is legal.'[3]

David Lord, who handed the Mosman club captaincy over to Barry Knight, when the Englishman emigrated to Sydney, and later became Thommo's manager, adds to the drama of that club match at Bankstown Oval:

We were nine down and our off-spinner Johnny McKenzie, who batted in thick horn-rimmed glasses and, like the NSW spinner David 'Cracker' Hourn, he couldn't see very far and Thommo bowled him a bouncer and McKenzie just stood there, he didn't see it. Fortunately it whistled past his nose and Knight yelled out 'declaring, declaring'. He waited at the gate for Thommo and he said threateningly to him, 'Wait until you bat'.

Sandy Morgan had about four for nothing, bowling beautifully and in came Thommo. Barry Knight grabbed the ball off Sandy, who protested, wanting to keep bowling. 'No,' said Knight, 'give me the ball.' Knighty had steam coming out of his ears. Thommo took guard and Barry bowled from the northern end and he went back about 50 metres which is about three times as far as he usually ran in his approach and he ran straight through the crease with the umpire screaming 'no ball' and he propped about 15 yards from Thommo and he threw it straight at his head. I was at first-slip and the ball passed me on the up. Thommo threw the bat and got out of the road as the ball whizzed past his head and one bounce and it was over the fence. Len Pascoe was at the other end and Lennie got the bat by the splice. 'You Pommie bastard,' he yelled, and he started chasing Knighty around Bankstown Oval. I just stood there trying to believe what I was witnessing. I think he might have wrapped the bat around Knight's head if he had caught up with him. For about five minutes it was a highly explosive situation, but thankfully Lennie ran out of puff and Knighty, who was pretty quick anyhow, survived and things cooled down, the game resuming in about ten minutes.

It was always the same when Mosman played Bankstown. You'd get in your car in a buoyant mood, for somehow this day it would be different even though you knew you were about to face Thomson and Pascoe, the most dangerous pace attack in Australian club cricket. You'd be feeling on top of the world . . . then you'd return looking like the old black telephone, blackened and bruised all down your left side from the pounding of that fearsome pair.[4]

Sydney University's experienced captain Ian Fisher echoed Knight and Lord's sentiments:

These days we give batsmen who haven't faced Thomson the warning to take a black arm band, wish them luck and tell them to get out quick. In the last six games only one batsman has done well against him and that was Tony Carroll who stood there for three hours and made 70.[5]

Since the last couple of years at Punchbowl High School, Jeff Thomson and Len Pascoe were firm friends—new ball partners, teammates in the soccer team, and mates who went surfing and fishing together. But sport still took precedence over anything and everything for Thommo:

Lennie and I used to love surfing—Maroubra Beach, The Entrance, Nora Heads, Soldiers Beach and Garie Beach. We'd go away for weekends, doing the usual teenage thing where you go to parties, booze on and get drunk. It didn't affect our cricket. We still bowled flat out for Bankstown, but we used to roll up late occasionally and we got into trouble.

When Thommo reached the age of seventeen, he and Lennie discovered the opposite sex and they began to chase girls. Lennie recalls:

On the morning of a match we'd often be down at Maroubra, chatting up the birds. And all too often we'd be late for the match. There we were rushing into the ground, the spinners were on and the captain was looking daggers at us.

Bankstown Cricket Club annual year books are full of comments from various captains talking about Thomson and Pascoe as good emerging talents, but any criticism was always the same—'need to apply themselves and to train more frequently.'[6]

As teenagers they were invited to practise with the NSW squad. They'd usually turn up to training in their board shorts and thongs, their surfboards slung on top of their cars. Thomson and Pascoe were from the western suburbs, traditionally a working-class area of Sydney. They didn't wear suits and ties like some of the squad such as David Colley and Kerry O'Keeffe. As Thommo says, neither man believed that clothes maketh the fast bowler:

> *Lennie and I would turn up to State training straight from the beach. We'd have salt in our hair and our cricket boots under one arm, our creams under the other. We wouldn't have a cricket bag and we had our shorts on—no shirt—and a pair of thongs. It's always been my motto that it doesn't matter what you look like or what you're dressed like so long as you get results and deliver the goods. The captains didn't like it. They'd say, 'Why don't you do this or why don't you do that?' but I just told 'em to piss off.*

Lennie remembers one night at NSW training, coach Peter Spence put down a rectangular piece of plastic on what he considered a good length so he could observe the consistency of the fast men:

> Thommo was all over the shop, but the others, including me, were consistent, yet compared to Thommo we were all bowling half-rat power. He was slinging them down just short of a length, scaring the hell out of the batsmen and knocking the pickets off the fence behind the nets.
>
> And there is Spence saying to Thommo, 'You're not bowling accurately enough Jeff.'[7]

Thommo and Len Pascoe started together at Bankstown, became legendary figures in Sydney grade cricket, and have remained close mates ever since. In the summer of 1970–71, when John Snow was ripping through the Australians for Ray Illingworth's England team, Thommo started to slip off the rails. Len Pascoe remembers it well:

Thommo started missing training more than usual. He was spending time at the Oceanic Hotel and slipping into the grog. [8]

The club was about to suspend Thommo, but Lennie stepped in and said to his mate:

'Thommo, if I go to the club and explain your disappointment in your own attitude and not training enough and how you will make amends and come back and train hard, will you agree?' Thommo nodded.

So I went to the Bankstown management and they said they would agree to the deal, but Thommo had to be punished. He would have to play one game in third grade, then he'd be reinstated. What punishment? Thommo took 10/31. [9]

While Thommo agreed to the club's terms, he reveals that he still had a rebellious streak:

I'd taken a few wickets, but when things went wrong I started to bludge. I decided not to worry about the slump. I'd rather go surfing. My attitude didn't impress the club and I found myself in the third grade. We were due to play the St George club that day. It was a really hot day and I said to my brother Greg, 'I'm not going to cricket. Let's go fishing, or to the beach.' Greg tried to talk me out of it and go to the game. 'No, stuff cricket,' I said. 'I've been dropped to thirds. I can't be bothered.' My mum stepped in and had Greg take me to the match in his red EH Holden car. We got there late, but luck was on my side for the umpires had been delayed.

It was good to knock off St George with an outright win because that club usually won all of the lower grade competitions. I took all ten wickets in the first innings, having bowled in four separate spells and no-one else in our attack looked like taking a wicket. I think I clean-bowled eight and had two blokes lbw. In the second dig I got 5/10 or something like that . . .

Thommo won pride of place in the local Bankstown newspaper, *The Torch*, in an article headed 'Sports Star':

Sports star of the week fast bowler 20-year-old Jeff Thomson won his award for his performance in a Bankstown-Canterbury District Cricket Club's third grade match against St George when he took 10 wickets for 31 runs.[10]

The seasons came and went. Thommo, made the State side, then he was picked for the Test side and played with a broken foot. Then came frustration in not being picked for NSW and finally getting the nod. But Thommo had already decided to leave for Qld, weeks before his belated return to the State side and his match-winning 7/85 against Greg Chappell's men at the Sydney Cricket Ground.

During Thommo's frustrating summer of 1973–74, Mosman batsman and journalist David Lord had a chat with Thommo one day and learnt of the fast bowler's frustration in playing cricket in Sydney. Thommo was being tipped for a return to the NSW team, but he was already thinking of moving interstate. South Australia was one option, but Qld had more appeal. Lord recalls:

> 'I'm not that happy here, Lordy,' he said. I asked whether he'd like to move to Queensland and he said he would definitely consider a move.[11]

More than a year later Lord helped organise a lucrative ten-year contract for Thommo with a Brisbane radio station which made him the highest-paid sportsman in Australia. Lord says:

> Others were involved in Thommo's initial move to Brisbane and the big contract—while it was a tremendous thing for the fast bowler— didn't happen until he established himself back in the Test side and had become a world champion.[12]

In cricket terms Thommo quickly made his mark but not without controversy. Thommo raised a few eyebrows when he was quoted as saying:

> *I enjoy hitting a batsman more than getting him out. I like to see blood on the pitch.*

But Thommo's main target was the stumps, to get the batsman out, not cracking heads.

Early on when playing for Bankstown I was out to show people what I could do, how fast I could bowl. I hit a bloke, you know the umpire Reg Ledwidge, well, it was his son. It wasn't really a bouncer, just short of a good length and it reared and smashed him straight in the eye. It was frightening to see this bloke just screaming and shaking and the pitch was spattered with blood. He was in the intensive care unit of the hospital for a week. Like so many blokes who batted against me, he just didn't have time to move out of the way of the ball, even though the Bankstown wicket was pretty dead. I never let this sort of thing put me off, alright, this is my aggression. The batsman's got a bat and he can hit the ball and do what he likes to me. I don't mean to hit him, even though I could if I wanted to—especially later in my career when I was bowling faster and more accurately than ever in my life. I'd rather bowl 'em out than knock 'em out.

A supreme athlete, Thommo was a man of immense natural strength. This approach, drive through the crease, and follow-through seemed so effortless, as if it was part and parcel of the man himself. Here was the most natural bowler I had ever seen. Thommo probably has come closer to anyone to possessing the perfect bowling action.

That extraordinary and disarming amble up to the crease preceded the way he glided into what he always called his 'load-up' position. He was perfectly sideways on to the batsman and in no time at all his front leg raised threateningly like a baseball pitcher and Thommo had the ball rocketing towards the batsman like a bullet: he was cricket's version of a human catapult.

Mike Denness's England team of 1974–75 watched SA play Western Australia in a Sheffield Shield match in Adelaide upon their arrival and Denness noted that Dennis Lillee, who was coming back from his back injury, 'did not now employ the high kick and jump which he had used before delivery' and 'he doesn't look as quick as he was in England in 1972'.[13]

At their peril England discounted the effect Lillee would have that season and they were virtually dismissive of Thomson. Denness did, however, note in the Queensland v England lead-up match to the First Test at the Gabba that Thommo made it 'a little difficult to pick up the ball, because when the arm goes back the ball is hidden behind the body and could not be seen again until just before he released it'. Most of the English batsmen thought Thommo quick but wayward and unlikely to get selected in the Australian team. What they didn't know was that Qld captain Greg Chappell had played a master psychological hand by imploring Thommo to bowl within himself.

'Just fuck around,' Chappell told him. 'Don't show the Poms what you can do.'[14]

Thommo says:

I followed orders and just bowled very much within myself, although I let rip with a few in the Pommie second innings.

England fast bowlers Bob Willis and Peter Lever showed intent by bouncing the Qld tail.

Thommo was duly picked, but England thought it was Alan 'Froggy' Thompson, the gangly, wrong-foot Victorian fast bowler who played a few Tests under Bill Lawry in the 1970–71 Ashes series. Most players on the international scene are so familiar with the opposition that their abilities are well known in advance of the big matches: surprises are rare. Twice in the 1950s one Australian and one England bowler sprang surprises.

In 1950–51 the mystery spinner, finger-flick merchant Jack Iverson, who bowled in a style that Johnny Gleeson would later copy, destroyed Freddie Brown's England team taking 21 wickets at an average of 15.73 in five Tests. He held the ball between his middle finger and thumb and he bemused and befuddled the Englishmen as much as he took their scalps. Then in 1954–55, Frank 'Typhoon' Tyson bowled extremely fast all series to take an Ashes-winning 28 wickets at 20.82 for Len Hutton's team. Now it was Thommo's turn to spring his own special surprise:

I was a man on a mission. This was my second Test match, but it was really my first because when I played that time at the MCG I was not 100 per cent fit. There would be no excuses. I was ready to go and it wouldn't have mattered who I was playing against, I was just going

*to give them a work-over. It just happened to be the Poms. Bad luck
for them.*

The night before the First Test match in Brisbane, Lillee found his new Test
opening bowling partner in the bar drinking scotch. Thommo explains:

*When I go out to bowl, I want a hangover from hell. I bowl really well
when I've got a headache.*

Australia batted first and Thommo had to cool his heels. Ian Chappell's
men scored a useful 309, before England took their turn with the bat.
During Australia's innings medium-pacer Tony Greig got a ball to rise off
a length, striking Dennis Lillee on his gloved hand and the ball ballooned
to keeper Alan Knott. As he stormed off Lillee said to Greig, 'Just remember
who started this, pal.'

There was more than a hint of fire in the wind.

Lillee opened the bowling and Chappelli was going to have Max Walker
bowl into the breeze, but instinct took over and he chucked the ball to
Thommo, saying 'Good luck, mate'.

Thommo's first couple of deliveries whistled past Dennis Amiss's nose
and smacked hard into Rod Marsh's gloves.

During that first over Marsh leapt for a ball from Thommo which
climbed off a good length and thudded into his gloves and he exclaimed,
'Hell that hurt—but I love it!'

Ian Chappell was delighted for Lillee was making a successful return to
the crease and his partner was hitting the scene like a tornado. He said:

I don't think the Englishmen knew what hit them. Thommo was
the fastest into-the-wind bowler I'd ever seen.[15]

Thommo took 3/59 off 21 overs in the first innings and in the second he
blitzed the Poms with 6/46 off 17.5 overs of the most blistering pace. Keith
Miller, the great all-rounder, wrote the next day:

Tornado Thomson! Jeff Thomson, lured from Sydney to Brisbane,
spun England into a real whirlwind with the most exciting fast

bowling spree since Dennis Lillee's brilliant burst on the 1972 Australian tour of England.

Exciting, did I say?

Frightening surely is the operative word. I was seeing the ex-Sydney cricketer for the first time. I was told he was erratic and would soon run out of puff after a few overs. How wrong can the good oil be? He even frightened me sitting harmlessly in the press box with some of his nasty rising deliveries.[16]

Tony Greig batted bravely, hitting a fine hundred in the England first dig, then Thommo bowled him with his famous 'sandshoe crusher', the fast Yorker aimed to hit the point of the big toe. The ball crashed from Greig's toe into the stumps: talk about rubbing salt into the wound.

Australia won the Test match easily by 166 runs, Thommo found his niche for this was the start of a great Test match career and the Poms were left to contemplate what they could expect in the matches to follow. It could not have been a joyous prospect.

In the Perth Second Test match of 1974–75, the first day dawned a hot and cloudless day. The temperature was expected to hover above the old century mark and Ian Chappell wanted early England scalps. Thommo had scared the hell out of the Poms in Brisbane, taking 6/46 in the second England innings, and Chappelli wanted to tighten the screw. Dennis Lillee had made a successful return from the near-crippling back injury. He took 2/73 and 2/25 in Brisbane, gradually easing himself into top gear. Thommo hit the Poms like a hurricane and he had left an imprint on the England team both physically and mentally.

John Edrich had a broken hand and bruised ribs, and opener Dennis Amiss had broken a thumb, so the England team management urgently called for a replacement batsman to be sent to Australia. They settled on an old warrior: Michael Colin Cowdrey, who played for Kent from 1950–1976. Cowdrey had not played a Test match since 1971, but here he was, just a few days short of his 42nd birthday and having been whisked away from the warmth of his Kentish log fire to play a Test match in the scorching Perth sun on the other side of the world. When told of Cowdrey's surprise recall, England opener Brian Luckhurst, a county player with Cowdrey's beloved Kent, said: 'I wish I had known, I could have saved 18 cents. I just sent him a Christmas card.'[17]

Cowdrey had shown his mettle in playing the fearsome pace of a number of Test combinations including Australia's Keith Miller and Ray Lindwall; the West Indians Wes Hall and Charlie Griffith; and South Africans Peter Heine and Neil Adcock. Cowdrey came in at the fall of the first wicket, when Brian Luckhust, after sustaining a broken finger courtesy of a Thommo flyer, went for 27.

Cowdrey, whose nickname of 'Kipper' was derived from his liking of a kip in the dressing-room while his England teammates were batting, meandered to the wicket looking like a big plum pudding in flannels. As he neared the centre of the WACA Ground, he nervously touched the peak of his dark-blue England cap, the one which depicts St George slaying the dragon.

Thommo recalls that he was about to start a new over when the next man in made his presence felt:

As I handed my hat to the umpire, Kipper came up to me and said, 'Ah, Mr Thomson, I believe. Colin Cowdrey's the name, lovely to meet you.' It was the best intro ever. I got the shock of my life. Up walks Cowdrey, introducing himself in the middle of the ground in the most jolly way, shaking hands and wanting to have a chat, and here I am about to dismantle somebody—I couldn't believe it.

Mind you, Cowdrey was a good player. I worked that out pretty quickly. You know a class player when you see one; when you come up against a bloke who's old but you know that they were very good once.

But Cowdrey's jovial introduction didn't stop Thommo from bowling like the wind. Yet the old man, who once batted one-handed (his left arm was broken and encased in plaster) against the fire of Wes Hall to famously save England a Test match at Lord's in 1963, got behind everything Thommo threw at him and played with great conviction. He was showing plain old-fashioned guts and the Australians admired the man's courage.

After a particularly torrid over where he was pummelled in the chest and the upper arm and copped two blows to the hip, Cowdrey waltzed up the other end to his batting partner, David Lloyd, and said: 'I say, David, this is all rather fun, don't you think?'

'Fookin' fun? You're bloody mad, Kipper,' was Lloyd's reply.[18]

The next Thommo over saw Lloyd cop one in the nether regions. He went down like a shower of shit and lay on the pitch writhing in agony. It is one of the quaint oddities of the game of cricket that when a batsman is hit square in the testicles, the fielding side rushes to the stricken man's side, then, as the victim writhes on the ground in agony, the opposition players stand about giggling and smirking, giving silent thanks to the Lord above that the victim was indeed 'him and not I.'

What we didn't know was that Lloyd was wearing a pink, plastic abdominal protector and the strike on the box had split the protector, leaving one of Lloyd's balls in the box and one out of it. He was in excruciating pain. The experience facing Thommo at full-pelt left Lloyd physically and mentally knackered. Denness made the observation that after his innings Lloyd just sat and stared.

Cowdrey's two innings in that game were magnificent in the context of his age and considering that he had not played Test cricket for years. He defied all that Lillee and Thommo could throw at him. In the first dig he hit a brave 22. He was so intent in getting back and across behind the line of flight that he went too far to the off side and lost his leg stump. Thommo got him lbw for 41 in the England second innings. He says:

In the Poms' first dig I bowled Cowdrey round his legs. The other Poms I bowled in front of their legs because they were running the other way.

I'll never forget Keith Fletcher, the little Essex right-hander, who was a tidy player against anything other than genuine pace. Thommo fired one down which might have decapitated a left-hander. Luckily Fletcher was a right-hander and his batting gloves were the only things in line with that rearing ball, for he got the faintest of touches on his gloved right hand and the ball sailed through, on the up, to Marsh standing some 35 paces back behind the stumps.

Fletcher didn't wait for the umpire's decision, he almost broke into a trot on his way back to the refuge that was the England cricket team's dressing-room. When I mentioned the name of Keith Fletcher, Thommo's eyes lit up:

Did you see that painting on my wall at home? Yeah, it's a big oil painting of me hitting Fletcher in the head. A mate of mine—Mick Hart—bought it at an auction in Sydney and he gave it to me. He paid something like $4000 or $5000 for it. You won't see too much cricket shit in my joint, but there it is—a painting of Fletcher getting hit on the head adorning my lounge-room wall.

In January, 1975, Chappelli's men had just won the Ashes after winning the Fourth Test in Sydney. Thommo took 4/74 and 2/74, and he was bowling at his absolute fastest.

The English press were critical of what they called Australia's 'bully-boy' tactics. Thommo's thunderbolts were anything but 'inspired bowling' to the English press covering the Ashes tour. Clive Taylor of the *London Sun* wrote: 'And Dennis Lillee went on television to discuss in clinical detail the parts of the body he aimed to hit when he was bowling short of the batsmen. Lillee and Thomson . . . brutal . . . the name of the game is intimidation . . . condemn these tactics.'[19]

In the midst of the furore about short-pitched bowling and unfair Australian tactics, Crawford White of the *London Daily Express* interviewed Thommo. Under the heading, 'Thomson: I don't bowl for blood', White wrote:

Jeff Thomson, the Aussie express bowler who has bruised and battered England's batsmen, told me: 'I don't aim to maim anybody.' And he pleaded, 'For heaven's sake kill that blood on the pitch rubbish in England. I bowl fast and play it hard, but I'm just a fast bowler trying to make the batsmen hop around.' Today Thomson rejected the fearsome image the Aussie press have given him. 'I'm not the blood and guts Thommo these stories have made me out,' he said. 'When I hit David Lloyd and Colin Cowdrey I was up with the rest of the lads to see if they were alright.'

How fast is Thomson?

'They put a computer on me in Melbourne and worked it out at 87 miles an hour, but I'm faster than that now. A lot faster.'

In the 1960s Wes Hall and Freddie Trueman were tested for speed and their figures were just about the same. But as Thomson is quick to point out, 'It all depends on the pitch. A dead wicket can kill pace. A quick one can build it.'

Cowdrey rates Thomson as fast as any bowler he has played.

'I was defending my face when he hit me smack on the spot where my arm was broken by Wes Hall at Lord's in 1963,' he told me.

'And I reckon if I hadn't been wearing a piece of special rubber padding on the break spot, it would have gone again and I might have been home for Christmas.'[20]

The former great leg-spinner of the 1930s, Bill 'Tiger' O'Reilly, the man Don Bradman always regarded as the best bowler he had played with or against or had seen in more than 60 years of playing and watching the game, came out in the Australian press lauding the efforts of Thommo:

The man of the series has been Jeff Thomson whom I congratulate for several reasons. He never shirked one invitation to bowl, a big point when one considers the tremendous demands made upon him. And this, probably above all, Thomson has taken his success without any visible 'swelling of the head' and has never shown the slightest hostile reaction when an umpire's decision has gone against his appeal. I have been proud of him.[21]

A few days after the Sydney Test where the Ashes were regained, SA played Qld in Brisbane and our new opening bowler Andrew Sincock, whose hair seemed to be his biggest concern in life, was blow-drying his mane when Chappelli walked past and through the dressing-room door to lead us on to the field. After having led Australia into Test battle with the likes of Thommo and Lillee, Chappelli was furious: 'Rowd, you'd better open from the other end. No bastard who blow-dries his hair before we hit the field is going to open the bowling for my team.'[22]

Thommo bowled at incredible pace in that match and I found myself at the non-striker's end watching Sincock trying to hook the fast man; a ploy which I feared might lead to a fatal outcome. I walked down the pitch and said to him: 'Now Andrew, Thommo is not a man to be hooked. Keep trying to hook him and they will be carting you off in a pine box.'

The very next ball Sincock tried to hook, the ball hit his bat high on the splice and a little dolly of a catch ballooned towards forward square leg where David Rathie got under it. He dropped the ball. Meantime Sincock had reached my end. I hadn't moved a muscle. I looked at him with disdain.

'Get back to Thommo's end, Andrew, or you'll be run out!'

In another South Australia–Queensland clash at the Gabba, Thommo trapped SA batsman Rick Darling lbw and he collapsed in a heap, having to be carried off the oval on a stretcher. That probably tells us as much about the quality of Darling's pads as the breakneck speed of Thommo.

Was Thommo quicker in the Ashes series of 1974–75 than at any other time? He doesn't think so, in fact he believes his speed increased over the next few summers:

> I reckon I was getting quicker each time I bowled. Not every game, but each summer.
>
> Remember the Poms, then the West Indies [1975–76]—I knew I had to bowl quicker against the Windies because of what happened in the World Cup. I was really on my mettle, ready and waiting for them. Then we started against Pakistan. I bowled a million miles an hour that game. I'm not joking, you ask the guys who were there; the Paki batsmen were shitting themselves.

Thommo bowled mighty fast against Clive Lloyd's West Indians in 1975–76, but during the Perth Second Test match he heard tragic news that his flat-mate Martin Bedkomer, who had gone north to try and find a Sheffield Shield place with Qld, was killed when hit in the chest batting for Toombul in Brisbane grade cricket in December 1975. After the Test match, Thommo flew to Sydney to attend his friend's funeral.

> When I think back at all the blokes I have hit, it is amazing that no-one was seriously injured. No helmets in those days and how tragic that Martin was killed when struck in the chest by a medium-pacer. He collapsed at the wicket and died two hours later in the Royal Brisbane Hospital. His death really hit home and changed my thinking towards bowling. I didn't mean to hit anyone, even though I knew I could have done.

To his eternal credit Thommo remained true to himself. He refused to slow down to achieve more accuracy. He was a fast bowler and he was to do it his way. He would not bow down to convention.

There was something in the spirit of ANZAC about this lovable larrikin. Thommo had great affection for his mates, to whom he was fiercely loyal. His rise in the game eventually came, but only after years of frustration and conflict with those who reckoned he should go about his cricket in a more conventional manner. By the time he got back to the Test stage for his second crack at the big time, Thommo was the fastest bowler in the world. I say he was the fastest bowler to draw breath.

All out pace was his motto in cricket, but in life itself Thommo lived in the fast lane.

In the wash-up of the Ashes series, cartoonist Paul Rigby's famous drawing with the caption 'Ashes to ashes, dust to dust, if Thommo don't get ya, Lillee must!'[23] provided Australians with a sense of achievement and pride. But for England Rigby's cartoon was a haunting reminder of a brutal campaign which ended in batsmen hell-bent upon survival of the personal safety kind.

Mike Brearley, the Middlesex captain who led England during the World Series Cricket incursion, said of Thommo:

> Broken marriages, conflicts of loyalty, the problems of everyday life fall away as one faces up to Thomson.[24]

2 THE BANKSTOWN BOY

There I was at the nets trying out for the school cricket team. The selector was our music teacher . . . This teacher just didn't pick me because I didn't cotton on to his music lessons . . . I like music okay, but not the theory of music. I just didn't understand the music teacher's raving on about crotchets and quavers and all that stuff—I thought a crotchet was something a sheila had in her pants!

Jeffrey Robert Thomson was one of five boys reared by Don and Doreen Thomson. In chronological order they arrived: Donny, Raymond and Gregory, then Jeff, then Kevin.

Don Thomson played a good deal of cricket in his youth and he had the same action his son later made famous on the international sporting stage. Don Thomson hailed from Newtown and Doreen came from Redfern, both old, established inner suburbs of Sydney.

Mum used to take me out to watch Dad play. Money was short and Dad didn't want to play representative cricket. He always wanted to play the game with his mates and that was in the Bankstown district,

A-grade juniors. We'd watch games every Saturday in Bankstown and the surrounding districts.

Dad opened the bowling and he batted about number five. He used to win lots of trophies. I'd sit there at the trophy cabinet and clean them and I used to say to myself, 'I'm gonna get more trophies than you Dad'. Honestly though, I never dreamt of playing cricket for Australia, I was only thinking of all the trophies I was going to win. I just played for the next trophy.

Jeff often helped his dad prepare for his job as a plasterer. In those days Don Thomson plastered over the fibres to make plasterboard and Jeff helped. He remembers all the fibres which seemed to stick to his hair and get down his throat.

It was like asbestos and I guess all those fibres couldn't have been too healthy for either of us.

Thommo attended Condell Park Primary School and when he was aged about ten, he met a kid named Lennie Durtanovich, whose father later changed the family name to Pascoe, after Thommo's grandfather on his mother's side. Lennie remembers Thommo as the 'kid with a crew cut and a funny bowling action':

We played a match and I think I got five wickets and Thommo got six.[1]

Thommo meeting Lennie Pascoe proved to be a turning point in his life.

Probably the best thing that happened to me in those days was when Lennie came along. He was playing for North Bankstown Public School and I was with Condell Park. We played near Bankstown Airport at a place called Dimpell Park. This young, skinny wog bloke got a few of us out and I thought, 'How good's this bloke'. Anyhow I got more wickets than him and that was the start of the rivalry. Bugger this, who's this prick? Before this I used to measure myself on how quick I bowled.

Anyway Lennie came along and we became mates, but I guess the real friendship didn't start until high school.

Thommo can't remember who got the most wickets that day but he does remember getting this feeling of wanting to outdo his bowling partner. He discovered then that he possessed within him a fierce competitive spirit.

Thommo played for Padstow Pirates in the Saturday morning competition and the hero at the time was a kid named Billy Palmer.

Before the school stuff I'd only really bowled in the backyard, but I remember thinking: 'I'm gonna knock this bloke Billy Palmer off.' He was getting all the wraps, Billy Palmer this and Billy Palmer that. He was about twelve and I was ten. Billy would play for the Padstow Pirates in the morning and then for the C-grade with the men on the Saturday afternoon.

His dad, Don, a stalwart of the North Bankstown Club, took Jeff to play with him and his mates. The club didn't have a junior team until the early 1960s, so when Jeff was about eleven he played with and against the men. Every year Jeff dominated the bowling aggregates and averages, bowling a two-piece ball on those concrete, matting-covered pitches which seamed and bounced alarmingly.

Dad's A-grade mates helped, taking turns to umpire, saying, 'Look Jeff just bowl to this bloke this way, or that way' and I could always bowl where they wanted me to bowl. I got millions of wickets.

Unlike most kids growing up in cricket-mad Australia, Jeff never had that burning ambition to play Test cricket.

I used to watch cricket on the TV, seeing Davo [Alan Davidson] and McKenzie [Graham McKenzie] and sometimes it was a bit like watching fuckin' paint dry, especially when they were bowling on those flat pitches. You know, it wasn't my cup of tea. They weren't quick enough, they were medium-pacers. The cricket wasn't exciting enough

*for me. You know, ya just watched it and I never went to a game
ever—no I tell a lie, I did go to a game once from school, when I was
ten; MCC v NSW, Harvey and all them, Simmo. I thought Freddie
Trueman was going to play. And the prick wasn't playing. I probably
saw Normie [Norm O'Neill] bat, but the big disappointment was
Trueman not playing.*

Freddie Trueman missed the first two Tests of Peter May's 1958–59
England campaign Down Under, but played in the final three matches of
the rubber. The first Test match Thommo saw 'live' was the first Test he
played in, at the MCG against Pakistan in December 1972.

In those early days at primary school Jeff used to play in three separate
competitions every Saturday in the summer months. At the age of 12 he
played in the Under-14s, from 8 a.m. to 10.30 a.m.; then for the Under-16s
from 11 a.m. to 1.30 p.m., then the C-grade men's match from 2 p.m. to
6 p.m. And if his dad couldn't pick him up, he would run a mile and a half
from one ground to the next.

*Some days with the luck of the toss I'd bowl in all three matches
and bowl more than 50 overs in the day and I never even felt
tired. I also won a few trophies in batting—the most runs. Those
trophies are still at home. My highest score was 89 not out, made
for the first grade at school, and that remained the highest score
of my career, in any form of cricket. I never worried about making
a century. I just liked to help the side along and I liked to make
runs quickly.*

Thommo got his highest Test score, 49, at Egbaston in July 1975, against
England. Thommo and I (3 not out) put on 16 for the last wicket.
He holed out to Geoff Arnold at deep mid off from the bowling of
Derek Underwood.

While never destined to become an academic, Jeff finished with good
marks, among the top five students at Condell Primary School, and he
won the chance to choose from three secondary schools. His brother,
Greg, had previously won a scholarship to Punchbowl High School, so
that's the school Jeff decided to attend.

At Punchbowl High, Jeff hardly knew anyone. All his mates had gone to schools elsewhere, so he had to form new friendships. He ran into an old cricket foe, Len Pascoe, but their friendship didn't really blossom until about the third year of high school. Lennie recalls:

> Poor old Thommo didn't get in the school eleven first up. The music teacher apparently didn't like him, so he had to play house matches.
>
> I heard that Thommo gave them buggery in the house games, smashing the bowling everywhere and getting wickets galore, along with breaking a few limbs.[2]

Thommo took his relegation to playing house cricket at Punchbowl High to be an absolute insult.

> *There I was at the nets trying out for the school cricket team. The selector was our music teacher, a bloke named Clarke. He had the glasses on and a beard; he looked like fuckin' Rolf Harris, and I can't stand him either. Here is me and Lennie terrorising these pricks in the nets. I didn't get picked. Lennie got picked. I had to go to house cricket. House cricket is for the kids who can't play. If you want to play cricket and you are not good enough to make the team, you play house cricket. I was keen to play so I was happy to carry the kit down to Roberts Park.*
>
> *Well, I used to smash 'em all over the park and get wickets galore. I could have gotten 'em out blindfolded. Eventually I got picked in the school eleven. This guy just didn't pick me because I didn't cotton on to his music lessons. I didn't disrupt the class. I like music okay, but not the theory of music. I just didn't understand the music teacher's raving on about crotchets and quavers and all that stuff—I thought a crotchet was something a sheila had in her pants!*
>
> *The music teacher's attitude helped me become more determined. When anyone puts shit on me, it always helps me in a big way because I just say 'I'll prove you wrong'.*

While Thommo didn't see eye to eye with his music teacher, he loved music, especially the likes the Rolling Stones, Elton John, Black Sabbath, Led Zeppelin and the ageless genius of Beach Boys.

Thommo reckons he wasted a year playing house cricket, but the second year of high school saw him join Lennie in the fifth grade. Their coach was Joe McCann, a former Mayor of Bankstown who was also their English teacher. Lennie sat next to Thommo in class and one day he became intrigued by his mate's feverish activity on the school desk. Thommo was drawing a Mini Minor on the desk. Next day he carved it out. Lennie recalls:

> The teacher got a bit peeved and had a go at Thommo for 'disfiguring the desk' and on the third day Thommo coloured it in. Next day came the saga of the big, fat grape. Joe McCann was writing on the backboard. He had his back to the class and Thommo picked up a plump, juicy grape. He was always eating grapes in class. He threw the grape with tremendous force, the grape narrowly missing the teacher's head and splattered the blackboard next to him. The teacher was delivering a lesson on Shakespeare. He turned to the class and with all the anger he could summon with the spirit of a Caeser who had escaped the assassin's knife, gave his students a resounding thumbs down: 'Everyone will be kept in until such time as the person who threw that grape owns up.'
>
> Thommo stood up immediately, his desk fell forward with a loud crash and his chair fell backwards as he stood. Thommo then said with dramatic tone, ''Tis I, Sir—I cannot tell a lie. 'Tis I who threw thouest grape.' And with that Thommo walked out of the door and we didn't see him for two weeks.[3]

When Jeff returned to the English class he got another one up on poor Joe McCann. Thommo recorded the sound of the bell which was used to signal the end of a lesson and for students and teachers to move to the next class. Lennie recalls that one day:

> We'd been in class for less than five minutes when Thommo switched on his recording of the bell and everyone packed and hurriedly left the room. No-one seemed to twig.[4]

Schoolwork bored the hell out of Thommo. He would rather go fishing or surfing, or play cricket or soccer. By the second year at Punchbowl

High, Thommo and Lennie were in the first-grade cricket team blitzing all opposition. They were also in the school soccer team.

Thommo was a talented footballer. He was strongly built and fit as a Mallee bull. He could run all day and was agile and skilled. He tried out for the Melita Eagles in Newtown, making their second-grade first up. He was on the verge of playing first-grade when he decided to hang up his boots on professional football.

To play for the Melita Eagles meant my having to train three nights a week, driving all the way into town, Camperdown Oval. I couldn't be bothered. So it was goodbye to serious football and from then on I would play only semi-serious soccer.

Sport always took precedence over schooling and Thommo demonstrated his lack of interest in academia by bringing along the same 'empty' exercise book to all of his classes. Len Pascoe will never forget the day Thommo upstaged the geography teacher:

Thommo could draw very well. And here we are with the geography teacher doing a map of Australia on the blackboard. Thommo leant back in his chair and yelled out, 'Call that shit a map of Australia? I could do better than that left-handed and with my eyes closed.' The teacher called his bluff and said, 'Alright, Thomson, you're on.' And with that Thommo waltzed up to the board, closed his eyes and drew, with his left hand, the best map of Australia you've ever seen. He brought the house down and teacher said, 'Now get out of my class, Thomson!'[5]

Thommo enjoyed metalwork classes and was often seen filing steel sheeting. At one time above his work station were some 50 Ninja stars, deeply embedded in the plaster ceiling. However, he did have a particular dislike for ancient history. The students didn't care much for the ancient history teacher's odd-ball appearance. They called him 'The Moose' and, whenever he appeared in the classroom, they would collectively set the tone with a sustained 'moo-ooo-ooo-oose'. The teacher trimmed his side-burns way too high on his head, according to his students. Thommo didn't take a single note in all the ancient history lessons, but students became very aware of Thommo frantically writing in his famous exercise book on the day of the examination. Lennie thought Thommo may have been studying on the sly and not really going to Maroubra Beach every day.

Thommo's exercise book was hanging out of his school bag the day he took 9/3 for Punchbowl against Belmore. Lennie reckons Thommo would have taken all ten had not the last man 'ran to square leg and the ball ricocheted from his pads onto the stumps' off Lennie's bowling. Kenny Scully, who went on to become a successful lawyer, was intrigued as were all the players about Thommo's apparent great effort in the ancient history exam paper. What could he have written in his exercise book? Scully asked to see Thommo's book and he showed them. A day before the ancient history exam, there had been a dangerous siege at Glenbrook, where the crack police Z squad had to disarm a man with an armour-lite rifle. Thommo had mixed ancient Greek history with the siege and wrote a screenplay of the event. He stayed true to the Greek connection, for every person in his screenplay had the tag 'opolous' on their name and they also knew all about A–47 automatic rifles, pistols and knives.

Lennie says Thommo copped a 'minus one, for his ancient history paper—because he spelt his teacher's name wrong'.

Thommo was in the Punchbowl High School first-eleven for three years, and captained the side in the last couple. The school magazine reveals that his 9/3 against Belmore included a hat-trick, the first of a total of ten he took in his career. He also got a hat-trick in Canada on the way to England in 1975. Thommo's opening partner at Punchbowl that summer, Lennie Pascoe, also got bags of wickets, including 8/21 against Birrong and 7/45 against East Hills.

Playing for North Bankstown with his dad was a joy for Thommo, but others saw his potential for great things and battling away in second division wasn't going to get him very far. A bloke from Bankstown RSL came around to the Thomsons' house one night and talked Thommo into playing for them. And there he opened the bowling with the fiery young Len Pascoe. Thommo says:

With Lennie and me in their side the Bankstown RSL Under-16s ruled the roost. We had some great tussles with the only other good team in the competition, Bankstown Sports, and round that time I was picked for the A.W. Green Shield team, coached by Dickie McDermott, who played first-grade rugby league for Canterbury-Bankstown and Bankstown grade cricket. This is where I once again joined forces with Billy Palmer. We opened the bowling and Lennie was sometimes 12th man, that's how good a side we had. Billy scored most runs and took most wickets, but my 17 wickets at 10.53 per wicket was the best average. The NSWCA Year Book shows a young bloke, St George's Kerry O'Keeffe, at the top of the bowling with 33 wickets at less than 10 runs apiece with his leg-spinners. My name is spelt with a 'P' in the Yearbook; people getting the spelling of my name wrong is something I've had to put up with all my life.

Thomson and Pascoe then progressed to playing for Bankstown C-grade in the Municipal and Shire competition.

Lennie and I were told to go to the net trials at the start of the season and we found ourselves practising with fellas like Ian King, the Aboriginal fast bowler, Grahame Thomas, who played for NSW and Australia, and Ronnie Briggs, who played for NSW.

At the end of the 1966–67 season, team captain, Alan Tyson, wrote in the club's year book:

Jeff Thomson and Len Pascoe carried the brunt of the opening attack and with their different styles became perfect partners. Jeff with his quick and accurate deliveries always placed the batsmen on the defensive and Len with his express deliveries and 57 wickets.
Len shows promise as being a good all-rounder.'[6]

That cricket year was very much a springboard for both Jeff and Lennie.

At school Thommo was still excelling at sports and totally ignoring his studies. He'd often turn up to class with flippers hanging on the top of his school bag. His mates knew it wouldn't be long before Thommo took off to Maroubra Beach for the rest of the day. Lennie remembers the time Thommo took on the school bully, a big kid they called Socco:

Socco was big and strong and no-one, not even the teachers, messed with him. A few people were trying out for a place on the javelin team. Socco was the school champion, but Thommo was hell-bent upon knocking him off. We all went down to see the contest. Socco would throw, then Thommo would get a few inches ahead, then Socco would outdo him by a bit and the thing went on. We were all thinking, 'Thommo don't beat Socco—beat this bloke and you're dead!'

But Thommo didn't care. He had no fear. After a while, with one just scraping ahead of the other, Thommo lost patience. He said, 'Give us the bloody thing' and he hurled the javelin way past all the lines, out of the school oval and onto the road. It was incredible. We all ran like hell, because Socco wasn't one to mess with. As it turned out Thommo's throw was not counted. The lines to measure the throw weren't out far enough, so his javelin toss was considered out of bounds. I've no doubt if Thommo had been coached in proper technique in throwing the javelin he could have been in the Australian Olympic track and field team.[7]

Thommo survived the contest with Socco and next summer (1967–68) he played for Bankstown second eleven, taking 20 wickets for 376 at 18.8 runs apiece. The next season he was taken straight into the A-grade side. And how he performed, taking bags of wickets including hauls of 7/34, 6/44, 5/48, 5/62 and 5/55.

His A-grade captain, Bob Madden, wrote in the club yearbook for 1968–69:

Jeff Thomson: first year in first-grade cricket and captured the most wickets at the best average; a commendable feat.

He had the knack of cleaning up the tail with the old ball. A little hint, Jeff, when you get the opportunity to practise, hop straight into it. Well done.

That season Lennie bowled well too, taking two decent hauls of wickets— 5/45 and 4/64. Madden said of Lennie:

Len Pascoe: Like Jeff another fast bowler and will improve if he listens and practises more. Keenness is a password to cricket.[8]

In November, 1968, Thommo was included in the Australian School-boys' Cricket Team to play against the touring Indian team in Canberra. Among his team-mates was Alan Turner (Randwick High School), who later opened the batting for NSW and Australia. Thommo only hung about at Punchbowl High School just to get the chance to make the side. Lennie says:

You didn't have to ask Thommo how he went with his HSC. In the final years of school you saw more of his parents round the classrooms than Thommo. He'd be off fishing or surfing and when he was at school it was usually only on sports days.[9]

There was a recurring theme in the club reports. While Thommo and Lennie were tremendous fast bowling talents, their lack of application to training had become an increasing annoyance to club officials. When they were invited to train with the State squad, they'd turn up in boardshorts and thongs and then proceed to terrorise the batsmen with their tearaway speed. Then they'd be off for a couple of weeks, returning only when the fish weren't biting, it was too cold or too hot for the beach or the girls were off the boil.

In the summer of 1969–70 both Thommo and Lennie struggled with the ball. Thommo took only a total of 5/234 and, although better in terms of figures, Lennie too wasn't cutting the mustard.

Bob Madden said of them: 'Jeff and Len, both quickies, need more and more practice and keenness.'[10] While Lennie recalls:

We were sort of on a journey. I went surfing and he went car racing and drinking.[11]

Thommo's eldest brother, Donny, used to be a rally driver and Jeff decided to give it a go. He bought a Mini Cooper S and had lots of fun racing with the Liverpool Car Club, screaming around the old Warwick Farm Raceway. Thommo was always in his element in the fast lane. That Mini Cooper S also had a history. He bought it from a local policeman and all the residents in the area identified the car as the 'local copper's wheels'. Thommo decided to turn that knowledge to his advantage. He used to play 'cop' with the couples on Black Charley's Hill, a popular parking place-cum-lover's lane. In the early hours of the morning Thommo would cruise up to Black Charley's Hill, sneak up in the car to a necking couple and turn high beam on.

One night Thommo, with Lennie and a mate in the back seat, drove up to a parked FJ Holden. Thommo turned on the lights full bore, scared the hell out of the couple in the FJ and then turned on the power and sped off. At the bottom of Black Charley's Hill there is an acute dogleg to the left. Thommo failed to fully negotiate the turn and hit the gutter, somehow putting the right front wheel of the Mini Cooper S under the sump.

> *I was paying the car off and I couldn't afford to have it fixed, so when I got the car back home, I pulled it apart completely and rebuilt it. I got the panels straightened out and rubbed them back. Kevin, my younger brother, is a top mechanic. He's come first in every exam he's ever done on the subject and Donny was the boss of a big car dealership and service place when he was 21.*
>
> *British Leyland were racing a few Minis out here at the time and I rebuilt the Mini Cooper S to their specifications. I put it together myself and raced it for a while.*

According to Lennie, Thommo's rebuilt suped-up Mini Cooper S was like a mini-rocket. But Thommo soon gave up car racing. He sold the car to a Bankstown-based man who used it for rally driving.

Apart from fishing and surfing, cricket and soccer were Thommo's two greatest sporting loves. But by the time he was twenty, Thommo had given up hopes of a professional soccer career. Yet, one day he found himself playing with Lennie 'in some church side', affiliated to the Protestant Churches League. Thommo's brother Greg was playing full-back and he was sounded out by the referee for a misdemeanor. Thommo recalls:

> I was pretty shirty all day. I felt the referee was cheating and I have always hated liars and cheats.
> When that happens I'm on a short fuse and this day I felt the ref was cheating.

Len Pascoe played half-back that day and he believes the incident occurred due to a misunderstanding:

> Thommo's brother was nailed for something or other and I reckon the ref mistook Jeff for Greg. He threatened to book Thommo and Thommo said, 'I'm not going for that. If you take my name I'll deck you.' The ref started writing in his little notebook and Thommo punched him in the nose, knocking him to the ground. It was very much out of character for Thommo. I know everyone, including Thommo, regretted what happened that day.[12]

Thommo was handed a life ban from soccer for his assault on the referee, but the ban was lifted after a few years and he played for the Trident Football Club in Brisbane in 1978. He still takes a great interest in soccer and is a fan of English club, Manchester United.

Recently Len was at a sports show he had co-ordinated and he met up with 'a bloke with a bent nose; a former soccer referee in the Protestant Churches League'. However, Lennie says:

> Thommo was a brilliant athlete, strong and he could run all day. He certainly could have made a career in football.[13]

While Thomson could well have played professional soccer had he chosen that path and signed with the Melita Eagles, he decided to throw in his sporting lot with the Bankstown Cricket Club.

In their school days, Thommo bowled a ball so fast that it bowled over the wicket-keeper, Garry Manuel, who within a few years became the Socceroos full-back in the 1974 World Cup. Lennie recalls:

Thommo's delivery beat the batsman, beat the stumps and hit Manuel in the guts, knocking him out cold.[14]

By the time the 1970–71 season was upon them Thommo and Lennie were still on what Lennie called 'a journey'. Thommo took 16 wickets at an average of 24 and Lennie took 16 wickets at an average of 27. Bob Madden wrote in the Club Yearbook:

Jeff Thomson: At times batted and bowled very well.
But Jeff, don't forget our talks.

Madden said of Lennie:

Well, we all know what Len can do. Now come on Len it is a team game.
    Let's give it all we have.[15]

That summer, when Bankstown played Manly at Manly, Thommo and Lennie rushed out to the beach in Lennie's suped-up 350 V8 Monaro. Lennie says:

We used to love the beachfronts because you'd pick up the hitchhikers and any girls you picked up you'd stay overnight and party on. Anyway this day we jammed five birds in the car and when we got to the ground the spinners were on. We were ten overs late. The captain wasn't happy, but Thommo let fly. I'll never forget his bowling to Terry Lee. One ball, just short of a length, whizzed past Lee's head flew over the keeper and hit the concrete base on the boundary at Manly Oval. That was the fastest I've seen Jeff bowl.[16]

Perhaps their attitude may not have changed if Dion Bourne hadn't taken over the Bankstown captaincy. Bourne is Steve and Mark Waugh's uncle and it was Bourne who helped both Thommo and Lennie with their cricket, especially their attitude to training.

Thomson and Pascoe are just two of some famous cricket names to hail from Bankstown. They include NSW and Test batsman Grahame Thomas, Ian Davis, Steve Smith and Steve and Mark Waugh. Former Prime Minister Paul Keating was like Thommo, a man who grew up in Bankstown. Thomson, the Waughs and Keating all became household names in Australia and they all reached the pinnacle of their chosen walk in life.

Thommo took a record 52 wickets at 13.9 off 260 overs and Lennie grabbed 42 wickets at 18.69. And in so doing they terrorised batsmen in Sydney grade cricket. Bourne wrote in the Yearbook:

Jeff holds the first grade record with 52 wickets this season. Has the ability to maintain speed and accuracy for long periods. Jeff's application, enthusiasm and ability should win him State honours next season.[17]

Thommo took 6/75 against Mosman and was fired up because David Colley was wearing the NSW State sweater that he wanted. It inspired him to bowl as fast as he has ever bowled.

The season had a steadying effect on Thommo in more ways than just the game of cricket. He got engaged, and surprised his fiancée with an engagement present, a 427 bridge-to-bridge racing boat. Lennie, who was waiting in the car for Thommo when he took the boat around to show her, remembers:

The door opened slightly, and his fiancée eyed the boat on the trailer and the door quickly closed.

I sensed something was amiss. Maybe she expected Thommo would put a deposit on a piece of land. That speed boat Thommo took around to show her didn't seem to impress her at all. I seized the opportunity and asked her out for a date. We were going out for some time when I felt a bit guilty about it and I said to Thommo, 'Mate, I have to confess that I have done something very wrong. I have been taking your fiancée out for two weeks.'

'Oh, that's fine Lennie,' Thommo laughed, I've been taking your girlfriend out for three months!'[18]

Lennie was working at Bankstown Council and Thommo's fiancée was secretary to the Town Planner, Dave McInnes, who just happened to play A-grade cricket for Sydney University. One day Lennie was fielding in the bat-pad position. Thommo was about to bowl when Lennie rushed up to him and had a few words:

> I told Thommo that Dave McInnes, who was about to face the bowling, was taking his fiancée out. And I was telling Thommo all the things McInnes was doing to her. Thommo was trying to get back into her good books and I don't think he was too impressed with McInnes. Boy did he give the batsman a working over.[19]

Thommo hit McInnes in the legs, the chest, the arms and the jaw. Dion Bourne eventually went up to Thommo and said, 'Jeff, this is getting embarrassing. Can you just get him out?'

Despite Thommo's fire that day on the cricket field, the engagement was soon over. He went back to playing the field and concentrating on his cricket.

Jeff Thomson's brilliant summer of 1971–72 gave him the platform to make the NSW State side. He bowled only 57 overs for Bankstown in 1972–73, taking 9 wickets at 24, but he made the State team.

Finally, the NSW selectors picked this bowler of genuine pace.

3 GOODBYE QUAVERS AND CROTCHETS

I got to the stage where I sat down and thought to myself, 'You can't spend the rest of your life as a wharfie, you'll end up a moron.'

Thommo stayed on at school for one reason: to win a place in the Australian Schoolboys Cricket team. Attending class seemed a meaningless exercise to him, yet it was his top-flight academic results in primary school that gave him the opportunity to choose which high school he wished to attend. However, the call of the sea became too much in the last few years. Schoolwork was a bore and Thommo loved to do his own thing. As high school wore on Thommo did less and less in the way of study. Here he was, an intelligent and articulate young man with a free spirit; a young man who lived within a loving family environment; a young man perceived by authorities in education and cricket circles as a bit of a 'rebel'; a young man who didn't quite realise his great potential to make it big time in cricket.

I only stayed at school to get into the Australian Schoolboys' side. For the last couple of years there I hardly opened a book and I just walked out whenever I wanted and went surfing.

And once that mission was accomplished Thommo was keen to get out into the working world.

At Punchbowl High School he was the school athletics champion, cricket captain and he was picked in the zone side for soccer and for the Combined High Schools representative team, but he didn't turn out for that team because soccer just didn't have the attraction for Thommo that cricket could provide.

One year, when injury kept Thommo out of cricket at school, he played hockey and he was picked in the zone team.

That was the first time I played hockey, but I found it pretty easy. As the team cricket captain I was a bit lazy and let Lennie do it all. At one stage—with two years to go—they changed headmasters. The new one was from the North Shore [of Sydney] and you know what I thought of North Shore people. He hated me, this bloke, but he couldn't do anything about it. Apart from the cricket, I was the athletics champ, a footballer, the whole deal. I used to win everything for them. I loved athletics. I used to do hop-step-and-jump, long jump, shot put, javelin and the 880 metres—and I used to win them all.

Thommo's schooldays were full of sports. It was all go and days were packed with outdoors action. Early on Thommo liked surf-boarding, but he eventually preferred body surfing.

Fishing, however, always played a big part in Thommo's life. When he was around the age of fourteen he joined the NSW Amateur Fishing Association.

My brother Greg and I were so keen we used to go to the association meetings in the city and, after Greg finished work and I'd got out of school, we'd go fishing. Sometimes we'd fish all through the night. We'd start late in the afternoon and go through to about 3 a.m. We used to go out and stand on the ocean rocks, hanging on to a metal spike while the surf rolled over us. Cape Banks is so treacherous that some 38 people have perished there, just washed away off the rocks. If you get taken there, you can say goodbye, unless you are a bloody channel swimmer or something. You'd have to swim right around the bay and the current is usually against you. If you asked me to fish all night these days, I wouldn't do it. But I'd go out in the boat, anywhere you like. Once at Narrabeen Greg and I went out on this ledge. There was a channel running alongside it, a couple of feet wide. Much of the channel was shallow, with a deep hole in one part. We'd caught a few fish, then as the wave came at me I took the shortcut too quickly and fell into the hole in the channel. There I was suddenly eye to eye with this bloody great wave. I've never moved so quickly, I was up and out of there like a rocket. My brother laughed his head off. We had a few hairy moments fishing off the rocks, but that was the worst one.

One day Thommo and Lennie were fishing off the rocks but the swell got up and it became too dangerous to hang about, so they headed for the nearest jetty. Lennie recalls:

Thommo's come along with a seventeen foot rod, huge sinker, the works. There was a bloke disrupting the fishing by making waves in the wake of his speed boat and Thommo said, 'I'll fix that bloke'.

He cast out a long way, knowing the line would get tangled with the boat's propeller and sure enough the boat conked out—it was time to go.[1]

It was not all smooth sailing for Thommo that night. Fate took a hand when he jagged the inside of his right calf muscle with a huge hook. Lennie immediately saw the danger. He fumbled through the tackle bag full of hooks, a fishing video and other paraphernalia until he found what he sought: a razor blade. Lennie held it up in the light of their car headlight and Thommo winced.

'Jeez, Lennie, the blade's rusty,' he protested.

'Now I have to sterilise this, mate,' Lennie said confidently.

He discovered a cigarette lighter in the tackle bag and he put the flame to the rusty razor blade.

An eight-inch lure was hanging from the hook which was imbedded in Thommo's leg. Lennie motioned for Thommo to put his foot on the fence and by the glow of the car headlights Lennie went to work on the offending hook. Len Pascoe was no surgeon but, as he explained to Thommo, he had seen film of fishermen getting hooks out of their arms and legs when snagged in a similar way to the fate which befell his friend. Lennie hacked into his mate's leg with the determination of a man hell-bent in getting the job done as fast as possible.

'Shit, Lennie, that's killing me.'

'No, you'll be right, mate.'

The more Lennie cut into Thommo's leg, the deeper the hook went and the louder his mate complained. Eventually Lennie drove Thommo home, the lure still dangling from the hook, which was by then deeply embedded in his calf muscle.

Thommo slept overnight with the hook in his leg, then the next morning the pain in his calf was so intense that he belatedly sought medical treatment. Lennie says:

> Thommo still had the lure hanging from his leg went he walked into the surgery. The doc removed the hook easily and Thommo copped a tetanus shot in the arse.[2]

That same day Thommo opened the bowling in tandem with Lennie. They bowled fast and accurately to have the opposition 6/50 at lunch. Next door to the ground was the local bowling club and the pace pair ducked in to have lunch. To their dismay, there was no food to be had, so Thommo suggested they have a few beers. Lennie recalls:

> When we got back to the ground, I think our skipper wondered why Thommo was struggling a bit to the get to the wicket. We both laboured in the wake of those beers and the other mob scored more than 250.[3]

Having dumped his school books, Thommo, then aged eighteen, headed for the wharves in Darling Harbour, where he built on his immense strength, heaving as a wharf labourer.

> *As a wharfie I used to work from 4 a.m. to midnight. You'd load these wool bales and beer kegs and it would make you incredibly strong.*

I used to load a couple of hundred 18-gallon kegs in a day—picking up a full one on my own. As for the wool bales I could roll them around on my ear. I was never so fit as when I worked on the wharves. We started early and finished early. After lunch I'd be home. I'd wake up early and that didn't worry me, the hours were okay. It never affected me at all. I enjoyed the work and it was pretty good money.

While Thommo was loading bales and kegs at the wharves, his Bankstown pace bowling partner, Lennie Pascoe, worked as a brickie's labourer for his father. Lennie reckons their respective stints at hard labour helped enormously with their stamina for the hard work of fast bowling. But Thommo was never going to become a 'lifer' as a wharfie.

I got to the stage where I sat down and thought to myself, 'You can't spend the rest of your life as a wharfie, you'll end up a moron.' You'd sit in the lunch room and you'd have a beer—it was like being in Long Bay Gaol, you'd look around the table and think, 'I can't have a conversation with anyone in this joint. I've gotta get out of here. Fuck this.'

So Jeff left the wharves and took a job on the city council. A lot of people would identify with his experience in that line of work.

All you had to do was check people's rates notices, but most of the people on our floor, all they did was have a race to see who could get to the shithouse first to read the paper. They did nothing. The best part of the day was sitting on the steps at midday when all the sheilas strolled past Town Hall. All the young blokes would perv on them and chat them up. That was the highlight of our day. Because when you walked back into the office, you had nothing to do. After a couple of days I said to my mate, 'You can stick this fucking job up your arse, this is worse than what I just left down at the wharves.'

Thommo turned from the public service to a career in banking. He joined the Wiley Park Branch of the Commonwealth Bank. It was a small

branch of five—the manager, second officer and three others, all male—
set in an industrial area.

> *I just joined the bank because there was fuck all else to do. Wiley Park*
> *was close to home, only a couple of railway stations up the track from*
> *where I lived. There was Bankstown, Punchbowl, then Wiley Park.*
> *The branch was run brilliantly, because we'd open at 10 a.m., close at*
> *3 p.m. and then balance everything and be off early. I was a teller and*
> *I'd do a load of other stuff as well.*
>
> *Then one Friday afternoon these fucking goons walked in and*
> *robbed us. They wore masks and held sawn-off shotguns, but I guess I*
> *wasn't a little bit scared because we've always had guns about the place*
> *at home and gone shooting, so blokes wandering around with guns,*
> *even during the hold-up, didn't faze me. The first officer just about shit*
> *himself. I think he's in a mental asylum now.*
>
> *One of the robbers pointed the gun at the teller, who was pooping*
> *himself. He reminded me of Wizard—you know Ian Davis [who*
> *played for NSW and Qld and opened the batting for Australia]. Geez,*
> *I thought, what's going on here? A bloke's got a gun trained on my*
> *teller mate at the front counter.*

Thommo sensed that he had not been noticed by either of the two gunmen.
He had his back to the wall at the rear of the bank chamber and he began
to slowly edge his way towards the doorway which led to the staff lunch
room. His confidence grew. He planned to slip away unnoticed then raise
the alarm. He had reached the door undetected, then as he was about to
slip through the opening, one of the armed men spotted him.

> *This bloke saw me and he swung his gun around. 'Hey you! Back! And*
> *get your hands up!'*
>
> *'Don't shoot,' I shouted. I had my hands in my pockets and I didn't*
> *want them to think I was going for something. It was then that I got my*
> *hands in the air pretty smartly.*

While one of the bandits had his weapon trained on Thommo and his
mate, the second gunman walked boldly into the bank manager's office.

The door was open and Thommo could see and hear all that was being said and done in the office.

> *We had been trying to get the boss's attention. He had his head stuck in the newspaper unaware of what was going on in the outer office. When I first started, he gave us a lecture on how 'I used to be in the army, don't ever fuck me up and we'll build a great team'—one of those sergeant major talks. And when we were robbed that day and the bloke walked into the office with the gun, the boss absolutely froze. He was shitting himself and it looked so funny I almost broke out laughing. Our war hero went to water. When the cops came, the other young bloke and I were the only ones who could tell 'em what happened. I signed the boss's name on statements. He couldn't even hold a pen.*

The bank robbers held up a number of banks in Sydney until they were eventually caught at Palm Beach.

Thommo was given a merit award for his calmness during the hold-up and he received other good reports as an able and diligent bank officer.

> *I had a short banking career, about two years. When they transferred me to the Wentworth Hotel branch in the city, I started to think about some other sort of work. I told the bank that I never wanted to work in the big office in town. That was the downfall of my banking career. It was a drag. There was shift work and you had to get into the Sydney CBD every day. The work in the bank was boring. Those bloody lists of figures we had to add up, in your head, no calculators in those days. And the pay was terrible. I was getting $62 a fortnight. Shithouse money.*

The Commonwealth Bank traditionally was helpful to cricketers, but Thommo decided to quit the bank a couple of months after being sent to work at the Wentworth Hotel branch. Ironically, in later years during Sydney Test matches, Thommo stayed with the Australian team at the Wentworth Hotel.

A year on the wharves and a further two years in the bank wasn't Thommo's idea of an ideal working life. He needed some stimulating work. By the time he was twenty, Thommo was starting to get wickets consistently for Bankstown and long before he played his first big match for NSW, he was being touted as a coming champion.

So why didn't he play sooner for NSW?

Lennie and I used to turn up to the Bankstown games with our board shorts on. We were just casual.

Cricket was just a game we could turn up to and play. I mean, you have to play all afternoon, so what's the hurry to get there? We are going to get them out anyway, and our blokes weren't too good with the bat at Bankstown. When we turned up, we turned off because we hated bowling on a hot day when we could have been somewhere else—we'd rather be at the beach chasing shielas, but we had to turn up to cricket. Fuck me, that's a good way to fuck up a good afternoon.

We used to go to State training about once a week. That's because we had to get through all the heavy traffic from Bankstown to the SCG. We'd arrive in our board shorts and there were the likes of Skull [Kerry O'Keeffe] . . . in his suit and tie. I don't think he had a job then, but he always arrived to State training in a suit and tie. The selectors had to take us as they found us. When we hit the track we struck 'em like a mini tornado. We tore into them, hitting blokes all over the place and then we'd take off as fast as we arrived. They looked stunned and were probably thinking, 'What was that?'

The selectors played Steve Bernard, Gary Gilmour and David Colley ahead of both Thomson and Pascoe, but Thommo reckons he and Lennie were hard done by.

One of us—Lennie or me—should have played for NSW long before we eventually did. I first got into the State squad when I got into A-grade cricket, when I was sixteen. Blokes like Gordon Goffett, Bob Simpson, Barry Rothwell and Dougie Walters were there. At that time I got into some sort of practice game, but I told the old man that I didn't think I'd bother turning up. Dad said he thought I should go and play because by doing so I would be able to gauge how good they were and what I had to do in way of improvement to be competitive against them. I can't remember my stats, but I do recall having one or two of them hopping about and beating the bat a fair bit. That was pleasing. I knew I wasn't too far off the mark.

Later, Dad said, 'How'd you go?' And I said to him, 'You were right, dad. They're not as good as they think.' It was then I knew I could do it, because these blokes were Australian and State players.

The sooner the young blokes get to know how good they really are the better. They can gauge their progress by being pitted against the top players—the sooner the better. These days the older guys are hanging on too long, denying the youngsters a chance to play earlier. I think the Under-19s should be scrapped. If a bloke is good enough at seventeen to play State cricket, he should be thrown in then. Why do they have to wait? These days the older blokes are hanging on for the money. They are, in a cricket sense, going nowhere, just keeping young blokes waiting.

After Thommo left the bank, he continued to work hard on his cricket, but he needed a job, so he joined Monier Concrete, his last employment before he left Sydney to move to Brisbane. At that time Jeff's dad was a gatekeeper at the firm's Villawood branch. Jeff started in the office as a clerk with the view to becoming a sales representative. After a few months in the office, Thommo was elevated to the position of sales representative. Thommo stayed at Monier for two years. He greatly enjoyed his work, although eventually the job that was too good became the job he had to leave for the sake of his health and wellbeing.

I used to sell all the Monier products in the office, then I went out and sold all the products to the people on building sites. It was good. I used to call on the plumbers who laid the pipes, from the engineers to the council bloke, the town planner. I had an unlimited expense account and if I didn't spend up big, they used to say to me, 'You haven't been out this week'. So every week I was on the piss.

The 1971–72 summer was a big turn-around year for Thommo. His record 52 wickets won him adulation from not only his Bankstown team-mates and captain, Dion Bourne, but it made the State selectors at last sit up and take notice. For this surfie who terrorised batsmen in the State nets and kept smashing bodies and stumps in grade cricket was no layabout; this bloke was the real deal. Lennie, too, had a bumper season in club cricket that year, taking 42 wickets and the pair often went on the rampage, scaring the hell out of opposing batsmen. But it was Thommo who got the nod from the State selectors.

I felt a bit sorry for Lennie because he always seemed to be the next man chosen. He missed selection this time, like all the sides he missed being picked in along the journey. That seemed to happen to Lennie throughout our careers.

In the Bankstown Cricket Club Yearbook Dion Bourne lauded the efforts of Thommo and Lennie and did not make a mention of any lack of commitment by either man. In the first couple of grade matches with Bankstown in 1972–73, Thommo failed to take a wicket, but he was picked in the first Sheffield Shield team for NSW after the injured medium-fast bowler David Colley withdrew from the original side.

In the local newspaper, *Torch*, a single column appeared under the heading:

WE LIKED . . . the fact that after 12 years Bankstown-Canterbury Cricket Club has received a State cap following last week's selection of fast bowler Jeff Thomson in the NSW cricket team to play Queensland. The club has been living in the wilderness for a long time and it must be morale boosting for them to have this happen. Jeff, 22, is a born and bred Bankstown man who thrives on sport. Many cups adorn his parents' house in Market Street, Bankstown, and they are not just from cricket. Soccer, squash, golf are just some of his sporting interests. But cricket is in his blood. His father, Don, was a medium-fast bowler in the fifties for the North Bankstown Club. His abilities were acclaimed by many knowledgeable followers of the sport. Jeff has a lot of determination and it won't be surprising to see him in the Australian team in a few years.[4]

It seemed Thommo's years of frustration were over.

His becoming a State player was a belated selection, but Thommo was keen to do well and prove to some people, who seemed to think that he didn't have the necessary passion and commitment to make the grade, that they were a long way off the mark about him. And Thommo celebrated his State selection with a sensational pace bowling effort against Gordon, taking 7/44 .

The NSW team: Bruce Francis, 24; Alan Turner, 22; John Benaud (*captain*), 28; Kerry Mackay, 23; Doug Walters, 26; Ron Crippin, 25; Gary Gilmour, 21; Kerry O'Keeffe, 22; Brian Taber, 32; John Gleeson, 34; Jeff Thomson, 22; Hugh Martin, 25 (*12th man*).

An article appeared in the *Sydney Sun,* by David Lord, under the tag: 'New Cap Jeff is fast with questions too!':

'Is Sam Trimble short or tall?' That was State cricket new cap Jeff Thomson's first question this morning. Thomson, who makes his NSW debut at the Gabba at Brisbane against Queensland on Friday week, said 'I haven't seen any of them play.'

The elated 22-year-old still couldn't believe he'd won selection. 'I was at my girlfriend's place and didn't hear the news until late last night,' Thomson said. 'Do you reckon there'll be any pace in the wicket? When do we leave? I'm a bit nervous, but I want to bowl fast. How do they play the short stuff?'—the questions came thick and fast. If Jeff Thomson, one of the State's fastest bowlers, fires deliveries at the same pace as his queries, it should be an auspicious start.[5]

Thommo's selection coincided with the State selectors naming a new captain, ex-Test all-rounder Richie Benaud's younger brother John. Thommo recalls:

We lobbed up in Brisbane for the game, but it poured for days and the Gabba ground was very wet. I was never so keen to do well, but I didn't know what to expect. I made a lot of stupid, raw statements to the newspapers along these lines—you know, 'What's a bloke expected to do against a batsman whose weaknesses I don't know, and all that crap. I was rooming with the captain, John Benaud, and while I used to love having a drink I wouldn't have one. I didn't want to put a foot

wrong—I wouldn't have swallowed a beer if you gave me a hundred
dollars. I sat in that bloody motel room for two days until JB [Benaud]
said: 'Look Thommo, this is not doing you any good. It's raining like
buggery. Get out and get pissed tonight. It will do you the world of
good. You're a bundle of nerves.'

Thommo went to a disco with opening batsmen Ron Crippin, Alan Turner
and Steve Bernard and they stayed out all night.

It was a long session and we all got pretty drunk. I can't remember
when the place closed, but it seemed a long time. I hadn't had a drink
for a while. Anyway we managed to find our way back across the Storey
Bridge and up Main Street to the motel. It was about a kilometre, but
it seemed a lot longer than that, something I put down to the time of
night and the fact we were a bit unsteady on our feet. I awoke early,
hungover and feeling a bit dry. I got out of bed and had a look out of
the window. The sky was clear—usual Brisbane caper, flooded one
day and red-hot the next. It was bloody hot. About 7 a.m. I got down
to the pool to freshen up. 'Fitterun' Turner had the same idea. We got
to the ground. It was hot and muggy and I remember the captains
talking about when to start. The curator Clem Jones was telling them
that he didn't want a start just yet because he was still putting bags
about the pitch and running rollers everywhere. However, he did come
in with his two bobs' worth telling them that there was nothing wrong
with the wicket and they should get in and play. JB told Clem Jones
that when he wanted his advice, he would ask for it and added that
Jones should refrain from sticking his bib in.

NSW batted first, making 9/174, with Queensland's Geoff Dymock,
a medium-fast left-hander, getting a bag of five wickets. Then it was time
for Thommo to bowl.

JB looked after me, after all it was his fault, he told me to go out and
get pissed. I had Don Allen caught behind and Dougie Walters caught
Alan Jones and I think I had 2/8 off 4 overs when Benaud rested me.
I finished with 2/24 off 8 overs and the match ended in a draw.

Thommo had, by no means, cemented his place in the NSW team. He had to fight all the way to secure a spot. A haul of 5/79 in the Colts match against Queensland in Sydney won him another Sheffield Shield match, this time in the NSW team to play the strong Western Australian team in Perth. It was Thommo's first brush with Dennis Lillee and he has never forgotten it.

Lillee took 4/44 off 15 overs in the NSW innings, a paltry one ending when Benaud called a halt to proceedings at 9/147. Thommo was listed to go in last, but when the ninth wicket fell, Benaud declared the innings closed. Thommo reveals:

I'd heard a lot about Lillee. After football training they used to come back to my place and we'd listen to the Tests in England on radio, have a drink and play cards all night. My mates used to stir me up about Dennis bowling quick and all that, and the blokes on the radio were saying how quick Lillee was bowling—the fastest thing out. I think my mates thought I was pretty quick anyhow, but they enjoyed stirring me up. So I remembered all that when I first met up with Dennis in that Shield match in Perth. Our batting didn't go too well, but here was my chance to show who's who and what's what with the ball. In those days I really did sling 'em and spray the ball about all over the place. I opened the bowling in front of that one-eyed WACA crowd, the Fremantle Doctor [Perth's afternoon sea breeze] behind me and Graeme Watson facing. Watson was hit a terrible blow in the face by Tony Greig when playing for Australia versus the Rest of the World a year earlier, but I gave him a bouncer first up. It took off and came down miles on the leg side. Ron Crippin ran backwards and caught it at deep leg slip. The crowd gave me a huge serve over that bouncer. I was nervous as buggery.

That night Thommo sat down by himself and evaluated his performance. Why should he be nervous? He had bowled well to get into the NSW team and knew from a long time back that he had the ability to match it with anyone.

Next day Thommo bowled 18 fiery overs and took 4 wickets. He cannot forget the sight of Dennis Lillee coming out to bat.

He strutted to the wicket—real mean bugger, you know, the King sort of thing. I thought, 'I'll show you, mate!' Doug Walters was standing at cover, near me, with the rest of the blokes behind the wicket, catching. I wasn't going to bounce him, Doug made sure of that when he advised, 'Don't bounce him Thommo for Christ's sake'. In reply I told Doug not to worry, but 'I'll soon fix him up!'

Dennis got me away through the slip for 4. I got angry about that edged boundary and I really let one go. It got up off a length and struck Dennis on the gloves. He let go of his bat and ran a single and when he got up my end he said, 'I hope you can hold a fucking blade, pal'. I was grinning and I said, 'Listen pal, you've got the bat at the moment. Just get up the other end and see how fucking good you are!' And Doug had turned as white as a ghost. He must have been pooping himself!

Those were the only words in anger Dennis and I have ever had against one another. I had him caught by Brian Taber and later on, when it was my turn to bat, Dennis bowled a couple of short ones which whistled past my chin, but I got 16—all fours, slogging—before he clean-bowled me with a slower ball.

It was a fine double for Thommo—4/71 and 3/34—but despite his efforts with the ball and Walters' fine second innings 106, WA won the match outright.

Against SA in Adelaide, Thommo failed to take a wicket in the SA first innings, in which Greg Chappell hit a splendid 129 out of 9/225. NSW scored 222 in reply with Thommo getting 30 not out, an innings of full-blooded slogs. Batting a second time SA scored 265. Ian Chappell opened the batting, scoring a solid 90 before Thommo trapped him lbw. Thommo bowled with plenty of fire on that placid Adelaide Oval pitch, taking 4/65. I scored 29 not out and ensured that I stayed up the opposite end to the new firebrand from NSW. SA won the match outright, after Ian Chappell (5/29) and I (5/41) spun them out for 162.

Before the teams were announced for the first two Tests against Pakistan, Thommo played five matches. After Adelaide, he played against SA at the SCG, his first big game at the cricket ground, taking 1/61 and 1/43; then 1/42 and 1/61 against WA at the SCG. At that stage, Thommo's figures read: 17 wickets for 443 runs at an average of 26; modest numbers, but his pace and fire had impressed many good judges and Thommo was earmarked for bigger things.

Thommo was aged 22 and he had played six first-class matches. In between Sheffield Shield matches, Thommo was enjoying life. His work was more a lifestyle of the social kind and he figured he could not keep that going if he wanted to make his mark in cricket. At Monier Concrete he was selling plenty of produce. The company was happy to allow him time off to play cricket, but increasingly each day at work had become a big day on the booze. It couldn't continue.

I walked into the sales manager Fred Kemp's office. He was a big guy, nice guy and told him, 'I've got to give this job away'. And he said, 'Why Jeff? You're doing well.'

'Fred, if I keep drinking with you blokes, I'll never play any cricket.'

I gave it away because it was just too much of that stuff.

In December, 1972, Thommo took his mum, Doreen, to hospital to visit his uncle who had had a heart attack. They arrived home to Market Street, Bankstown, late that night and Thommo was surprised to see the car belonging to a Bankstown Cricket Club team-mate, Tony Radanovic, in the driveway.

Tony was excited. 'I'm not saying anything to you, Thommo, but it is absolutely vital you come with me to the club, right now. Trust me, Thommo. There's a few blokes who want to have a drink with you at the club. It can't wait, mate. Trust me.' I said, 'It's a bit late isn't it?' But Mum said, 'Go on Jeff, you might as well.'

When Tony Radanovic and Thommo walked into the club house, all the A-grade players were there. A rousing cheer erupted the instant Thommo walked into the room. What on earth was happening?

4 A TEST OF METTLE

. . . that season there were arms and legs and stumps flying in all directions. I hurled myself down in fury. Blokes just didn't want to face me.

Thommo was in the Test team. There were handshakes and backslaps all round for the popular Bankstown fast bowler. His team-mates were overjoyed at Thommo's Test selection and the club bar became the site of a big drink.

I was on top of the world, but I must admit hearing that I had been picked in the Test side really was the shock of my life. We celebrated big time.

Next morning, Thommo saw the story leading the sports pages of the *Sydney Morning Herald*:

NSW FAST BOWLER CHOSEN FOR TEST
NSW's young fast bowler Jeff Thomson was sensationally chosen for Test cricket last night after a first-class career of only five matches.

The 22-year-old right-arm speedster will partner Dennis Lillee in the Second Test against Pakistan on December 29.

In what is clearly an experiment with the five Test tour of the West Indies in January in mind, Thomson will replace champion swing bowler Bob Massie, who will play in the First Test in Adelaide on Friday week.[1]

But Thommo's form had tailed off in recent matches. He failed to take a wicket for NSW against Victoria in a one-day knockout match at the MCG and was keen to find form in the Sheffield Shield game with the Victorians at the same venue. He found the MCG wicket sluggish, with little or no bounce.

On Friday, 22 December 1972, an article, written by Bruce Matthews, appeared in the *Melbourne Sun*, entitled 'Jeff Keen to Atone':

Australia's new glamour bowler Jeff Thomson will strive for two personal objectives in the annual Christmas grudge match between NSW and Victoria at the MCG tomorrow.

He will be flat out to even the score with the Victorian batsmen, and to prove that his Test selection was not unworthy. The young NSW pace bowler will be keen to capture wickets on the ground where he will make his Test debut against Pakistan late next week.[2]

There was, however, something on Thommo's mind. He was carrying a niggling injury and he wasn't about to tell anyone about it. The Sheffield Shield match with Victoria was no easy task for him, as his match figures of 1/96 illustrate, but he was worried about how he might go in the coming Test.

I hurt my foot in one of the Sheffield Shield games in Sydney. I couldn't remember which one. After I bowled a short ball, I felt the pain. My left foot slammed hard and flat on the pitch. You know immediately when something is wrong. I knew. It was bloody sore. I could hardly walk on it. It was a big decision for me to make whether I should let on about my left foot. If I'd pulled out of the game I might never have played for Australia again. I made the wrong decision.

Thommo's attitude towards wanting to play in the Test despite a potentially crippling injury was not unlike that of Ross Duncan, the Queensland, then Victorian, medium-paced swing bowler who was picked in Bill Lawry's Australian team to play Ray Illingworth's England team in the Fifth Test at the MCG in January 1971. Duncan was nursing a badly bruised right heel and he decided to keep quiet about his injury and play the game. Duncan says:

> I understood Thommo's decision to play. I also believed that if I had pulled out of the match I may not have been given another chance to play for my country. As it was, I got none for 30 off 14 overs, scored 3 with the bat and didn't bowl in the England second innings. The game was a dull draw and I never played a Test match again.[3]

Thommo, of course, was destined to play more Test cricket, but he had to endure a little more pain than an injured foot in the wake of his ill-fated decision to play in the match. The MCG wicket was rock-hard, flat, a heart-breaking surface for any type of bowler. I doubt you could have made a mark on it with an exploding hand-grenade. Ian Chappell's men batted first and Chappelli declared with just 5 men out for 441. Ian Redpath led the way with 135 and Greg Chappell hit a majestic, unconquered 116. Walking on to the MCG from the confines of the air-conditioned dressing-room was akin to going from a cool-room into a sauna bath. The MCG was a teeming cauldron of thousands of sweltering fans watching intently under a blazing sun as Dennis Lillee took the new ball. His opening partner, Jeff Thomson, bowled the second over. He lacked pace as well as direction and all of us out there in the middle put that down to first Test-match jitters. I sensed there was something wrong with Thommo for he seemed to be, as they say in Australian Rules Football parlance, 'favouring' a leg.

We didn't learn the truth of the matter until days after his 17 fruitless overs in the Pakistan first innings in which he conceded exactly 100 runs. Thommo recalls:

> *I just couldn't bowl properly. I kept falling away to the left and the ball went immediately to the right. It was a dead wicket too. Six centuries were scored on it—four by Australia and two by Pakistan. I took none*

*for 100. I bowled one session pretty well, but then the foot just gave out
on me.I couldn't even walk back to the Hotel Windsor from the ground
after play ended for the day.*

Amazingly, Australia still won the Test match by 92 runs—and that was
after declaring their first innings closed at 8/574. Lillee took 1/90 off
16.6 overs, I took 3/124 off 38 overs and Max Walker, also making his
debut Test, took 2/112 off 24 overs.

On day four Paul Sheahan, who had announced that he would not
be available to tour the West Indies later that month, scored a brilliant
127 in what turned out to be his last Test knock. The Test selectors had
already announced their team for the Third Test against Pakistan in
Sydney. Sheahan and I were dropped from the Third Test not due to
lack of form (Sheahan had scores of 44 in the Adelaide match and 23
and 127 in Melbourne, and I had taken 13 wickets in the first two Tests)
but because we had both made ourselves unavailable for the tour of
the Caribbean, neither of us was considered for the next Test against
Pakistan. Even news of Thommo's injured foot did not save him from
the selectors' axe. He was dropped, along with John Benaud, who hit a
brilliant 142. On the very day news broke that Benaud had been dumped
for the final Test, he brought up his maiden Test century with a straight
six over the sight-board off leg-spinner Intikhab Alam. He raised his
bat to the crowd and gave a Churchillian-style two-finger salute in the
direction of the Test selectors sitting in the stand. While he missed
the third Test, Benaud was sensibly reinstated with his selection in the
touring team to the West Indies.

On the last day Pakistan needed only 292 runs to win the match, but
as the day wore on they became embroiled in a tense struggle to survive.
The visitors collapsed for 200, thanks to some tight bowling and good
fielding. Walker starred with the ball, taking 3/39 to take his match figures
to 5/151, a fine debut for any bowler on that deadest of dead tracks. The
Melbourne Sun's headline, emblazoned in bold 96-point letters across
the back page, read, 'Panikstan'.

For the disconsolate Jeff Thomson the Test match was a disaster. He
had bowled only 2 overs in Pakistan's second innings, taking 0/10; a match
analysis of 19 overs, one maiden, none for 110.

Back in Sydney I got my left foot X-rayed and the doctor told me there was a broken bone. He said, 'The only way you can fix it up, Thommo, is to rest it. You can't play cricket for the rest of the season.'

The *Sydney Morning Herald* of 17 January 1973, blurted out the headline: 'Thomson hurt, out of cricket':

Opening bowler Jeff Thomson has a split bone in his foot and has been advised not to play cricket again this season.

He was not considered for the State Sheffield Shield team to play Queensland at the SCG from January 26. Thomson's injury and the return to first-class cricket by Dave Colley were the highlights of a 'surprise' side announced by the selectors last night. Thomson's Bankstown-Canterbury Club secretary, Mr Tony Radanovic, discussed the injury with State selector Mr Jack Chegwyn on Sunday.

They thought it best that Thomson step down for the rest of the Sydney grade season.

Thomson will decide whether to undergo surgery. An operation would put him out of the game for a year. Thomson injured the foot last season and has apparently been unconsciously carrying a further complication. NSWCA doctors examined Thomson during the weekend and found a split bone in the instep of his left foot. The foot was badly swollen at the base of the big toe.[4]

However, the newspaper's head cricket writer, Phil Wilkins, gleaned more information when he dug a little deeper into the episode:

It may have puzzled a number of people why NSW's Test speedster Jeff Thomson delivered so few bouncers this season, despite his openly hostile attitude to batsmen. It is a puzzle no longer. The foot injury which has forced Thomson out of cricket for the remainder of the season prevented him from slamming the foot down in his delivery stride. Thomson suffered the cracked bone near the ball of his left foot last FEBRUARY but because he wanted to break Bankstown club's wicket record of 48 in a season he said nothing.

Thomson went on to capture 52 wickets despite the painful injury and then won Test selection after five Shield matches this summer. Apparently the bone has calcified, leaving a protuberance. Thomson's foot was so sore after the Melbourne Test he could barely walk for a week. A talk with a Macquarie Street surgeon in the next few days should clarify the situation whether an operation will solve the problem.

Thomson has been warned off all sport for the winter but four weeks in plaster now would be preferable to a belated operation at the height of the next summer.[5]

Thommo had a frustrating winter of 1973. He was forced to rest up, but lounging about doing nothing never did sit well with him. He resolved to make amends for his performance in his first Test match. Typically, he never found an excuse for his poor form.

Okay, so next summer I was ready to make up for it. After my foot healed I trained and built myself up. I'd show 'em what I could do, because I had let a lot of people down—or at least I had let myself down. Now I went to Sheffield Shield training and I was bowling quick, beautifully, you name it, bowling everyone out. But the day the first NSW side was picked [at the start of the 1973–74 season] Kerry O'Keeffe came up to me and said, 'Bad luck, Thommo'.

I said, 'What?'

And he replied, 'Don't you know?'

'Know what?'

'Oh. It doesn't matter . . .'

The selectors weren't big enough to come up to me and tell me I was dropped. My last game was a Test match. I was good enough to play for Australia then. I'd been told by the medics to rest. Now I didn't even make the Shield side. That was a grand how'd ya do!

The NSW selectors had given the young fast bowler a reason to become very angry indeed. When Thommo was in a good mood he was always quick enough for any batsman. An annoyed Jeff Thomson was something else. Thommo's Sydney grade cricket opponents soon found themselves looking down the barrel of a fired-up Thommo at his furious best.

> *I went home from the SCG that night as disappointed as hell. And when I cooled down, I thought, 'Right, that's it. Now it's on for young and old.' And that season there were arms and legs and stumps flying in all directions. I hurled myself down in fury. Blokes just didn't want to face me.*

That was the summer David Lord's Mosman team copped Thommo in full flight; blokes were battered and sent to hospital; there was the spectacle of Barry Knight trying to brain Thommo when he chucked a ball at his head from fifteen paces, and Thommo's batting partner Lennie Pascoe chasing Knight about the ground trying to scone him with his cricket bat. Lord recalls:

> Facing Thommo at any time was a frightening experience for any batsman. That year, however, he was quicker and meaner than ever before.[6]

Lord believes the grade cricket in the 1970s was far superior to what it is today:

> In those days we played against the Test players and the State men turned out regularly for their clubs. Today in Australia, State cricket is like club cricket and today's club cricket is like the park cricket of old.[7]

Mosman and NSW all-round David Colley, who played three Test matches on Ian Chappell's Australian tour of England in 1972, remembers playing against Jeff Thomson in the Poideven Gray Shield Under-21s:

> Thommo . . . mmm . . . thin, long-haired lout, with a rather strange action. One day I was batting number four and cruising along towards 70 when this lean fellow with the funny action, who had seemed so disinterested before, suddenly produced two balls from nowhere—they were terrifyingly quick. The second such thunderbolt knocked out my middle 'dolly'. I departed somewhat

bemused, but that scruffy individual certainly had my undivided attention from that moment on.

Thommo's bowling had an underlying theme with me—total and utter fear![8]

Colley had more to consider than his Mosman team-mates because Thommo saw him as a man to be removed for he was one of the bowlers keeping him out of the NSW Sheffield Shield team. According to Thommo, he had something to prove to the selectors:

Mosman's Greg Bush wasn't the only fella I sent to hospital. I had taken some 45 wickets that year and I figured that the State selectors could no longer ignore my efforts.

There had been rumours that Jeff Thomson was a chance to go to Adelaide, given that SA didn't have a bowler of genuine pace. A story appeared in the *Sunday Mirror* in January, 1974:

THOMSON MAY TRY HIS LUCK SOUTH
Former Test fast bowler Jeff Thomson, who helped Bankstown to an exciting four-run victory over Petersham at Marrickville Oval yesterday, could be playing his last season in Sydney.

Thomson has been unable to force his way back into the NSW side this season and will probably try his luck with South Australia.

'It looks more than a 50–50 chance that I will be leaving for South Australia next season,' Thomson said.

'There just does not seem any way I can get into the NSW side.'

Thomson, despite nursing a slight thigh muscle injury, bowled well to take 3/21 off nine overs and [Len] Pascoe 4/56 off 13 overs.[9]

Cricket writer Norman Tasker had long championed a campaign for a return to State cricket for Jeff Thomson. Heralding a return for Thommo, he wrote in *The Sun*:

A seemingly certain inclusion for the game against Queensland, at least, is the 1972–73 Test bowler Jeff Thomson, who has been terrifying grade batsmen with his blistering pace. Thomson is gathering an awesome reputation among grade players as the fastest in the land, and it is no secret South Australia are keen to see him in their ranks next season.[10]

Through the sheer weight of Thommo's on-field performances and public opinion, the NSW selectors simply had to give the Bankstown fast man another chance on the first-class stage.

Thommo was belatedly picked for NSW's final game of the summer, against Queensland at the SCG.

A few weeks before that belated recall to the State side, Mosman batsman David Lord had sounded Thommo out about a possible move interstate. Lord arranged for Thommo to meet with business executives from Brisbane. Despite the State recall, Thommo was still keen to further his cricket elsewhere.

But first, he would show the cricket world just how fast and how well he could bowl. Instinctively he wanted to prove himself to all and sundry, especially the selectors who didn't have the faith in him to pick him early in the summer.

It was not the best of fortune for the visitors, for Thommo was in his most hostile frame of mind when he happened to be selected for the very game Queensland so desperately wanted to win outright to claim the Sheffield Shield trophy for the first time in its history. NSW wasn't in the hunt for the trophy, so they had a nothing-to-lose attitude when they went into the game.

Queensland captain Greg Chappell won the toss and sent NSW in to bat first. He was pleased that his bowlers managed to bowl NSW out for a moderate 249; Marshall Rosen getting 94, Tony Dell 3/49 and leg-spinner Malcolm Franke bowled immaculately to return the fine figures of 5/81. Thommo was left stranded on 0 not out; the calm before the storm, or perhaps more fittingly the hurricane that was Jeff Thomson.

He had the old hands at the SCG harking back to the days of Harold Larwood, then Frank Tyson and more latterly, the big West Indian Wesley Hall. Thommo's pace startled everyone, not least the Queensland batsmen. NSW wicket-keeper Brian Taber couldn't believe how far back he had to stand to take the Thommo deliveries. In his career, Taber had kept to Graham McKenzie in Tests and Dennis Lillee at full tilt in England in 1972. He stood much further back to Thommo than any other bowler.

Thommo scythed through the Queensland batsmen like a hot knife in a cake of butter, taking 7/85 off 20.5 explosive overs. Thommo got the prized wicket of Greg Chappell, but he also won Chappell's admiration and his pace and fire prompted the Queensland captain to say to his deputy, John McLean, that he wanted Thommo in Brisbane because it was better to have Thommo in their team than to have to face him.

Thommo dismissed Sam Trimble with a steep delivery which took the seasoned opener by surprise. The ball reared alarmingly and Trimble took evasive action only to knock the ball on to his leg stump.

Greg Chappell looked in imperious form until he touched a Thommo fireball down the leg side and Taber completed a neat catch.

In his last big match, the MCG Test in December, 1972, Thommo struggled to come to terms with a broken foot and the superb batting of Majid Khan on a perfect batting strip. Majid was facing a much tougher Jeff Thomson this day. Thommo was fit and bowling like the wind. The SCG wicket had some life to encourage the fast men and Queensland were up against it. Twice Thommo sent balls whizzing past Majid's outside edge and the third ball the batsman flashed at recklessly, sending the ball hurtling over third slip and into the third man boundary fence.

Despite giving Majid a torrid time of it at the crease, Thommo didn't get his man. Kerry O'Keeffe had Majid caught by Gary Gilmour at backward square as the Pakistani swept lamely at a wide delivery down leg-side, succeeding only to produce an easy, top-edged chance.

Majid's fall was much an aside, for all eyes were on Thommo and his lethal speed. His pace was an irresistible and compelling magnet for the sea of delighted SCG patrons.

Thommo bowled 20.5 overs of the most amazing pace, taking 7/85, to skittle the much-vaunted Queensland batting line up for 205.

Under the headline, 'Thomson, 7–85, Shatters Q'LD Shield hopes', Phil Wilkins wrote:

Understandably, after Gary Gilmour's neat, low catch of Bill Albury, there were comparisons being made of the speed of Thomson and

Dennis Lillee. It is a hard argument to settle but Thomson's bowling seemed to me the fastest I have seen since Lillee put the World XI to flight in Perth in the second International in 1971–72. Lillee took 8/29 on that extraordinary occasion and some of Queensland's swaying batsmen, flashing and waving outside the off-stump, reminded me of the World XI's shell-shocked players.

It is not difficult to imagine both Lillee and Thomson playing vital roles in the Test series against England next summer in Australia when Australia will attempt to wrest the Ashes from the tourists.

Lillee is quietly preparing for his own comeback after the stress fracture in his back suffered in the West Indies last year. Thomson, 23, was making his first appearance for NSW in a first-class match since last summer.[11]

NSW skipper Doug Walters said:

Jeff turned in the best fast bowling we've seen this summer. Those deliveries he really lets fly must travel at 100 miles an hour.[12]

And the Queensland captain Greg Chappell admitted that he had not seen any bowler as fast as Thomson in this match.

Thommo also won plaudits from Bill O'Reilly, that tough, old campaigner who wrote a regular column for the *Sydney Morning Herald*, the *Sun-Herald* and its interstate stablemates, *The Age*, and *The Sunday Age* in Melbourne:

BOOST TO OUR CRICKET STOCKS
In one of the most spectacular comeback performances any bowler could wish for, young fast bowler Jeff Thomson raised Australian cricket stocks enormously at the SCG yesterday.

Had he been given the chance to show this form earlier in this first-class season, Thomson would have played in the three recent Tests in NZ.

Since his Melbourne Test against Pakistan when he performed disappointingly, Thomson has managed to change his whole attitude to his tough job.

Foremost among the change is his obvious zest for it.

It is easy enough, I suppose, to be enthusiastic when the day is cool, the wind encouraging and the wicket slightly responsive— just as things were yesterday. But other quite obvious changes emphasised the startling fact that the young Bankstown speedster had really and truly been doing his homework.

His direction was almost faultless, and his knowledgeable use of his blistering bouncer were infallible signs that the young man has matured fully in the past twelve months.

At this moment I unhesitatingly class him as the most lethal fast bowler in Australian cricket. I think he is unlucky not to be in the Australian side right now. But he may be assured that yesterday's performance has presented him with a green light passage straight into the all-important series with England next season. If he does not then develop into a punishing bowler of the John Snow type I shall be wrong and deeply disappointed.

Bowling to [John] McLean yesterday he gave a clear indication that he knows the telling advantage to be taken from the surprise element in speed, a feature upon which Snow relied heavily.

Thomson bowled so consistently yesterday that even a Doubting Thomas would be convinced that this was no flash in the pan.[13]

Greg Chappell, hurt that Queensland were again denied the Sheffield Shield, was keen to talk to Thommo. Chappell says:

There was a big statement from Thommo in the newspaper that the match against Queensland would be his last for NSW.

Then he bowled faster than anyone I'd seen. His performance prevented Queensland winning the Shield. I think we only needed first innings points. Over a couple of beers in the dressing-room, I asked Thommo if he was interested in moving to Queensland.

'Are you serious,' he said. 'I'll go anywhere.'

I rushed upstairs to the executive suite above the SCG dressing-rooms and spoke to QCA official Norm McMahon, who had connections with Toombul Cricket Club. I told Norm that I had spoken with Thommo and 'We've got to get him to Brisbane. I don't ever want to face him again.'[14]

A few weeks after his brilliant 7/85 against Queensland, Thommo was offered a job in Brisbane, with a view to playing regular Sheffield Shield cricket for the Queensland team.

While Thommo planned his move to the northern State, Ian Chappell had to make-do on a brief three-Test tour of New Zealand with three medium paced bowlers—Gary Gilmour, Max Walker and Geoff Dymock. He lamented the fact that Dennis Lillee was still sidelined with his back injury and a Victorian fast bowler, Alan Hurst, a man Chappelli specifically asked the selectors to include in his Australian squad, was not picked.

Back in Perth Lillee was nearing a full recovery and had begun on the long road back to fitness.

In Sydney and in the wake of all the frustration of non-selection and injury, the tide had turned for Bankstown's Jeffrey Robert Thomson.

5 CYCLONE JEFFREY

Just before I left Sydney there was that big article about me in a cricket magazine where I was portrayed as being a brutal killer and all that caper. Although it wasn't true that I enjoyed seeing batsmen twitching about on the ground and bleeding all over the place after I'd hit them, it probably didn't do my image any harm.

In February 1974, cricket fans in Brisbane got a taste of things to come; more than a hint of the young NSW fast bowler who would take Brisbane by storm. Tornado Thommo played in a charity knockout match. Queensland University was to play Valleys in an invitation one-day match. University planned to bolster their ranks with SA leg-spinner Terry Jenner and Balmain all-rounder Robert Wilkinson. Valleys included former Australian great all-rounders Alan Davidson and Richie Benaud, both then in their mid-40s. Wilkinson dropped out of the Queensland University team and he was replaced by Thommo. It was only a few days since Thommo blitzed Queensland at the SCG in what was destined to be his final match for NSW. Benaud had marvelled at Thommo's pace in that match and upon hearing the news that Jeff Thomson would be playing in the charity match and on the opposing side, he immediately rang Davidson:

'Davo, I'll tell you the good news first. Wilkinson's not playing. Now the bad news. They've got Jeff Thomson.'[1]

At a function to open Barry Knight's restaurant above his Kent Street, Sydney, sports complex, Mrs Daphne Benaud, put in a good word for her husband Richie and his mate, Alan Davidson:

'Now, Jeff. Remember they [Richie and Alan] are old gentlemen— you've got to be gentle.'[2]

Former Queensland wicket-keeper Lew Cooper led the university team. The university captain asked Jenner to go to the gully and as Thommo was about to start his approach, Lew was astonished to find that Jenner was standing at a very deep gully, some 20 yards from the bat:

'Terry, you are far too deep, come up a lot closer.'
'Lew, do you know how quick this bloke bowls?'[3]

Cooper wasn't alone in discovering Thommo's unbelievable pace. That day he bowled quick alright, but Benaud and Davidson survived the ordeal. No-one got hit by Thommo, but those who watched the fast man knew that a new speed phenomenon had emerged. Within a few months Davidson was lauding Thommo as the fastest bowler of all time, some accolade from a man who batted against Frank 'Typhoon' Tyson, the balding Englishman who won the Ashes for Len Hutton's 1954–55 team Down Under, and Wes Hall the fearsome opening bowler for Frank Worrell's outstanding West Indian team, at his peak in 1960–61.

Early in July 1974, an article by David Falkenmire appeared in a Brisbane daily newspaper. On the back of Thommo having had talks with the Queensland Cricket Association, Falkenmire wrote that he had been offered a job with the Sharp Corporation:

. . . and the outcome of talks with the company's manager, Mr D Hayes, will virtually decide whether he comes to Brisbane.
'I think we can fix him up with a job and I hope Queensland cricket benefits,' Mr Hayes said.

Thomson could not be contacted at his Bankstown home last night, but his mother answered the telephone.

'Jeff is keen to go to Brisbane, but is waiting for word of a job,' Mrs Doreen Thomson said.[4]

But the job offer that would count did not come from the Sharp Corporation. A job was promised, but the big contract with 4IP was more than a year away. Thommo needed work, for apart from the fact that he would always reject going on the dole, he needed to keep himself active away from cricket.

Even when he left the Commonwealth Bank and then Monier Concrete, Thommo did not register for unemployment relief. He always possessed a strong work ethic, and never considered accepting a government handout while he was between jobs.

Late in the summer I had no job, but I was deadly serious about my bowling and I was dead keen to get back into big cricket. I think that's why I really went berserk in grade cricket that summer and then they gave me that final Shield game against Queensland.

Earlier in the winter a concrete job offer did find its way to Thommo from the northern state. Former Toombul and State player Errold La Frantz owned the Whatmore Sports Store in Brisbane. La Frantz recalls:

NSW batsman Tony Steele was an agent for the cricket bat manufacturer, Gray-Nicholls, and he was in my store looking at a bat order. We were talking cricket and he told me that Jeff Thomson wouldn't play for NSW again. He was apparently going to Western Australia.

I then asked Tony if Thommo would consider a move to Brisbane if he could be offered a job. And Tony said that he probably would. So I rang Thommo and he indicated that he would be interested in coming to Brisbane, playing for Toombul and for Queensland, so long as he could be guaranteed a job. Mind you he took a long time to make up his mind. I rang a few times a week for a month, before he confirmed his decision to make the move.[5]

A Queensland State selector from 1953–1968, Errold La Frantz played representative cricket for Queensland in 1941 and, having played for Toombul 1931–54, he was a life member of the club. La Frantz organised Thommo a job with Austral Motors:

> Austral Motors was a large company, dealing with the sale of high-priced cars. Managing Director Doug Collier was a guy who loved his cricket. He was a personal friend and he readily agreed to give Thommo a job. Thommo didn't have to sell cars, just meet people on the floor. For this he was paid an attractive salary and given a new car for his personal use. He was given time off work to play cricket on full pay.[6]

It was July 1974 when Thommo boarded the plane bound for Brisbane. He looked mournfully out of the window of the jet. He was saying goodbye to everything in his beloved Sydney, his family, Maroubra and the other Sydney beaches where Thommo and his great mate Lennie Pascoe used to chat up the girls before grade matches, his mates at Bankstown Cricket Club, the NSW team and the State selectors who did him no favours.

> *It was a lonely feeling. It was a big step for me because I'd never been away from home before, or hardly ever. I remember looking out of the window of the plane and thought, 'Hell, but I've got to do it!'*
>
> *I started work in Brisbane as a car salesman. I sold a few but it wasn't really a go. I used to spend heaps of time at the Gabba training, bowling to Sam Trimble. Eventually I had to give the job away, because I had it in my mind that I was going to absolutely slay 'em. There were no two ways about it, I was set to fire.*
>
> *There were lots of things promised—they were going to give me this, going to give me that. It all turned out to be bullshit. As it turned out I began work in Brisbane as a bloody car salesman.*

A few weeks after Thommo moved to Brisbane, his NSW team-mate, youngster Ian Davis, nicknamed 'The Wizard', was sounded out by the Queenslanders. So too was yours truly. Curiously, at the same time I received a job offer from the Brisbane City Council. The job offer was pretty good for an aspiring journalist like me, for it meant my being the Brisbane Lord Mayor's press secretary. The Lord Mayor of Brisbane, Clem Jones, wielded a lot of power. He was big in political circles and he had great influence in Queensland cricket. Becoming Clem Jones's press secretary was an infinitely better employment proposition than working for Messenger Newspapers, a local throw-over-the-fence weekly newspaper in suburban Adelaide.

Twelve months earlier, just before Greg Chappell left Adelaide in 1973, he spoke with State selector Sir Donald Bradman and co-selector Phil Ridings over lunch at the Adelaide Stock Exchange. According to Chappell, Bradman advised him not to venture to Brisbane and told him that Queensland cricket was in a bad state. But Chappell decided to move from his home state.

I also sought Sir Donald Bradman's counsel about my Queensland offer and he told me in no uncertain terms how futile it would be for me to move to Brisbane:

Ashley, the SACA cannot prevent you from leaving Adelaide to go and work and play cricket in Brisbane, but I would strongly advise you to stay in SA. This State gave you your chance in big cricket, you have established yourself in the State team and your wife's family are all here. And, I am duty bound to say, Clem Jones is not a man to be trusted.[7]

Brisbane Lord Mayor Alderman Clem Jones was, in fact, a staunch Labor man, so Bradman, a strongly committed conservative, was politically and ideologically opposed to him.

Alderman Jones was a man of many parts. Curiously, the Brisbane Lord Mayor was also the curator of the Brisbane Cricket Ground. So when he wasn't preparing the famous Gabba wicket, Clem Jones was laying down the law in the chambers of the city council. When Thommo first played for NSW at the Gabba, his State captain, John Benaud, had a brief altercation with Jones over the condition of the pitch. Jones seemed to have a penchant for rolling mud into the surface of the track and declaring alternative methods as unsatisfactory. He seemed somewhat of a tyrant, yet he was also compassionate and a good organiser. Clem Jones was the Brisbane Lord Mayor from 1961 to 1975 and while he presided over Brisbane, it grew from something like a sleepy country town to a vibrant sub-tropical city. During his tenure he mixed his Lord Mayoral duties with rolling the Gabba wicket and he often turned up at the ground in his suit and tie. He discarded his suit coat, rolled up his sleeves and got to work. A hands-on role was Jones's way in public life and he gained universal acclaim when he chaired the Darwin Reconstruction Commission following the destruction of that city when Cyclone Tracey hit on Christmas Eve, 1974.

My wife Christine and I talked it over and we decided to stay in Adelaide. I doubt if the South Australian Cricket Association would have made a counter offer if I had decided to go to Brisbane because that was not their way at the time. Bradman ruled the roost and despite his own efforts to build a good income from the game during his playing days, he appeared to act as if any money from the Association or the Australian Cricket Board was his own and he zealously guarded any outlay of funds. Whether he was the chairman or not, Bradman seemed to lead SACA and the ACB during his long administrative years. Bradman's fellow committee members had him so high on a pedestal his head was forever stuck in the clouds.

It seemed to me that Queensland was all about building a Sheffield Shield trophy winning side and they were not shy in asking players from other States to join them. Thommo's blitz at the SCG denied Queensland the winning of their first Shield trophy and Greg Chappell was hell-bent upon having Thommo in his State team. Thommo's situation in his home State was vastly different to Greg Chappell moving to Brisbane, for Greg was an automatic pick for his State team and he was going to Queensland to get some captaincy experience. Incumbent skipper John MacLean offered to stand down from the Queensland captaincy to allow Greg to take over the team, paving the way for him to one day take over from brother Ian as the Australian Test captain.

Thommo had been ignored by the NSW selectors and was belatedly picked for the last match of the season. Despite his magnificent bowling against Queensland in that match and the likelihood that all was forgiven and the selectors would consider him an automatic pick for

NSW, Thommo had made up his mind. He yearned to prove his mettle and as much as he would miss his family and friends and the lifestyle in Sydney, the Brisbane move was something he instinctively knew he had to do.

Just before I left Sydney there was that big article about me in a cricket magazine where I was portrayed as a brutal killer and all that caper. Although it wasn't true that I enjoyed seeing batsmen twitching on the ground and bleeding all over the place after I'd hit them, it probably didn't do my image any harm. Blokes who'd played against me knew what I was like and the Poms were soon to find out.

In his first grade match for Toombul, Thommo bowled erratically, taking two expensive wickets against University. Unbeknown to many, Lennie Pascoe had ventured north to join his mate in Brisbane. Lennie had been disillusioned playing for Bankstown, getting wickets but having to be content to play representative cricket of a standard no higher than NSW Colts. He decided to go to Brisbane in the lead-up to the 1974–75 summer. Lennie had heard that there was every chance Tony Dell, the burly Queensland left-hand opening bowler, was about to announce his retirement from big cricket. Understandably Lennie was excited. Here was the chance for him to bowl in tandem with Thommo on the big stage for Queensland. It would be like the old days at Bankstown when the pace pair terrorised all opposition. Despite Queensland having some good fast bowlers in Geoff Dymock and Dennis Schuller, and with Thommo about to play for the Shield side, Pascoe possessed an unshakeable belief in his ability to perform at the highest level.

Lennie had followed Thommo through thick and thin, even volunteering a few months earlier to be the 'catcher' in an egg-throwing competion in Sydney. The thrown egg had to be taken cleanly for the throw to be measured and perhaps ending up in the *Guinness Book of Records*. Thommo hurled some 65 eggs, most of which covered a distance beyond 400 feet; however, the only one Lennie caught intact was a throw measuring 269 feet. By that time Lennie Pascoe was covered in egg and he looked like unmade oeufs Florentine.

But while the odds were that Thommo was a certainty to join Dell and Geoff Dymock in the Queensland team, Lennie's future was less certain. Thommo recalls:

Lennie talked me into shifting house, to a place nearer the city. Later we realised the place, which was a lot smaller than the house I had, was situated in Fortitude Valley, smack in the heart of the Brisbane's red light area. You couldn't swing a cat in the place, but Lennie reckoned he was low on cash, no job, and with Tony Dell staying on to play again he didn't think he'd get a go for the Queensland State side. All through our careers I seemed to get a go ahead of Lennie. That was always the case, going right back to our school days. I'd get picked and he wouldn't, then he'd catch up.

Errold La Frantz has a chuckle these days when he thinks of the first game Thommo and Lennie played for Toombul:

It was hot and the wicket was flat and both of our new fast bowlers copped a bit of a belting. University scored 425, Thommo got a couple of wickets for plenty and Lennie was hammered. In fact, he didn't front up for the next Saturday of the match. He'd gone back to Sydney.[8]

After his first unsuccessful stint at the bowling crease against University, Thommo soon made amends. Against Greg Chappell's highly rated Souths, Thommo excelled. The *Courier Mail*'s Jack Reardon wrote of Thommo's claim to a Sheffield Shield spot:

Thomson captured 6/75 for Toombul against Souths at Fehlberg Park. Thomson, whose victims included Test bat and Shield captain Greg Chappell (6), was watched by another selector Peter Burge.[9]

Thommo's sustained paced over 17 overs impressed everyone at the game, especially State captain Greg Chappell.

A few days after Thommo's stirring 6/75 against South's, all eyes were on the NSW import in a State trial at the Gabba. But in the wake of an indifferent performance in that game he copped a blast in the local newspaper from former Queensland and Australian all-rounder Tom Vievers:

THOMSON'S TRIAL FORM NOT UP TO STANDARD
Sheffield Shield prospect Jeff Thomson showed little of his expected fire in the State Trial match at the 'Gabba yesterday.

It was a disappointing effort by the former Test speedster on the eve of the first Shield match against NSW this week. Admittedly the wicket provided him with little or no hope but there seemed no 'zip' in his bowling. Both Thomson and Dennis Schuller found the going hard. Thomson, in particular, was very erratic and will need to lift his game against NSW next week if he is to live up to the reputation that preceded him to Brisbane.[10]

A few days before Thommo's Queensland Sheffield Shield debut, he flew to Sydney to visit his family. He also turned out to bowl at practice with his old Bankstown club. Cricket writer Norman Tasker wrote of Thommo's bowling:

His former NSW teammates could draw cold comfort from the recommendation of Bankstown captain Dion Bourne.

'Thommo bowled two hours non-stop and without doubt he has built pace even on last year.

'He is fitter and seemingly keener. I did not think it possible that he could bowl any quicker than he did with us, but he is. He is quite frightening. Our batsmen could not really lay a bat on him. Fortunately, he kept the ball well up, otherwise he would have been a real danger.'[11]

However, Thommo wasn't a sure-thing to play in the minds of two State selectors—former Test players Peter Burge and Ken Mackay. Both men, stalwarts of some of Richie Benaud's best Test elevens, were impressed with Thommo's speed, but they had reservations about Thommo's accuracy. How could they pick a bloke who bowled them all over the shop? State captain Greg Chappell was adamant, though, about Thommo. He wanted him in his team and he was the one bowler Chappell demanded play against NSW. Chappell said:

> I don't care if 'Thommo' hasn't a clue where they are going, he'll frighten these blokes out. They'll be so desperate to get down the other end they'll run themselves out.[12]

Messrs Burge and Mackay were also worried about how the keeper, John MacLean, would cope with Thommo spraying the ball at high pace. But Chappell assured them that MacLean would handle the situation.

Greg knew, as most first-class cricketers in Australia at that time knew, that MacLean was not dissimilar to Rodney Marsh, not the most stylish of glovemen but mighty effective and he rarely missed anything. MacLean proved a fabulous ally for Chappell. He stood down from the State captaincy to allow Greg to take over in 1973, and his splendid keeping, stout batting and wise counsel helped bring Queensland to the brink of winning the Sheffield Shield for the first time since the State entered the competition in the summer of 1926–27. MacLean was as talented and as tough as the incumbent Test keeper Rodney Marsh. The WA-based keeper was more agile standing back to the fast bowlers, but MacLean did have the edge on Marsh when standing over the stumps to the spinners.

Thommo was hell-bent upon turning on an explosive performance to impress all and sundry with his immense speed. There was an instinctive need for him to dominate and ensure that he became a fixture in the Queensland team.

On the day of Thommo's Queensland debut, an article, by Howard Rich, appeared in a Sydney newspaper:

FIERY THOMSON SHIELD THREAT
Tear-away fast bowler Jeff Thomson is the player NSW will fear most in the Sheffield Shield match against Brisbane which starts in Brisbane today.

Thomson, 24, is said to be bowling faster than at any stage in his career. And that spells danger for NSW. Thomson, who forms a formidable pace trio with Tony Dell and Geoff Dymock will be under close scrutiny from test selector Neil Harvey. Success in this match would bolster his chances against England. So NSW batsmen can expect plenty of 'treatment' from Thomson in his first game for Queensland.[13]

Thommo was, by far, the quickest bowler about, but he knew he had to perform to maintain a regular place in the side. NSW skipper Doug Walters won the toss and decided to bat first. Thommo drew early blood getting Alan Turner (7) and Rick McCosker (1) to have NSW reeling at 2/28. Dell got the wicket of Ian Davis (10) and Dymock removed Walters (10). Marshall Rosen (91) batted bravely to top-score in his side's paltry 222. Thommo bowled 13 overs of extraordinary pace to take 4/65. He was expensive in terms of runs per over, but he cut a swathe through the batting line-up and struck fear in the hearts of the batsmen. Queensland replied with 277, with debutant right-hander Martin Kent scoring a maiden century and going on to hit a superb 140. Kent's team-mates were soon calling him 'Super' and Super remembers Thommo in that first hectic summer in Brisbane:

I played only one club game against Thommo. He was with Toombul and I played for Sandgate-Redcliff. Harry Frei was up one end and Thommo the other. I was giving Harry a bit of a touch-up, then I faced Thommo. I tried to hook one, it took the top edge and flew high past the keeper for six. It was a flat wicket.

Boy was he quick. The hardest thing about him was his cartwheel action. You didn't see the ball until the last split-second. He was a shade quicker than Andy Roberts at his absolute quickest. Batting against him in the nets was a bloody nightmare. All the quicks were off about 16 yards, but Thommo was quick enough for anyone from 22 yards. I remember him for his extreme pace and turning up at training in a Beige Dino Ferrari, talk about life in the fast lane.[14]

Thommo didn't open the bowling in the NSW second dig because he was laid low with sunstroke.

It was a pretty warm day that first day and I came off the field feeling a bit daggy, a bit funny in the stomach. I was also more tired than I should have been after having not bowled a helluva lot of overs. They called in a doctor and he had me rushed off to hospital and they diagnosed it as sunstroke. I was released from hospital and I spent the night at Greg and Judy Chappell's place. I wasn't going too well. I couldn't move. I sat down and I couldn't move my neck or anything. Luckily it passed, but after that I often wore a hat when the tropical sun got a bit too much.

Tony Dell and Geoff Dymock opened the bowling and they both got among the wickets; Dell 3/26 and Dymock 2/47. Thommo bowled only 4 overs, but he again unleashed his mighty speed to take 2/7, including a steaming yorker to skittle Doug Walters's stumps. It was Thommo's famous 'sandshoe crusher' as the Englishmen were soon to discover.

Senior cricket writer Jim Woodward of the *Daily Telegraph* wrote of Thommo's devastating spell of just 4 overs in the NSW second innings:

The former New South Welshman took the ball for the first time in the second innings yesterday after being laid up on Saturday with sunstroke. In four deliveries the erratic 24-year-old had NSW's Test batsmen Doug Walters (2) and Ian Davis (4) back in the pavilion. Bowling at tremendous speed, Thomson moved one away from Davis who snicked an easy catch to keeper John MacLean off the sixth ball of the morning. Yet Thommo was so much astray at times that one delivery went to MacLean on the full. Walters, who came to the crease with NSW tottering at 3–61, was dropped by Malcolm Franke at cover point before scoring off the second delivery he faced. Thomson got his reward with the first ball of his next over by way of a superb Yorker which sent Walters' leg stump cart-wheeling.[15]

NSW was bundled out for 97 in their second innings and Queensland won easily by 9 wickets.

And Thommo's season was off to a flying start.

Thommo played two more matches before the First Test; taking 2/24 and 0/50 against WA at the Gabba and 1/22 off 11 overs and 1/29 off 10 overs versus MCC at the Gabba. He had bowled just 62 overs and had taken 10 wickets for 197 runs before the selectors sat down to pick the Test match squad. There might well have been raised eyebrows over Thommo's 10 no-balls in the MCC first innings and 9 no-balls in total against WA at the Gabba, but they knew that Test captain Ian Chappell dearly wanted a bowler of genuine pace. With Dennis Lillee coming back into top form after his back injury, Chappell looked forward to having two genuine pace bowlers in his attack, especially after having had to try and beat New Zealand on sluggish wickets without so much as the fast-medium bowlers in Walker, Dymock and Gary Gilmour.

Chappelli was without his champion fast bowler Dennis Lillee and before the NZ tour he had requested that the selectors pick the Victorian fast bowler Alan Hurst. Walker, Dymock and Gilmour were all quality bowlers, but none of them were fast bowlers and he wanted at least one genuine strike paceman. The Australian selectors went for the three medium-pacers and Hurst stayed at home.

However, reports of Lillee having fully recovered from his near-crippling back injury and his likely return to big cricket in 1974–75, together with the cricket player grapevine talking about the extra-ordinary pace of Jeff Thomson, gladdened Chappelli's heart. In an article in *The Australian* on Thursday, November 21, 1974, headed 'Chappell rates Thomson's speed a danger', the nation was alerted to the new speed demon:

'Against Western Australia Thomson bowled as fast as any other speedster I've seen in my career,' Queensland cricket captain Greg Chappell said.

'He was very quick through the air. He was hitting the bat and the gloves hard and he hit a couple of players as well.'

Chappell said comparison between Thomson and Dennis Lillee was difficult because Thomson has a slinging action and Lillee a more conventional action which caused greater bounce from the wicket.

When Lillee was used downwind against Queensland in the game which ended in a draw at the Brisbane Cricket Ground on

Monday, his speed was as great as when he took his record 31 wickets
on the tour of England,' Chappell claimed.[16]

England's Test squad had been in Australia for more than a month as the
campaign for a Test recall for Jeff Thomson began to gain momentum.
The England camp was skeptical. They didn't believe all the hype about
Lillee being back to his pacy best and about this new bloke Thomson,
who couldn't possibly be as fast as people were saying. The Poms were
convinced: the Australians' unsubtle attempt to get into their minds was
psychological warfare gone balmy.

6 AMAZING PACE

> The high point of my performance was the wicket of Tony Greig in the
> second innings . . . The night before, Ian and Greg Chappell had a chat
> with me and pointed out that as he had such a high back-lift, I might
> be able to run a yorker under his bat . . . that's exactly what I did . . . My
> immediate reaction was to laugh and I did so for some time, although I
> can assure you Tony Greig wasn't too amused.

England came into the 1974–75 Ashes series without John Snow and Geoff
Boycott—its two key performers who helped Ray Illingworth's team wrest
the Ashes from Australia in 1970–71. Snow had been unceremoniously
dumped and Boycott was unavailable for the tour. However, England had
a fine pace attack, led by Peter Lever and Bob Willis and backed by Mike
Hendrick and the ebullient Tony Greig, who strutted about like a tank
commander in Rommel's Afrika Corps. Even without Boycott, the England
squad had experience and depth in the batting with Dennis Amiss, John
Edrich, Mike Denness, David Lloyd, Brian Luckhurst, Keith Fletcher, the
all-rounder Greig and the diminutive wicket-keeper-batsman Alan Knott
leading the way. But there was something of the calm before the storm in
the lead-up to the First Test.

There was the usual pre-Test banter, claim and counter-claim, but the England squad was ill-prepared for what was the come: no-one in the England party could have envisaged the savage attack which they were about to face. Thommo was desperately keen to erase the demons of his debut Test disaster. He picked up the wicket of Dennis Amiss in the England–Queensland match, but because his State captain Greg Chappell had urged him to bowl within himself in that match and 'not show the bastards anything', Thommo was hell-bent upon letting fly in the First Test.

When I was chosen to play again for Australia, I remember saying to myself, 'Hell, I've worked so hard. Between the last time I played for Australia and this time, what if it went wrong?' This thought flashed through my mind, but almost as quickly the negative thought disappeared. I was ready to go. Super fit and bowling at the fastest of my career. Sure I had bowled a few no-balls in the lead-up matches but I was confident of making my mark in this game. I had a lot to prove. It was great to be there and I was really confident this time. Against Pakistan two years before, I was raw, and I thought I was lucky to be there. This time I knew no other bloke was better than me. I didn't know any of these Pommies but I was confident I'd get them out.

November 30, 1974, was a day of reckoning for Jeffrey Robert Thomson, for in just 5 overs of blistering speed, Thommo had taken 2/5, sending the nation wild with excitement. His figures were almost inconsequential for it was the devastation of his attack which had the Poms in desperate survival mode, ducking and diving, and the nation's pulse racing. His last stint on the Test stage was a disaster. Thommo was keen on making amends. His first-innings haul of 3/59 wasn't sensational by any means, but he captured the imagination because of his terrifying speed. Time and again deliveries leapt from a good length to strike the batsmen, who could only fend off the rising balls and hope they wouldn't lob gently to provide the short-leg fieldsman with an easy catch. All batsmen were the prey. And Dennis Lillee also tore in like a man possessed. He had been out of Test cricket for more than a year and he was desperate to show his mettle on cricket's highest stage.

During a promotional tour of England Ian Chappell alerted the Poms to the likelihood of a savage battle in the coming Ashes series Down Under. Dennis Lillee would return as good as ever and he 'warned' of a new fast bowling threat when he wrote:

Maybe Lillee won't be flat out every ball as he was in England in 1972, but he springs a really fast one now and then as a shock delivery. Max Walker and Jeff Hammond will be around after injury and we have lively left-armers Gary Gilmour and Geoff Dymock as well as the new Queensland acquisition Jeff Thomson. That lot should more than match England.[1]

The England squad was unconvinced that Lillee could return as strong as ever after his back injury. They had watched him bowl in the SA–WA Sheffield Shield match in Adelaide a few weeks before the Brisbane Test and they believed that Lillee was only a shadow of his former self.

Some, including the left-hand opening batsman, David Lloyd, thought the press had somehow got the name wrong and that the Thomson they were writing about was none other than the gangly Alan 'Froggy' Thompson, who came into Test cricket for four matches against Illingworth's Ashes-winning side in 1970–71. The English squad had read that Thommo liked to see blood on the pitch and a batsman squirming about after being hit by him, but they took little heed of the reports.

During the build-up to the series, Lillee was quoted widely about his plans for the England batsmen in the coming Ashes battle:

You have to steel yourself and whip up within yourself a feeling bordering on hatred for your opponent. I try and hit a batsman in the rib cage when I bowl a purposeful bouncer—and I want it to hurt so much that the batsman doesn't want to face me any more.[2]

How wrong could the England camp be about the champion fast bowler? Here was Lillee, fit and tanned and back to his best, paired with a man hell-bent upon bowling the fastest stuff seen on earth and proving the knockers wrong. Thommo always thrived when people said he couldn't do something or he wasn't good enough. He only had to recall the negativity of the man of quavers and crochets, his music teacher at Punchbowl High School.

There was high drama in the days leading up to the start of the game. Brisbane Lord Mayor Alderman Clem Jones had single-handedly breathed life into the Gabba pitch, which, because of heavy rain storms, was short on preparation. After one particular period of torrential rain, two days before the scheduled start of the match, the wicket was under water.

Lord Mayor Jones provided the 'miracle' which cricket writers said would be needed for the wicket to be in a reasonable state for the start of play. *The Australian* newspaper of Friday, November 29—scheduled first day of the Test match—bore the headline 'Players face a "phantom" wicket for First Test':

Alderman Jones has done a tremendous amount of work since Wednesday morning's storm flooded the ground. Where there was a drying quagmire is now a reasonably hard 36.58 metres (40 yard) strip of unevenly-textured turf from which he will cut the Test strip. Strong winds and bright sunshine have brought a remarkable transformation.

Australia's selectors Neil Harvey, Sam Loxton and Phil Ridings, arrived at the Brisbane Cricket Ground yesterday to see Ald. Jones sprinkling the pitch with a yellow watering can and scrubbing mud from the turf with a wire brush. The mud fell on the wicket during rolling on Wednesday morning and would have killed the grass if not removed.

A 10-ton roller on the wicket yesterday helped to harden the pitch and with so much grass remaining Australia's selectors will be tempted to carry out their original plan of attack and use all three pace bowlers, speedsters Dennis Lillee and Jeff Thomson and swing bowler Max Walker.[3]

Only days before the announcement of Australia's Test squad for the First Test, Thommo had made quite an impression in the Queensland–Western Australia Sheffield Shield match at the Gabba. When Ian

Chappell arrived in Brisbane to prepare for the First Test, he sought the company of his mate and drinking partner, Test wicket-keeper Rodney Marsh. Over a cold beer they discussed the make-up of the squad. Chappell recalls:

> 'What's Thommo like?' I asked Rodney.
>
> 'He is unbelievably quick,' he said, relating how Thommo had been operating on a line of about off stump and the odd one was wide of off stump, giving Rodney room to cut.
>
> 'Then he got smart. He started to bowl across my body, angling from a line of outside leg stump. Most deliveries came at my body and lifted off a very good length. Then came the death ball. The ball was heading straight for my head and it would have hit me between the eyes had it not struck the handle of my bat.'
>
> I guess after speaking with Bacchus [Marsh] I realised that Thommo was obviously something special.[4]

A robust series was in the wind for even dear old Aunty, the ABC, decided to get with it by announcing that it would provide colour telecasts of all six Australia–England Test matches. The Ashes battles brought consistently big crowds and with it truckloads of entrance money that was to fill the coffers of the Australian Cricket Board.

Australia batted first against the much-vaunted England pace attack which comprised the gangly Bob Willis, Peter Lever and Mike Hendrick, none of them express pace, although Lever was quick and aggressive, the fastest of the trio.

Then came the medium-pace of Tony Greig and the quick, left-arm cutters of Derek Underwood. Lever and Willis, keen to impose their will on Australia's batsmen, bounced the Queensland tail in the MCC match before the Test. Australia scored 309, but it was tough going for the Englishmen bowled with professional accuracy and determination. Ian Chappell top-scored with 90 and much to the Gray-Nicholls' bat-maker John Newberry's initial dismay, Chappelli chose the first day of this Ashes Test to 'trial' the revolutionary 'Scoop' bat. Newberry had hoped Chappell might use the bat in a lesser match, less the 'Scoop' shatter into little bits in full view of millions of cricket fans on TV. Valuable contributions to the respectable total came from Greg Chappell (58), Ross Edwards (32), an unbeaten 41 by Max Walker and Thommo who scored 23 before being run-out in a 52-run last wicket stand with Walker. Tony Greig bounced Lillee in the Australian innings and had him caught behind for 15, but the Australian retaliated with a few choice words along the lines of England's need to remember 'who started this', a none-too-veiled message that their batsmen might cop a few bouncers.

Fast bowlers are like elephants—long memories.

Thommo had a vivid memory of the England bowlers bouncing the Queensland tail only days before. The English had gravely miscalculated. They were keen upon launching a bouncer war, expecting Lillee to be only half the pace bowler that he was and that the speed and hostility of Thomson was just psychological hogwash emanating from the Australian camp. While Chappelli was happy enough with a score of 309, the innings had taken 499 minutes and time was the element in his strategy to set up a first-up Test win in the series.

Chappelli gave Dennis Lillee the first over. Lillee had made a successful return to big cricket, although he bowled within himself in the Sheffield Shield match against South Australia at Adelaide Oval. Would his back stand up in the more vigorous demands of the Test arena? Lillee recalls:

I had bowled within myself in the matches leading up to the Test, but I decided to bowl flat out in the big game. This, after all, was the first Test of a new Ashes series.[5]

As the first over got into full swing, Australian captain Ian Chappell weighed up his options as to which of his bowlers would share the new ball with Lillee:

I had planned to bowl Lillee downwind and to use Max Walker into the breeze. When I got to the middle and during Lillee's first over, I began to think how I might feel facing two genuine quick bowlers first up. As a batsman you are at your most uncomfortable against a bowler of genuine pace. So against two genuine pace bowlers you'd be doubly uncomfortable. So why not use both fast men together, first up? I signalled to Thommo to warm up. He didn't do a thing. There was no flexing of muscles or stretching you associate with a fast bowler. At the end of Lillee's over I threw the ball to Thommo and said, 'Good luck, mate'.[6]

The hurt and frustration of being ignored for so long by the NSW selectors manifested itself in Thommo's initial assault upon the poor, unsuspecting England batsmen. He soon had them ducking and diving in survival mode and the crowd on the edge of their seats. Thommo's sheer pace was electrifying. The youngsters loved it and the oldies recalled the pace of England's Frank Tyson and the West Indian Wes Hall, both of whom were like the tornado that was Thomson. Ian Chappell was at one with the rest of slips cordon; they all sported wide grins. Chappell says:

I watched in awe. Thomson was the fastest into-the-wind bowler I had seen. Rodney Marsh probably summed it up best. He leapt for a ball from Thommo which climbed off a length. The ball thudded into Rodney's gloves and he said, 'Hell that hurt—but I love it.'[7]

After two balls, Thommo discarded his sleeveless jumper. Brian Luckhurst almost played on to Thommo, the ball careering from the bottom edge, just missing leg stump, in that first hectic over. The fast bowler vented his frustration on the next ball, which flew at tremendous speed off a good length just outside off stump, Marsh having to reach high to take the ball and that's the one that brought forth the keeper's telling exclamation about the agony of taking his deliveries and the sheer joy of Thommo's express speed. Among the throng of press men at the match sat two who formed the greatest opening bowling partnership for Australia in the immediate post-War period: Keith Miller and Ray Lindwall. Miller was covering the match for the *London Daily Express* from within the safety of the press box and he wrote of the impact Thomson's pace and lift had on the ducking and weaving England batsmen:

He frightened me with some of his nasty, rising deliveries and I was
sitting 200 yards away.[8]

Thommo made a ball kick venomously and had Brian Luckhurst caught
by Marsh. It was Thommo's first wicket and the team gathered around
him. Instinctively, they all realised that they were seeing first-hand a
bowler at work that would be one day be recognised as the fastest Test
bowler to draw breath.

On the second day, Thommo blasted out three key English batsmen—
Dennis Amiss (7), Brian Luckhurst (1) and the tough and competitive
John Edrich (48), to pick up 3/59 off 21 overs. Max Walker bowled well to
take 4/73 off 24.5 overs and Lillee was effective without storming through
the line-up, taking 2/73 off 23 overs and the good news was that he had no
twinges of pain in his back. England scored 265.

With a lead of just 44, the Australians set about getting quick runs
so Chappelli could set England a target. They compiled 5/288 with
Greg Chappell (71), Ross Edwards (52), Doug Walters (62 not out) and
Rodney Marsh (46 not out) showing the way. England needed to score
332 runs for victory, but in the end they fell way short. On the eve of an
almost certain Australian victory, the British press was giving its own
version of events.

'Thomson is the terror', 'Thomson's Fire Burns up England', and 'How
to Stop Speed-man Thomson' were the headlines that greeted Britons
when they opened the sports pages of the nation's papers. Henry Blofeld,
writing for the *Daily Telegraph* wrote:

On a slow pitch he found tremendous speed and an unpleasant lift.
The English batsmen were shaken, but they must not panic.[9]

Thomson's incredible ability to get the ball to rear at the batsman's face
from a fulsome length even had the umpires struggling to come to terms
with this speed phenomenon. In the final couple of overs before stumps on
the fourth day of the Test, England had to negotiate a tricky little batting
session of twenty minutes against Thommo and Lillee in fading light. Phil
Wilkins reported:

Umpire Robin Bailhache spoke to Thomson after the Australian speedster had delivered only seven balls of the first over, three of which had whistled past England opener Dennis Amiss' head.

The light was poor because of the approaching storm and Australian captain Ian Chappell ran from first slip position to the umpire and Thomson, obviously annoyed at the intervention.

Thomson bowled the last ball of the over and before Dennis Lillee could begin his second over umpires Bailhache and Tom Brooks conferred about the deteriorating light for the third time and decided that play should end 19 minutes early. According to Chappell, Bailhache had told him he and Brooks were considering the light and Chappell said, 'The umpire said something about short-pitched deliveries.' Chappell responded to the umpire. 'They're not bouncers, Robin. They're just short of a length.' Chappell went on: 'He virtually told us to keep the ball up to the batsman. It was pointless being out there. In my opinion the balls were just short of a length.' Amiss, a vastly experienced opener, obviously did not agree with Chappell's assessment. Each one of the three seemed as genuine a bouncer as he would have received in his career.[10]

Thommo bowled faster—if that was possible—in the second innings, but it was his famous sandshoe crusher that accounted for the big, gangly blabber-mouth, Tony Greig, which provided the icing on the cake for the fast man, who took a magnificent 6/46 off 17.5 overs of sustained and often frightening pace bowling. Thommo says:

The high point of my performance was the wicket of Tony Greig in the second innings. After his century in the first innings he was a danger man, but also he'd been saying a few words to some of our boys on the field so I particularly wanted his wicket. The night before, Ian and Greg Chappell had a chat with me and pointed out that as he had such a high back-lift, I might be able to run a yorker under his bat. The next day that's exactly what I did. The ball hit his boot and took his leg stump. My immediate reaction was to laugh and I did so for some time, although I can assure you Tony Greig wasn't too amused.

Tall and blonde and arrogant, Greig got up the nose of the Australians. Every time he struck a four in the England first innings, Greig mocked the bowlers by signalling a four. Greig was wearing a pair of specially designed rubber-soled cricket shoes and the Australians immediately dubbed them 'sandshoes'; thus the term, 'sandshoe crusher'.

Dennis Lillee didn't dominate in terms of wickets, for he got only 2 in each innings, but Lillee bowled with fire and showed that he was back on the Test stage as a big force. He, too, was impressed with Thommo's speed:

I wasn't surprised that Thommo was rushed into the First Test to open the bowling with me at the Gabba, for in the Sheffield Shield match I played for WA against Queensland, Thommo revealed his amazing pace.

At the time I didn't realise just how quick he was, but you knew that it was extremely fast given the way the ball reared off a good length and, perhaps more enlightening, was how the batsmen reacted. In their desperate attempts to get out of the line of fire, you could see that their whole being was in survival mode.[11]

In the wake of the First Test drubbing, England found a number of players injured including opening batsman Dennis Amiss, who had his right thumb broken by a Thomson fireball. Few of the England players came out of the Test without sustaining some injury to their fingers which were bruised by the Thomson–Lillee flyers. All the casualties were sustained at the one end of the pitch—the very end that Alderman Jones predicted might be a bit 'crook'.

Only two England batsmen that summer—wicket-keeper Alan Knott, arguably the best gloveman the world has seen, and Tony Greig—played Thommo with any confidence. Their method was often crude, slashing at rising balls outside off stump, backing and cutting with the idea that if they swung hard enough, the ball would be mighty difficult to catch and it may bring a boundary.

Knott was very effective. He stood at the wicket as if he was playing French cricket, very front on, his bat held low about midway between the popping crease and the stumps. He revealed after the series that the reason he stood so far back behind the popping crease was to give himself that extra split second to sight the ball. Even from the regulation stance on the crease, a batsman had precious little time to sight the ball, let alone get his feet in the right position to play a shot. But Knott was also a great improviser. He latched onto anything on the line of the pads which he would whip to the square leg boundary and he slashed at everything wide of off stump. Knott wasn't a strong driver, but he had an eye like a hawk and he swooped on anything slightly off-line.

Greig's height was an advantage against Thommo, but he too decided that the best way to survive was to hit out and get as many runs as possible before the fast bowler struck. He slashed at wide deliveries and sweated on the full-pitched ball which he would drive fiercely. Although not a gifted cricketer, Greig made absolutely everything of his ability; he worked hard and he tried to get under the skin of the opposition with his continual banter, most of which bordered on the inane.

The rest of the Poms were pummelled into submission. Batsmen of the calibre of John Edrich, Dennis Amiss, David Lloyd and Keith Fletcher were hit all over their bodies; they were shell-shocked and defeated in the mind long before the Ashes changed hands at the SCG Fourth Test match.

Thommo's match figures of 9/105 were grand enough, but it was the quality of his bowling which so enthused his team-mates and lifted the nation.

In the wake of England's flogging by 166 runs at Brisbane, team manager Alec Bedser sent an urgent SOS to Lord's for a replacement batsman. John Edrich and Dennis Amiss had both sustained hand injuries and were ruled out of the Second Test due to start in Perth in eight days.

The man they chose was the old war-horse Colin Cowdrey. The former Kent and England batsman, who was about to turn 42 on Christmas Eve, was a veteran of 113 Tests played between 1954 and 1971. He had led England 27 times and had scored 7700 Test runs; 2268 against Australia at an average of 36.58. Bedser asked specifically for Cowdrey to join the touring party:

'We considered everyone and we felt that experience was necessary. The fact that Cowdrey had been here before was a major consideration.'

'It is a gamble, but we are not thinking of the future, we are thinking of now,' he said.

Cowdrey has played in more Tests than any of the players and will be making his sixth tour of Australia. His first was in 1954–55. After the announcement at Lord's, Cowdrey said: 'It is nice to be remembered and naturally I'm delighted. It is quite a challenge, but I don't want to say too much at this stage. I have not had any cricket practice since the season ended, but I play a lot of golf and squash and I'm quite fit. It won't take long to sort things out.'[12]

A day later there were images in the newspapers of the portly Cowdrey at the Lord's indoor centre practising with his teenage son, Christopher.

When Thommo learnt that the veteran Cowdrey was coming out to Australia as a replacement England batsman, he was totally unconcerned and he delivered a faintly veiled warning:

Cowdrey will cop it as fast as anyone.

Thommo's words had a huge impact back in the home country, for the English had been fed a diet of half-hour highlights of the Test in Brisbane. There was the cream of the England batsmen reduced to ducking for cover in the face of hostile pace before a ceaseless howl of approval from a crowd that was more in keeping with a blood-lust collective at the ancient games of Rome's Colosseum.

But not everyone was convinced that Thommo was the man Australia could rely on to wrest the Ashes from England. Some argued that the exaggerated bounce Thommo got from the Gabba pitch was due to Alderman Clem Jones's wicket preparation. Keith Miller reported from the press box:

TOM THUMB THOMSON
All you Aussies think the Second Test is as good as won by Ian Chappell and his merry men.

And with England walking wounded and grand pappy Colin
Cowdrey back from the ARK, it sure looks another walkover. But I
recall the walking wounded at a small French coastal town named
Dunkirk bouncing back for the greatest victory of our time. So
take a tip from an old campaigner who used to sling them down
a bit. Tornado Thomson won't have the English batsmen's knees
knocking next time. The Perth pitch is certain to be better and have
more even bounce than the pock-marked one in Brisbane where
Thommo got extraordinary lift.[13]

On the same day, Sydney's *Sunday Telegraph* ran a story under the heading
'Thommo's not so genial':

In the business of dark scowls, new Australian bowling firebrand,
Jeff Thomson, can't match it with an angry Dennis Lillee.

But in the occupation of high speed bowling, Thomson is cur-
rently upstaging his famous partner. Lillee may glower at the luckless
English batsmen, but Thomson approaches him with disarming
innocence.

Nobody is deceived.

Thomson is pure dynamite.

The English batsmen were forewarned, of course, but that hasn't
made the shock any easier to handle.

They read some time ago a rather hair-raising interview in
which Thomson confessed a rather gory desire to see the blood of a
writhing batsman on the pitch.

Unlike Lillee who generates his pace from his long, rhythmic
run, Thomson's approach is as casual as the local postman's. One
suspects he could cut it down to a few strides. But on that final
delivery stride, then—POW![14]

There was less than a week to the start of the Second Test in Perth.
Already there had been talk of a bumper war and Thommo and Lillee
were about to be cut loose on the WACA pitch—the fastest wicket in
the world.

The England batsmen had every reason to be very afraid.

7 NEW TEST HERO

I can't remember Chappelli talking about the green light to bowl flat out.
That's what I planned to do anyway. That's the only way I could ever bowl,
flat out . . . And that's what I planned to do in the second innings against
the Poms, bowl as fast as I could, flat to the boards.

Thommo was now our latest Test hero. The kids wanted to emulate his pace and athleticism and the girls loved his laid-back style and surfer-boy looks. Enroute to Perth for the Second Test match, Thommo was pictured with Suzi Quatro, the US rock-star, with Suzi testing Thommo's muscled right arm, 'the arm that rocked England'.

In the wake of the First Test drubbing, ex-Australian Test batsman Lindsay Hassett further rocked the England boat with his revelation to eminent English journalist E.W. 'Jim' Swanton, of London's *Daily Telegraph*, that one particular Jeff Thomson over in the Gabba Test was 'the best I have ever seen from any fast bowler'. Hassett played against some of the best fast bowlers of them all, including Ray Lindwall and Keith Miller, England's Frank Tyson and Fred Trueman. Hassett knew genuine pace when he saw it and Thommo's pace in Brisbane was out of this world.

With John Edrich and Dennis Amiss nursing broken hands and David Lloyd returning to the fold after missing the Gabba Test with a finger break, the plight of the England batting was pretty much forgotten in view of the flood of publicity over the recall of England's ageless war-horse batting star, Colin Cowdrey. Talk of Santa Claus and Dad's Army emerged, but Cowdrey was driven to put on a good show. Many still had images in their mind of Cowdrey, his broken left arm heavily plastered, battling one-handed the speed of West Indian Wes Hall at Lord's in 1963. Such was his courage and skill, Cowdrey saved that Test for England, defending desperately with spinner David Allen, and the match ended in a draw after England were 9 wickets down and required 6 to win off the last ball of the game.

Despite the England batsman's former heroics, Keith Miller couldn't believe that Cowdrey would want to subject himself to the world's fastest bowlers in the stifling heat of Perth, but Cowdrey said at the end of the game that 'I did enjoy it so'. Due to a 19-hour delay at Bombay Airport on his way to Australia, Cowdrey had barely four days in which to prepare for the big game.

Meantime Thommo was sitting back, basking in the reflective glory of a magnificent First Test performance, confident that he could do it again, on any Test pitch surface.

After all the talk of the poor pitch in Brisbane and how I got the ball to rear off a good length due mainly to the pitch, I was determined to prove to everyone that I was no one-Test wonder. I was looking forward to getting into the Poms again. And I made the statement that I'd be around their ears again at the WACA ground in Perth.

Thommo told the press that he was really very quiet, but there were times when he simply had to say something. Poor old Jim Swanton, senior correspondent for the visiting press, a man who had survived a POW camp under the Japanese and had seen every Australia–England Test series Down Under since the summer of 1946–47, was taken aback when Thommo met him at a function later in the series: 'Are you one of those Pommie bastards who've been writing all that shit about me?'

Swanton was a big man, who always wore a pinstriped dark blue suit, matching tie and a large handkerchief which flowed gregariously from his coat top pocket. His steel-grey hair was brushed back and his bushy John Howard-looking eyebrows couldn't even hide behind his thick, black, horn-rimmed glasses. Seemingly, Swanton was not a man to shirk any sort of confrontation, but after his meeting with Thommo he didn't loiter and I am not sure he ever fully recovered from the experience.

Ian Chappell won the toss and had no hesitation in sending England in to bat. After the physical and psychological battering they received in Brisbane, England's batting line-up looked decidedly vulnerable. David Lloyd and Brian Luckhurst put on a creditable 44 for the first wicket, Luckhurst cutting a ball from Max Walker straight to me in the gully. This brought the man of the hour, Colin Cowdrey, to the crease.

I had just taken my cap from the umpire when up comes the roly-poly England batsman we call 'Kipper'. And he thrusts out his hand and introduces himself. I must admit it was a bit bizarre. This bloke has just turned up in Australia, Dennis Lillee and I had just dismantled his team in Brisbane and we were about to do the same here, and Cowdrey arrives at the crease all smiles and looking for a nice chat in the middle.

Cowdrey batted with grace and great skill. He moved back and across, usually before Thommo or Lillee let the ball go, and there was often a delivery which got past his broad bat and thudded heavily into his chest. After one particularly savage Thommo over, in which he copped at least four painful blows to the chest area, Cowdrey waltzed down the wicket to his partner, David Lloyd, and told him how much fun he was having, back in the Test arena and batting against the pace of Thommo. Cowdrey was so heavily padded in the chest area that Lillee jokingly referred to him as England's latest knight, 'all ready for a joust'.

With Thommo and Lillee bowling in tandem, fielding in the gully was something else. I had to very smartly develop a method to see the edges and slashed shots which were bound to come my way. With all the other fast bowlers—even Lillee—you could watch their delivery all the way from the time they let the ball go to the time it was about halfway down the track, then quickly focus your attention on the edge of the bat. With Thommo there was no time for that strategy. I found that I watched him until his load-up at delivery and a split second before he was about to release the ball, I directed all my attention to the edge of the bat. It gave me a split second more time to see the ball. I decided to get as close to the bat as possible and worked out that seven paces was the go. The closer you get to the bat, the tighter the angle and there are lots more catching opportunities. Gully specialists in later years, the likes of Geoff Marsh, Steve Waugh and Matthew Hayden, stood so deep you felt there was more a chance of batsmen running two rather than a chance in the offing.

At lunch England had lost only Luckhurst, with Lloyd surviving on 25 and Cowdrey on 9. At drinks the score had sneaked along to 1/99. Seemingly, there were no gremlins in the pitch, but then Thommo floored Lloyd with a brute of a ball which hit him squarely in the nether region. Lloyd collapsed in a screaming heap. Thommo's fireball had split Lloyd's protector and one of Lloyd's testicles was flopping out of the protector and the other contained within, thus contributing to his immense pain. Soon after Lloyd, who had batted bravely for 49, followed a Thommo delivery which had moved across him, succeeding only in edging the ball to Greg Chappell at second slip. When Lloyd staggered painfully back to the pavilion, Mike Denness was padding up nearby and he said, 'Well played, David'.

'Bloody hell, captain, you never get any balls in your half,' was Lloyd's reply.[1]

Out in the middle Cowdrey was left to face the fired-up Thomson who honed in for the kill. With the score at 119, Cowdrey went too far across to get behind a Thommo delivery and lost his leg stump. The Kipper's brave fight ended at 22. By tea England was 6–133 and was eventually dismissed for a paltry 208, the last 9 England wickets had fallen for 109 runs. Thommo had 2/45 off 15 overs; Lillee 2/48 off 16 overs and Max Walker grabbed 2/49 off 20 overs. Doug Walters chimed in with a handy 2/13 off 2.3 overs, getting Alan Knott (51) and Fred Titmus (10), both caught by Ian Redpath at fourth slip. Ian Chappell took the wicket of Chris Old, courtesy of a brilliant one-handed catch by brother Greg at a short and straight mid-wicket. But it was the pace and fire of Thommo and Lillee that did the real damage. England nicked, nudged and dodged their way to a meager 208 and the second day saw the complete domination of England by Australia's batsmen.

Doug Walters hit an amazing unconquered 103, which included 100 between tea and stumps. Walters needed exactly 6 runs off the last ball from Bob Willis and he launched himself into Test cricket folklore with an extraordinary pull shot off that last ball that soared over the square leg boundary, bringing the 6 runs he needed to complete his century in the final session.

At stumps Australia was 4–352 with Walters on 103 and Ross Edwards, 79. Walters fell soon after play began on the Third Day, snicking a ball from Willis to Fletcher at slip, but Edwards went on to notch a century (115), while Rod Marsh hit out for 41 and Thommo smacked 11 in just 12 balls at the end of the innings. Australia had 481, a lead of 273.

Survival was uppermost in the England batsmen's minds as Cowdrey opened the England second innings with David Lloyd. A change was forced given Luckhurst had a broken left hand and would bat, if needed, down the order. Lillee opened proceedings from the River End and at tea Cowdrey and Lloyd had taken the score to 35 without loss. England lost only 1 wicket, Cowdrey for a brave, fighting 41. He again moved back and across to a ball of full length from Thommo and the sheer pace beat him on the back foot. Cowdrey had played some classical shots against the fast bowlers and his innings confirmed his status as a great player of genuine pace.

> *I heard a lot about the ability and class of Colin Cowdrey and he revealed in the Perth Test match just how good he was and how great he must have been. He might have been pretty old and past his former brilliance but he showed enough to tell me that this guy was one of the very great players in Test history.*

At stumps England was 1/102 with Lloyd injured on the sidelines, Denness not out on 13 and Tong Greig not out 28. Long before Thommo wrapped up this Test match, the English press were bleating about Australia's intimidatory bowling tactics. Keith Miller in the *London Daily Express* was one of the lone Australian voices to back the English press corps:

Bowling? I call it intimidation.

PERTH, Sunday—Yes, this bumper war must stop.

I am staggered that the umpires have not cautioned BOTH sides for intimidatory bowling.

I used to hurl plenty of bumpers, as Len Hutton, Denis Compton and Bill Edrich know, but always my plan was to get the opposition out.

Here as in the Brisbane Test, it appears to me that the one aim of Thomson, Lillee and England's Bob Willis has been to hit the batsmen.

I agree with Crawford White [*London Daily Express* reporter] that unless umpires take more stringent measures someone could be seriously injured.

Colin Cowdrey has been the main target for this aggressive bowling. But hasn't the old boy been marvellous! He volunteered to open against this brutal attack and was a model to his team mates as he unflinchingly got behind every piece of shrapnel hurled down. His reactions for a 41-year-old—whether withdrawing his bat, dodging the bumpers, or pouncing on the loose ball—were marvellous.

Cowdrey has more cricketing ability in his little finger than most of England's batsmen. He's a genius and the crowd loved him. I admit I advised him not to come out here, but the crispness of his strokes, especially his cutting, turned the clock back 20 years. Had England 11 men of his courage and ability they would win the series. And yet Lillee and Thomson wasted the new ball so badly that Lloyd and Cowdrey rarely had to play a shot in the early overs. The Aussie fast bowlers are wild colonial boys trying to maim rather than defeat fairly, in my opinion.[2]

Praise for Cowdrey's performance was pretty much universal. Certainly the Australian team marvelled at Cowdrey's batting. Here was a man who was playing Test cricket before some of our blokes were out of short pants. Here was a man of middle age standing up to the fastest bowlers of the age. Thommo said Cowdrey would cop it as quick as anyone and he didn't let the portly Englishman down on that score. What the Australians respected was Cowdrey's total commitment to his team's cause and his courage.

Australia's senior cricket writer, Phil Wilkins of *The Australian*, wrote:

What an amazing cricketer England have in Cowdrey. He has been in Australia for less than a week and it is doubtful whether any opener in the world could have surpassed his handling of Thomson. Cowdrey might have been dismissed fifth delivery before he had scored, but Ian Redpath plunged across from fourth slip, probably spoiling any effort Doug Walters might have made for the catch. Despite his lack of match practice, Cowdrey seldom appeared ill at ease against Thomson's thunderbolts. At times he was so perfectly positioned that he played deliveries with grace and ease, as if Thomson were a medium pacer. No better stroke was played by Cowdrey than his superb square drive from Max Walker. Cowdrey made an unusual request midway through his innings when seagulls settled behind Walker's arm in front of the sightboard. Umpire Robin Bailhache complied by scattering the birds lest Cowdrey 'lose' the ball if the flock took off in fright.[3]

At the start of the fourth day I recall Ian Chappell talking about Lillee and Thomson having been given the skipper's permission—the green light—to really let fly. The day dawned brightly and the weather forecast was a century in the shade. Australia had to take 9 wickets to finish off the England batting on that fourth day.

I can't remember Chappelli talking about the green light to bowl flat out. That's just what I was planning to do anyway. That's the only way I could ever bowl, flat out. I wasn't one of those guys who could slow down and use all manner of cut and swing to suit the conditions. I was a fast bowler, always a fast bowler. And that's what I planned to do in the second innings against the Poms, bowl as fast as I could, flat to the boards.

And flat to the boards did both Lillee and Thommo bowl.

Lillee took 2/59 and Thommo a brilliant 5/93 off 25 blistering overs. Keith Fletcher came to the wicket in the morning session and he lasted one ball. Thommo let fly and the ball fairly screamed off a good length, just clipping Fletcher's batting glove on its way to a gleeful Marsh standing 30 yards back. Fletcher might well have thought that this first-ball dismissal was the luckiest duck of his career, for the Essex man didn't wait for the umpire to raise his right index finger, Fletcher was off, at a trot, towards the sanctuary of the England dressing-room. Thommo had dismissed Cowdrey, Fletcher and Greig before tail-ender Geoff Arnold drove at a wide ball and edged it between fourth slip and gully. I saw it early and dived to my left, taking the ball in my left hand while parallel to the ground. It was easily the best catch of my cricketing life, but no-one remembers it because the victim was a lowly tail-ender. Oh that it were Cowdrey!

Australia won the match easily by 9 wickets and with more than a day to spare. Thomson had taken 16 wickets in the first two Test matches. He also received an offer to join Tony Greig's county team Sussex.

At the time a lot of blokes were agitating for a better deal from the Board. There was hardly any money in the game and it was always a financial struggle to mix work with cricket. I thought I'd get a few more offers to play in England. I wanted to be a professional cricketer. I was hoping to get into the 1975 Australian tour of England for my first look at the Old Country and the chance of my playing county cricket might follow down the track.

During the Test match Barry Humphries and Barry Crocker marched into the Australian dressing-room, accompanied by a bevy of pretty girls. They handed out T-shirts promoting their new film, *Barry McKenzie Holds his Own*, and we were invited to the Perth premiere. Thommo immediately got into the swing of things by putting a sticker, with the words 'I'm pulling for Bazza', on the back of his bat.

The Boxing Day Test at the Melbourne Cricket Ground provided the closest match of the series. England batted first before a huge crowd of 77,165 spectators. David Lloyd drew one of the few smiles in the England dressing-room by telling all and sundry of a letter he was writing to his mother sitting by the fire in frosty Manchester, worrying about her son coping against the pace and hostility of Thomson and Lillee: 'Dear Mum, Today I got a half volley in the nets—and I didn't know what to do with it.'[4]

Again Lillee and Thomson made early inroads and despite good batting from John Edrich (49) and Alan Knott (52), England fell for a moderate 242. Thommo again got Cowdrey lbw (35), and David Lloyd (14), Knott and Bob Willis (13). Thomson took 4/72 off 22.4 overs, Lillee 2/70 off 20, I got 2/37 off 15, and Walker 1/36 off 24 overs.

The wicket was a little uneven in bounce and lacked a lot of pace. It really suited England more than Australia and Ian Chappell's men struggled throughout, finally being dismissed for 241, 1 run short of England's first innings tally. Bob Willis (5/61) bowled well to thwart any Australian really getting into batting stride. Ian Redpath (55), Rod Marsh (44), Doug Walters (36), Ian Chappell (36) and Max Walker (30) all got starts without going on to big scores.

In the England second innings Dennis Amiss and David Lloyd really got going. They attacked Lillee and Thomson to the tune of 115 for the first wicket. It seemed that on this sluggish MCG wicket, the faster Lillee and Thommo bowled, the easier the ball came on to the bat. Thommo had conceded 46 runs in his first 7 overs as the England openers cut loose; especially Amiss who hit 70 runs before lunch in what was a gem of a knock. For the first time in this turbulent series, the England openers looked assured and completely at home in the middle. Miraculously, it seemed, both Amiss and Lloyd were suddenly devoid of indecision. They moved comfortably on to the front foot and gave the Australian pace pair the only thumping of the series.

I dismissed Lloyd (44), caught and bowled, when the left-hander lofted his drive against the spin, then Ian Chappell accepted a catch off Amiss (90), again off bowling. Amiss fell 2 runs short of Bobby Simpson's runs tally record for a Test match summer and Chappelli really enjoyed letting the England batsman know all about that little statistic.

This opened the floodgates for Thommo and Lillee to take charge. Cowdrey fell to Lillee, courtesy of a fine catch at second slip by Greg Chappell, then Thommo had Edrich (4) caught at first slip by Ian Chappell.

Only Tony Greig (60) could muster any runs at all and from none for 115, England was all out for 244. Greig hit splendidly and came down the track to hit me over mid-off for a mighty six. Thommo had a fine double, taking 4/72 off 22.4 overs in England's first innings and 4/71 off 17 overs in the second. Lillee again took two wickets in each innings. Thommo got 8 wickets for the match; I got 6 and Lillee 4. So far in the series Lillee had taken a total of 12 wickets, while Thommo had 24 wickets and the record watchers were pointing to the distinct possibility that Thomson would eclipse Arthur Mailey's long-standing record of 36 wickets for Australia versus England in an Ashes series Down Under.

Requiring 246 to win Australia fell 8 runs short and the match petered out to a draw. It was an enthralling contest, but neither side really deserved victory and a draw was a fair result. Perhaps the slowness of the track limited the fast bowlers' effectiveness, and I believe the England camp took particular notice of the way Lillee and Thomson bowled on that slow MCG wicket, especially Thommo, with a view to the 1975 Australian tour of England.

Australia dropped WA opener Wally Edwards for the Sydney Fourth Test and brought in the tall, right-hander Rick McCosker, who had won selection through sheer weight of runs in Sheffield Shield cricket. Ian Chappell, won the toss and decided to bat.

McCosker hit a brilliant debut 80, the majority of his runs coming from deft cuts and workman-like shots off his pads. Ian Chappell (53) and Greg Chappell (84) batted grandly before the tail really wagged. Rod Marsh (30) and Max Walker (30) batted well before Thommo (24 not out) and I (31) put on 37 for the last wicket to take our score to 405.

During Australia's innings the England bowlers bounced our tail. Lillee was hit on the arm and I copped one on the bowling hand. There was a certain amount of talk in the middle and the crowd got involved. The Sydney Hill was packed with fans who frequently delved into their ice boxes to draw on another can of cold beer. By the time England batted, the crowd was in a frenzy. They began to chant 'Lill-ee, Lill-ee!' as Australia's opening bowler charged in from the Randwick End, and we all knew that this would be an eventful day.

England replied with 295, Thommo again bowling with pace and fire to notch 4/74 off 19 overs. He got Cowdrey (22), Greig (9), Knott (82) and Willis (2) to take his series wicket tally to 28. Knott played a wonderful, plucky innings, often backing away to slash the fast bowlers over the slips or through the cover point area. At 82 he chanced his luck once too often for Thommo slipped in his famous 'sandshoe crusher' and the express yorker sent Knott's leg stump flying.

Batting a second time Australia hit 4/289 with Greg Chappell hitting a masterly 144, well-supported by Ian Redpath (105), before Ian Chappell called a halt to proceedings, leaving England with 400 runs to win.

England survived late on the fourth day to be none for 33, with both Amiss and Lloyd surviving a chance apiece off Lillee and Thomson. But the anticipated England collapse began early on the last day, with three wickets falling for 74, and on the same score John Edrich was struck a telling blow in the ribs from a Lillee delivery which saw the stand-in England captain rushed to hospital for an X-ray. The crowd chanted as Edrich struggled to his feet and was helped off the ground.

The old Test player John 'Stork' Hendry stirred the pot in the local press by suggesting that the so-called intimidatory bowling by Lillee and Thomson was 'worse than the methods used by Harold Larwood and Bill Voce in the Bodyline series of 1932–33'. Keith Fletcher clearly didn't enjoy facing Thomson. Amiss (37), Lloyd (26) and Cowdrey (1) were back in the pavilion and Edrich in hospital when Fletcher faced another brute of a ball from Thommo. It reared from just short of a good length and spat at his head, cracking the batsman on the edge of the peak of his cap, via the bat handle, and ballooned towards cover point where Ross Edwards made a desperate dive to get his hands under the ball. Mercifully for the shaken Fletcher the catch went begging, but the experience had Fletcher on the ropes in the psychological sense. Mentally he was done. Thommo moved in for the kill. He knew he had his man. He served up a fast ball of full length outside off-stump and Fletcher meekly sparred at it, succeeding only in edging it to Ian Redpath at fourth slip.

One of Thommo's prized pieces of memorabilia is a huge oil painting of Fletcher being hit in the head in that Sydney Fourth Test. The painting depicts Fletcher, having dropped his bat, holding his head as his knees bend, his body slumped forward. Thommo has completed his follow-through and the slips and wicket-keeper are up in anticipation. Thommo says he doesn't have 'much cricket shit' on his walls at home, but the painting of Fletcher being hit on the head—given to Thommo by a mate—no doubt appeals to his sense of humour.

Lillee, Thomson and Walker all took 2 wickets and, despite having Edrich dropped at short-leg late in the England innings, I took 4–21 (including Greig who'd hit me for six in Melbourne) off 16.5 overs to notch the outright win and ensure Australia regained the Ashes. Thommo's 2/74 off 23 overs brought his series wicket tally to 30 and Mailey's record seemed certain to be broken by the 'Boy from Bankstown'.

In the reflective joy of the Ashes success, Ian Chappell said he was grateful that he had Jeff Thomson and Dennis Lillee playing for him and not against him:

> I think Thomson is a very good bowler but, at this stage, I couldn't say he's the best of my experience. He is still 24. Lillee is 25 and he isn't bad either. At times Dennis was a little quicker in this Test than Thomson. Lillee varies his pace these days. Fast bowlers have their moments. There is very little in difference between their pace. Thomson has a very good temperament. He gets angry but doesn't show it much. Dennis is a different type, he had a long lay-off with his back injury and perhaps you can put that down as a reason for his frustration when the wickets are not coming as frequently as he probably deserves. Maybe it's frustration with Thomson.[5]

Colin Cowdrey, a man I first saw fielding in a Test at the SCG when I was nine years old and who later became my first Test wicket at the Oval in 1968, revealed a batting technique against pace that was infinitely superior to any other England batsman in this Ashes series. Cowdrey had batted against Frank Tyson in county cricket and against Wes Hall and Charlie Griffiths at their fiery best and South Africa's Peter Heine and Neil Adcock. He'd also faced Gordon Rorke, the NSW speedster who often hurled them from about eighteen yards at the end of an elongated drag, but Cowdrey reckoned that Thommo had the edge on all of them for sheer pace. At the end of the Fourth Test, Kipper told me about three particular deliveries:

Thommo bowled me three balls on the trot which were unbelievable. The first took off from a good length. I felt as though I had it
covered, back and across, but the ball reared viciously and hit the
bat handle, and luckily it flew over the slips to the boundary. His
next ball seemed pretty ordinary. It was a bit short and I shaped
to turn the ball off my hip. It looked a good bet for an easy two,
but the ball again took off and smashed into my left arm. Those
two balls made me very wary indeed, although I simply didn't
have the reflexes to prevent the third ball getting me. The ball was
faster, if that's possible, and I played back, trying to avoid the ball,
but it came at me and I fended it away with the glove, only to put
it straight into the hands of Rick McCosker at short forward leg.
I doubt if I had ever faced three such difficult deliveries, three nasty
ones in a row, in my whole career.[6]

In the wake of England losing the Ashes, some of the English press were
up in arms about Australia's tactics and crowd behaviour. Even Murray
Hedgecock, UK-based Australian correspondent for News Ltd, wrote a
damning piece on the antics of many of the famous Sydney Hill. Under
the headline: 'Hillites jeers shock the English fans', Hedgecock wrote:

The fourth Test has killed a cricketing legend—that the Hill was
the home of all that was best in Australian cricket.

For years England cricketers, cricket writers and visiting
barrackers have told tales about The Hill and its passion for cricket,
its loud but golden-hearted barrackers. In the eyes of the English
cricket-lovers the Australian game has always been epitomised by
the Sydney Hill. E.W. (Jim) Swanton said in the *Daily Telegraph*,
'the atmosphere has been something after the manner of a bull-
ring' and Alex Bannister of the *London Daily Mail* said, 'England
endured a barrage of bumpers round their heads and beer cans,
fruit and pies hurled at them from the notorious Hill.' But the more
restrained John Woodcock, which befits a correspondent with *The
Times*, made the most significant assessment: 'For England it is
like being brain-washed. The Hill is not a place for old-fashioned
barracking any more, or for subtleties, but for taking as many cans

of beer as one can carry and consuming them until each voice becomes louder than the next, each remark more obscene.'[7]

At around this time Australia's leading cricketers had been agitating for better pay and conditions. Dennis Lillee was quoted as saying that he believed each Test player should be placed on an annual retainer of $25,000. The Australian Cricket Board was horrified by Lillee's boldness and through its chairman, Tim Caldwell, captain Ian Chappell was told to advise Lillee 'to back off' in his columns. The Board had only recently allowed players to write in the press and a ban on such things went back long before World War II. But Chappelli was not fazed, 'Turn it up Tim, I'm not going to tell Dennis anything—I happen to agree with what he's been writing.'[8]

Chappell had been talking to the ACB for some time, trying to get a better deal for Test cricketers in Australia. Chappell did win concession from the Board, with the players getting a $200 bonus per Test, which effectively doubled their Test match fee, and a bonus and a credit to their two-year provident fund. News of the deal came to Chappell's men during the course of the Fourth Test, and it came despite Sir Donald Bradman's long-term tactics to deny the players anything but the most basic expense money.

The ACB secretary Alan Barnes was quoted in *The Australian* on the morning of the first day's play in the Adelaide Test as saying:

There are 500,000 cricketers who would love to play for Australia for nothing.[9]

Every Australian player was incensed by Barnes's comments and some, including Chappelli, planned to take Barnes to task when they returned from the Adelaide nets. When they got back to the dressing-room they discovered Test opener Ian Redpath had Barnes by the throat, pressed up against the dressing-room wall, and he yelled at the quivering ACB secretary: 'You bloody idiot Barnes, of course 500,000 people would play for Australia for nothing, but how bloody good would they be?'

No-one else needed to have a go at Barnes. Redders had done the job perfectly.

Australia had won three of the four Test matches and was expected to go on to win the Adelaide Fifth Test, but a cloud hung over proceedings because Thommo, who took 3/58 off 15 overs in the England first innings—getting Cowdrey (26), Fletcher (40) and Denness (51)—badly injured his bowling shoulder during a game of social tennis on the rest day.

For much of the post-War period it was traditional for the players, wives, girlfriends and officials of both sides to travel to Angaston in the Barossa Valley and enjoy the hospitality of Wyndam Hill-Smith, owner of Yalumba Winery, one of Australia's oldest family wineries. Good food and fine wine abounded. The swimming pool beckoned, so too the tennis court, and it was on the latter that Jeffrey Robert Thomson found himself in a doubles match, teamed with local football legend Neil Kerley. Thommo and Kerls were pitted against Doug Walters and the ex-Australian wicket-keeper Brian Taber. Thommo was serving. As with his bowling, Thommo didn't have a medium-paced serve. It was flat out, or nothing.

I served the ball hard, as I usually do, and felt a terrible pain in my shoulder. I dropped the racquet and went straight to a specialist who diagnosed a pulled tendon and torn muscles. Mind you it made me feel a bit better when I realised that I served an ace.

Although Australia won the Fifth Test easily, Thommo was expected to be out of big cricket for the rest of the season. That big serve in the Barossa Valley tore fibres off the tendon sheath at the point of his right shoulder. However, Thommo, who had surprised the Englishmen with his great speed, also surprised with his powers of recovery.

8 ELEPHANT RIDERS DOWN ON THEIR LUCK

> Bertie *[Ian Chappell]* came up to me and said, 'Have a bowl Thommo.
> I don't care what you do. Brain 'em, bowl 'em out, but we have to win this
> match . . .' That's when the fun and games started.

Much of the gloss of the stunning Ashes win was taken away from the players when it was revealed that the Australian Cricket Board coffers were full to overflowing, yet the men who actually took to the field were paid peanuts. Take the Melbourne Third Test match. Gate takings were not far short of a quarter of a million dollars, yet the team payments totalled less than $4000. Even at that early stage of his career, Thommo wasn't backward in coming forward about player payments. He believed the players should have been getting a percentage of the gate, but Dennis Lillee believed that nothing would ever be achieved without the players forming a union.

In January 1975, just before he injured his shoulder, Thommo was considering offers from two county cricket clubs in England. Sussex was one. Australian selection for the 1975 tour of England would prevent him taking up such a contract, but it was always in the back of his mind to some day play in English county cricket.

With Thommo sidelined Australia lost the Sixth Test match convincingly. It was more an anti-climax than a lowlight as the players weren't keyed up for this final game because the result meant nothing. Thommo was confident that his shoulder would mend quickly and it did, for within a few weeks he was back, fit and rearing to go.

Thommo was covering the Sixth Test for *The Truth* and on February 9, just before the Australian and England teams trained in readiness for the third day of the Test match, he tested his shoulder by firing a few down at the MCG nets. He passed with flying colours, bringing broad smiles to everyone when one of his 'specials' broke a stump in two.

> *I felt fine after that little workout. My major problem was in the field. I knew that I needed to be careful and not throw hard in case I jarred my shoulder out of position. Other than that, I was confident that all would be fine and I would make a successful comeback to big cricket.*

During and after his enforced convalescence, Thommo was feted by the Australian press. On February 15, 1975, he featured in a Saturday edition of *The Melbourne Truth* under the heading 'Top-scoring bachelor gay, Thommo! I've taken out some real dolls.' The sub-title boasted 'Girls fling themselves at the handsome young Test bowling star who rates as cricket's Alvin Purple'.

Pictured wearing only a towel and lolling on the bed of a Melbourne motel, Thommo lapped up all the attention. He was quoted at the time:

> 'For some unknown reason, the birds throw themselves at me. It's good for the ego though. I've been caught a couple of times. I got pretty close to marriage, but luckily sport saved me. When we go on tour, we usually have a few beers at night and I often get hold of a bird or two. I choose the good-looking ones and take them out.'
>
> Does Jeff see himself as a sex object?
>
> 'I hope so, but I don't think I've got enough time to be one. It's flattering, you know, having women you don't know trying to meet you. I just hope it continues before I slow down.'[1]

'I'd just lope in and go whang!' Showing his style at Lords in 1981 in the Middlesex v. Australia match. [Patrick Eagar]

Sequence of shots by Patrick Eagar showing Thommo bowling in May 1981,
Australia v. Middlesex. [Patrick Eagar]

Colin Cowdrey facing Thommo, 2nd Test Australia v. England in Perth,
1974–75. [Patrick Eagar]

Fred Titmus after being hit on the knee by a ball from Thommo (walking towards Titmus with back to camera), 3rd Test Australia v. England in Melbourne, 1974–75. [Patrick Eagar]

'Ashes to ashes, dust to dust   if Thomson don't get ya, Lillee must . . .'   *Sunday Telegraph, Sydney*

Paul Rigby's cartoon that says it all. [Paul Rigby]

Dennis Lillee and Thommo talk strategy at Lords for the Prudential World Cup in 1975. [Patrick Eagar]

Thommo unsettles Greenidge during a hostile spell of fast bowling, 2nd Test
West Indies v. Australia at Bridgetown, 1978. [Patrick Eagar]

Thommo scores off Botham in the 4th Test, Australia v. England, Melbourne
1983–84. [Patrick Eagar]

Thommo and life-long mate Lennie Pascoe in 1980, Hampshire v. Australia at Southampton. [Patrick Eagar]

Rodney March and Thommo relax with a beer after retaining the Ashes,
4th Test Australia v. England, Sydney 1974–75. [Patrick Eagar]

One Jeffery Thomson takes to the microphone with Jonathan Agnew for the
Australian tour or England in 2001. [Patrick Eagar]

Thommo in 2009, before speaking at the Day of Difference Golf Classic, Terrey Hills Golf and Country Club, Sydney. Day of Difference is a foundation that raises money for critically injured children. [Suzanne Brown]

Most of the players had nicknames and Thommo was given the label 'Two-Up' when he played for NSW and the source of that sobriquet was Thommo's Two-Up School, a well-known haunt for certain types in Sydney of the 1970s and before.

Thommo returned to Sheffield Shield in sparkling form, bowling as fast as he had done all summer when he reduced the England batting to the brink of mediocrity. On March 10, 1975, Thommo decimated the Victorians at the Gabba, taking 6/17 off 12.6 blistering overs. Victoria was all out for 76, its lowest total in an innings in a Sheffield Shield match since 1927, when it scored 86 against Queensland in Brisbane. Thommo's blitz, and subsequently Queensland's outright win, ensured Western Australia won the Shield, with Queensland runners-up for the second time.

Both Thommo and Lillee took 62 first-class wickets in the summer, Thommo averaging 19.37 and Lillee 25.15. In the Tests they took 58 wickets (Thommo 33 and Lillee 25). I snuck into the frame to snare 57 first-class wickets at 22.05 to grab a spot on the tour with the famous pace pair.

Greg Chappell, who had marvelled at Thommo's recuperative powers following his shoulder injury in Adelaide, praised the fast man for his brilliant bowling in the match against Victoria: a Thomson performance that prevented Victoria from winning the Shield and, in effect, handed the trophy to the Western Australian team.

In *The Australian* of March 1, 1975, and under the heading, 'Thommo has a habit—winning the shield for the opposition', Chappell wrote:

Jeff Thomson sure has a habit of preventing teams from winning the Sheffield Shield. He did it to us [Queensland] last season in Sydney, playing for NSW, and this time his magnificent all-round ability has all but whisked the shield from under the nose of the Victorians.[2]

At the time Greg's article appeared, Thommo had 4/6 and had only to finish the job on Victoria, thus presenting the Sandgropers with the coveted Sheffield Shield. So long as his fitness was okay, Thommo was always a certain selection for the coming tour of Canada and the United Kingdom.

Ten days after he demolished Victoria's batting line-up at the Gabba, Thommo easily passed a precautionary ACB-instigated medical test, having already withdrawn from a short tour of South Africa with the Derrick Robins troupe. At that time there were rumours of Thommo looking elsewhere; a possible move interstate, perhaps returning to his home in Bankstown.

Featured on the front cover of *The ABC Cricket Book*, Thommo was the flavour of the moment. The book contained special articles from Jim Swanton, who reckoned Australia was the favourite to retain the Ashes almost exclusively because of its two fast men Thommo and Lillee, and from Keith Miller, who forecast England to bounce back and turn the tables on Ian Chappell's men on their home turf. Miller predicted that the effectiveness of Jeff Thomson would be drastically reduced on the soft, slow English pitches:

Thomson's erratic cannonballs will cushion into the soft pitch, reducing its pace considerably. Here on the harder pitches he gained speed, especially in Brisbane. I recall Ray Lindwall, the finest fast bowler I have seen, spending a season in Lancashire League cricket when at his peak.

He had everything a fast man needed—speed, accuracy, subtle change of pace and untold stamina. Yet in the lowly-rated cricket of the Lancashire League, on ill-prepared pitches, Lindwall had great trouble in grabbing wickets early on, even against very mediocre batsmen. He had to re-style his bowling, then the wickets came.[3]

Miller knew English conditions like the back of his hand. He also knew the English thinking and how the wickets were almost certainly going to be sluggish to combat the threat of the Australian fast bowlers.

England captain Mike Denness, despite his 188 in their Sixth Test victory at the MCG, was on the brink of being dumped as captain, and the old warhorse Colin Cowdrey was unlikely to retain a batting spot, despite his bravery Down Under. In nine Test innings against the pace of Thomson and Lillee, Cowdrey collected only 165 runs, his highest score 41, at an average of 18.33.

Thommo's shoulder had healed completely. He was ready for his first look at England, cricket's inaugural World Cup and another tilt against the old enemy in the 1975 four-Test Ashes series.

During the World Cup preliminaries I found myself in conversation with the old England fast bowler Fred 'Fiery' Trueman, who told me that Thommo reminded him of Frank Tyson, the express bowler who, under the tough command of Len Hutton, put Ian Johnson's Australians to the sword in 1954–55. Trueman said:

> The possession of excessive speed can turn a nonentity into a national hero in the course of a Test match. Never was this better illustrated than in the case of your Thommo. No-one had heard of Jeff Thomson, who had played, without success, in one Test against Pakistan last year and had been unable to establish himself in the NSW State team. To me Thommo had the blonde hair and the physique to be a girl's most romantic version of a surfie. Rather than for his bowling he had become well-known in Australia for his juvenile magazine article—ghosted, of course—about hurting batsmen.
>
> The more I think of it, Dennis Lillee is the Muhammad Ali of cricket, an artist, whereas Thomson is essentially a slugger with a knockout punch—not exactly subtle.[4]

The Australian team spent two weeks in Canada—a week in Vancouver, then a week in Toronto. It was more a promotional tour, although the players enjoyed the relaxed atmosphere and playing in matches with almost no pressure on them to perform.

Thommo took a hat-trick in the opening match at Vancouver, but the team was beaten by Eastern Canada in Toronto; the Canadian side was made up of West Indians, Indians and only one Canadian-born player. Matches were played on matting stretched over hard turf and the bounce was slightly erratic. Our leg-spinner Jim Higgs was described in the press as a 'slow screw-ball pitcher'.

When Ian Chappell's team arrived in England, the glare of publicity was again on Thommo. He amazed the English by telling of his admiration for Freddie Trueman.

If I followed anyone in the game it was Freddie Trueman. He went about his bowling in the right way.

He was a good entertainer and that's what I think you have to do these days. Garry Sobers was another great cricketer.

The Australian fast bowler also spoke to the English youngsters.

Practise all you can, and watch the top-class players. Watch the batsmen's footwork and note how they hold the bat. It is hard to generalise on bowling, but I would say that you should keep your own action and don't try to copy anyone. Concentrate on bowling at one stump and landing it at a certain distance.

The English press must have read *The Melbourne Truth* of February 15, for in no time at all pictures of Thommo surrounded by beautiful girls were being published. One photograph showed Thommo in a T-shirt that had the word 'SUPERTOM' emblazoned on the front, with three pretty girls. The headline read: 'A hat-trick for Jeff . . .' while the story read:

This is how the British see Australia's fast bowler Jeff Thomson— as Supertom, the guy who gets all the girls. Helping him to relax beside a swimming pool are, from left, Edina Ronay, Christine Donna and Michelle Deri. He says he's happy to share his interest between cricket and girls.[5]

Thommo may have had the old shoe-shuffle working, but he was having a lot of trouble with the English umpires. He was no-balled sixteen times for over-stepping the frontline in the Australian team warm-up match, a one-day benefit game for Middlesex wicket-keeper-batsman John Murray, and spectators were amazed that Thommo wasn't called by the umpires on more occasions.

Just before the Prudential World Cup got underway, all the teams congregated at Buckingham Palace where the eight teams were introduced to the Queen and Prince Phillip. But Thommo was a man of action. He'd much rather be fishing, chatting up the birds or bowling his thunderbolts to the best batsmen in the world than standing about being 'on his best behaviour' meeting the Queen on her home turf.

Australia played Pakistan at Headingly in its first World Cup encounter. While he conceded only 25 runs in 8 overs, Thommo was no-balled 12 times.

Australia made 278, with Ross Edwards getting 80 and Thommo hitting a more-than-useful 20 at the tail of the innings. In his first over Thommo was wild, with 5 no-balls called by Umpire Tommy Spencer. The crowd heckled Thommo and the Australian's knee-jerk reaction was a two-finger salute. Some in the English press welcomed Thommo's ill-conceived gesture and gave him a bit of stick in the newspapers, but it was all water off a duck's back. Thommo couldn't care less.

A second World Cup qualifier loomed—against Sri Lanka at The Oval, but first there were net practices at Lord's. Thommo recalls:

The press were there in their droves and loads of photographers, so we thought we'd have a bit of fun. I deliberately over-stepped the front line just about every ball and the photographers and writers fell for the fuse. They must have reckoned my habit of no-balling would be the end of me for the Cup and the Ashes series.

But something else was about to add to Thommo's woes. Only hours before the Sri Lanka match was about to get underway, Australian team manager Fred Bennett called Thommo to his room and dressed him down for a series of articles written by Thommo's manager, David Lord, stories which appeared in the British and Australian press under the fast bowler's name. They were stories which greatly angered the Australian cricket authority. 'The Australian Cricket Board has decided that you are to be sent home', Fred told me bluntly.

Bennett told Thommo that the stories written by Lord, and sanctioned by the fast man, were considered 'not in Australian cricket's interests'.

When I left Fred's room I bumped into Bertie [Ian Chappell]. *He was in the next room with Greg* [Chappell] *and Bacchus* [Rod Marsh]. *I explained to him what happened.*

'Fucking bullshit, Two-Up', he said and asked me to come to Fred's room with him. Bertie gave Fred a real gob-full.

'Now listen Fred, tell those fucking idiots back in Australia [ACB members] that if Two-Up is to be sent home they'd better send the lot of us back too.'

So that was it. I stayed.

Until his confrontation with Bennett, Thommo was seemingly content to be having a good time. In reality he hated the stuffiness of the official functions Ian Chappell's Australian team had to attend. He was as comfortable at those official functions as a rock star at a sewing class. He hated, as most of us did, the utter pretence of it all.

The thing was I hadn't been away from Australia before. I was very homesick. For me the tour was a bit of a party. Here I was drinking piss and carrying on with all the birds and that, but I wasn't enjoying things at all.

Thommo yearned for the big open spaces of Australia. He missed his fishing, pig-shooting and opening the top of an iced-cold XXXX beer after a refreshing dip in the Pacific Ocean.

Fred [Bennett] said it was the Board's decision to send me home and that was that. Thanks to Chappelli it was all sorted out straightaway. But the whole episode really got me motivated. I knew then that it was not going to be a good day for the batsmen who had to face me.

Ian Chappell's intervention prevented a player–administrator crisis, but the ACB's threat, which came via Fred Bennett, stirred Thommo. He resolved to bowl at break-neck speed. He was about to take out his wrath on the next lot of opposing batsmen.

I was fired up and the poor Sri Lankans copped the wrong end of the stick. It was just bad timing for them. I was really fired up that day and was going to bowl as fast as I had ever bowled and it just happened to be these little 'elephant riders' facing me in my most hostile mood.

Former Sri Lankan Test opening batsman Sunil Wettimuny was a pilot with Sri Lankan Airlines for more than twenty years. Sunil now trains captains to fly the giant airbus jet airliners for Indian Airlines. In more than 30 years of flying, where he had to weather hurricanes, electrical storms, mechanical breakdowns and terrorist bombs, Wettimuny has never known fear like the time he faced the sheer pace of Jeff Thomson at The Oval on June 11, 1975:

That was the day I faced Thommo in full flight.
   His first ball whizzed past my nose and a chill ran down my spine. I never saw the ball, just a streaking line—it was like a tracer bullet was coming at me.[6]

At that time Jeff Thomson was at the peak of his amazing powers to generate great speed with a cricket ball. The feared fast bowling pair Thomson and Dennis Lillee were leading Ian Chappell's 1975 Australians against the minnow cricketing nation Sri Lanka. Chappelli's men had belted the Sri Lankan attack to the tune of 328 runs for just 5 wickets down, Alan Turner, who was later named Man of the Match, hit 101, fellow opener Rick McCosker 73, Greg Chappell 50, and Doug Walters 59. Then Chappell unleashed Thommo and Lillee upon the unsuspecting Sri Lankans. Sunil says:

We [the Sri Lankan batsmen] had not seen speed such as this and with the way Thommo seemed to hide the ball behind his back, you couldn't pick up the ball at all.
   In his opening spell Thommo hit me twice in the inner thigh, a cracking blow to the hip bone and finally a crunching hit to the rib cage.[7]

The aggressive Australian fast bowlers were mighty quick and intimidating, especially Thomson. His pace was such that a ball just short of a length became a great problem for the batsmen, for most of them were relatively short, and Thommo's 'good length' came at them at chest height. But despite the aggression of Thommo and Lillee, the Sri Lankans batted bravely.

Fernando scored 22, Bandula Warnapura 31, and Duleep Mendis hit 32 before he was forced to retire hurt. Chappell had the field up early, two slips, gully, short leg, a fine leg, but no third man. There were plenty of boundaries scored in the early overs. The Australian bowlers were going for runs: I was at 6 an over; Walker and Lillee at 4 an over; Walters at 5 an over; only Thomson could put a brake on the scoring. Apart from Thommo, the Australian attack was coasting, even Lillee; a psychological effect of our massive innings of 328. We thought that a score in excess of 300 was way beyond the reach of Sri Lanka's inexperienced batsmen, but the runs continued to flow, even after Fernando lost his off stump to a Thommo fireball and Warnapura was stumped by Rodney Marsh off my bowling, the second wicket falling at 84. Wettimuny and Mendis were batting bravely and scoring freely before the reintroduction of Thomson. Australian captain Ian Chappell could read the warning signs. He knew Thommo was fired up and ready to bowl at his fastest. Chappelli turned to his fastest bowler.

Bertie [Ian Chappell] *came up to me and said, 'Have a bowl, Thommo. I don't care what you do. Brain 'em, bowl 'em out, but we have to win this match, so do whatever you have to do to win us the game. Chappell was determined not to let this match get away from us. That's when the fun and games started.*

Poor Duleep Mendis. He played a couple of balls from Thommo, then the fast man sent one down just short of a length. Mendis tried to fend it off and it hit him squarely on the forehead. The batsman staggered about the crease and fell heavily on the pitch. Then Mendis lay face down and not moving. All the Australians, except Ross Edwards at cover point, rushed to him fearing the worst and we gave a collective sigh of relief as Duleep moved.

As we stood looking down at the little bloke lying on the pitch, Edwards arrived, cursing his gallant diving effort in trying to catch the rebounding ball from Mendis's head, a ball that he had thought the batsman had snicked. A few minutes elapsed before Duleep slowly turned over and lay on his back; his eyes were wide open, like saucers. Tears were streaming down his face.

'How yar goin' mate?' someone asked as Thommo and the rest of Chappelli's men continued to look down at the stricken batsman.

Then Duleep opened his eyes wider, the tears continuing to roll down his face and he said, 'Oh, my God, I am going now!'

London-based English cricket writer Alan Gibson wrote in *The Times* that Mendis had been struck by a ball aimed at the body. However, Thommo explains the difference between his bouncer and the rearing delivery supposedly aimed at the body.

> *The Sri Lankan batsmen were only little fellas so you couldn't bowl a bouncer at them. A ball coming at chest height to a Tony Greig was head-high to these little fellas.*

Sunil Wettimuny, already nursing badly bruised ribs, watched his brave partner being carried off the ground on a stretcher. Thomson was getting his share of boos from The Oval crowd which was clearly on Sri Lanka's side, given the pounding they had received from the fast bowlers, especially Thommo. Sri Lankan captain Anura Tennekoon took an age to get to the wicket. He says:

> I came in at number five and I took a long time to get to the crease—I stopped to see if Duleep was okay. Not a very pleasant situation, having to face Thomson after he had just knocked one of our men out cold.
>
> I took guard and faced him. I must admit I couldn't pick the ball up from his hand. The first over I only saw the ball whizzing past my head. Luckily nothing hit my head and I was able to survive that spell. The ball was coming from behind his back and his arm-speed was so rapid you couldn't see the ball.[8]

At that stage of the innings Fernando and Warnapura were out and Mendis retired hurt. Tennekoon had joined the limping, sore limbed Wettimuny, who negotiated Max Walker's next over, taking a single off the last ball. Tennekoon recalls:

> Thommo bowled three full length deliveries, the third of which hit Sunil flush on the instep. I have this image of Sunil hopping about in pain and Thomson tried to run him out.[9]

But according to Thommo:

> *I had the ball in my hand and as the batsman hopped about, my team-mates were urging me to throw down the stumps and run him out. I threw down the stumps at the batsman's end with Sunil miles out of his ground. I appealed and no other bastard among my team-mates joined in on the appeal. They all stood about with their arms folded. I was done cold.*

The truth is, Thommo was lured into that little indescretion at the baiting of his own men. The 1975 Australians were ruthless and had a pretty warped sense of humour. Thommo later saw the funny side.

But with a ball in his hand Thommo wasn't in his most sympathetic mood that day. He had generated extraordinary pace and lift on this flat, slow wicket and often Thommo's flyers were taken by Marsh with a resounding thud as he stood some 30 paces back behind the stumps. Thommo had summarily dismissed Mendis with a missile to the head; now Wettimuny was writhing in pain. Thommo remembers saying:

> *Look, mate. It's* [Sunil's right foot] *not broken. But if you face up to the next ball, it bloody well will be broken!*

After a lengthy delay, Wettimuny bravely stood up to face Thomson's next ball. It was an identical sandshoe crusher and the ball screamed into Sunil's right instep, the exact same spot Thommo had hit the previous ball. This time the batsman collapsed in a heap and had to be carried off on a stretcher, to be taken directly to join Duleep Mendis at London's famous St Thomas's Hospital. Wettimuny says:

Never before or since that day did I know fear on a cricket field. When I got to hospital I discovered I had sustained a hairline fracture of the rib, my right foot was broken, I had a dreadful bruise on my inner thigh, my hip bone was badly bruised and I was completely numb in my left leg.

I thought I was paralysed. The numbness stayed with me for twelve hours.

Later on I remember Sri Lankan players telling me of the great pace of bowlers like Imran Khan. Sure Imran was a speed merchant, but compared to Thommo, Imran came at you at a gentle medium pace.[10]

Sunil Wettimuny's strategy against Thommo was to step back out of the line and slash at the ball, hoping he might middle it through extra cover, or edge it with enough power that it would be tough to catch and might go for a boundary. Sunil explains:

I had a 2.1 lb Duncan Fearnley bat and my method seemed sound enough.[11]

Don Bradman adopted a similar plan when he batted against Harold Larwood in the Bodyline Ashes series of 1932–33. Bradman averaged 55 in that series, while Weittimuny scored 53 before Thommo's last sandshoe-crushing finale. According to Sunil, getting out was the safer option:

My strategy generally worked, but after getting pummelled all over my body, I started to question my sanity. 'Sunil, what the hell are you still doing out here?' That second hit on the foot saved me from further punishment.[12]

Thommo's 12 overs (5 maidens) cost just 22 runs for 1 wicket. But what damage, physically and mentally, did his pace cause that June day?

Like all of his fellow batsmen, Duleep Mendis believes the curious sling-shot, catapult action of Thommo made it difficult to pick up the ball from his hand:

And you didn't have a lot of time when the ball was coming at that pace. No time at all to make up your mind the type of shot you were going to play. The biggest problem with Thommo was we could not follow the ball from his hand. With that slinging, catapult action, the ball seemed to appear from nowhere. With Dennis you could follow the ball right from his run-up. You can just imagine a bowler delivering at 95 to 100 miles per hour [153 to 160 kph] you haven't got a lot of time to play your shot. At the last moment, when the ball is delivered, that is the critical time to decide what shot to play and with Thommo you couldn't pick up the ball.

I was taken to St Thomas's Hospital and the hospital staff told me I had to stay overnight for observation, obviously because I had been struck on the head. It was lucky that I was hit right on the forehead because that is the hardest part of the skull.[13]

Unbeknown to Duleep a policeman, who was not on duty at the World Cup match, turned up at the hospital and asked the staff how Mendis and Wettimuny had sustained their injuries. He was told that they were hit by an Australian named Jeff Thomson. Duleep recalls:

Next morning a policeman walked into my room. He held his bobby's helmet under one arm and he asked 'Do you want to press assault charges against a Mr Jeff Thomson?'

When he walked in I was wondering what he was going to say. After he uttered those words, I was lost for a minute. 'Charges? No, constable, it is only a game.'[14]

The Sri Lankan batsman will forever be remembered as a brave lot. Wettimuny scored 53, Mendis 32, Tennekoon 48 and Michael Tissera 52, and the Sri Lankans in total scored 276 for the loss of just 4 wickets.

While Sri Lanka lost the match by 52 runs, they won great ever-lasting respect and admiration from Thommo and the Australians, as well as all the top cricketing nations and cricket fans the world over. June 11, 1975, was probably the very day Sri Lankan cricket first stood tall on the international stage.

Some nine years later—while playing for Sri Lanka against Queensland in a 50-over match at the Brisbane Cricket Ground—Mendis and Wettimuny again faced the bowling of Jeff Thomson. But while in January 1985, Thommo was still quick, he had lost much of his explosive power. It was long after his shoulder injuries and he sometimes was used as a first change bowler to Carl Rackemann and Harry Frei in the Queensland team. Queensland scored 5/212, with Glenn Trimble hitting an unconquered 100, but Sri Lanka hit off the runs easily, scoring 5/213 in 47.3 overs. Man of the Match was Duleep Mendis, now the Chief Executive of Sri Lankan cricket, top-scoring with 72 not out; while Sunil Wettimuny hit 28.

But Thommo's bowling that day at The Oval in 1975 has never been forgotten by the men Thommo calls the 'little elephant riders'. Sri Lankan batsmen of 1975, Duleep Mendis and Bandula Warnapura hold executive posts with the Sri Lanka Cricket Board. Anura Tennekoon still advises the Sri Lanka Test batsmen of today and whenever those men get together they talk in reverent tones of the day Thommo bowled at a furious pace. Mendis recalls:

> How fast was Thommo? If you go to the West Indies and talk to the old fellows in the stands they know the game backwards and they have seen all the great fast bowlers, including the most recent champions. And when you ask them who was the fastest of the lot, they will say 'J.R. Thomson'.[15]

J.R. Thomson is forever a talking point in Colombo among these men who continue to count their lucky stars for having survived the blitz. Thommo copped a lot of flak from the pro-Sri Lankan crowd, but he was certainly back to his hostile best, and bowled at perhaps the quickest he's ever bowled.

After the drama of playing Sri Lanka, Australia lost to the West Indies at The Oval, before facing England in the World Cup semi-final at Leeds.

The wickets in England seemed particularly sluggish. A number of the Australian touring party had been to England on a couple of occasions and all thought the wickets seemed very dead indeed. Personally I thought the wickets had been deliberately 'doctored' to eliminate the threat of

Thomson and Lillee's bowling. While there is no evidence that English groundsmen were instructed by officials at Lord's to 'doctor' pitches at all first-class grounds throughout England in 1975, the Australian team suspected as much. Given the history of similar suspected 'foul play' by groundsmen obeying the orders of the hierarchy at Manchester in 1956 and Leeds in 1972, our suspicions were probably well-founded.

At Old Trafford, Manchester in 1956 England off-spinner Jim Laker took a world-record match wicket haul of 19/90 against Ian Johnson's Australians. The pitch was a dust-bowl that stood like a small pitch-long desert in the middle of a sea of green. Johnson's men suspected that the wicket was prepared specifically for Laker. It was bone dry and stripped of grass. There was an investigation, but as with all 'in-house' inquiries, little or nothing underhanded was found.

When Ian Chappell's 1972 Australian team turned up to play the Fourth Test at Headingly, Leeds, they found the wicket to be completely devoid of grass, yet only four days earlier the track was lush green. The pitch was 'made' for the deadly left-arm medium paced spinner Derek Underwood, who had been brought to the England team for his first match of the series. He revelled in the conditions, taking 10/80 for the match, thus ensuring an England victory and his team retaining the Ashes. An inquiry found that the pitch had been affected by Fuserium disease and that the groundsman, George Cawthray, was in no way to blame for the condition of the pitch. Freak storms from the Continent had swept over the Leeds area a week before the Leeds Test and had flooded the ground at the weekend prior to the Test match starting. Curiously the Fuserium disease only affected one tiny part of the ground—the Test match pitch. The rest of the Headingly ground was lush green.

In 1975 the pitches were prepared to dull the pace and fire of the Australian pacemen, especially J.R. Thomson. All the England players had the luxury of playing well forward to Thomson and Lillee, something they would never have attempted on the fast and bouncy Australian wickets. England's David Steele played forward every ball and he got runs. Had he tried that technique on a fast pitch against Thommo he might well have had his head knocked off. Unlike the controversial wickets of 1956 and 1972 in England, the pitches in 1975 were 'euthanased'—dull, lifeless, dead as a dodo. My mind harked back to the Third Test in Melbourne where Dennis Amiss and David Lloyd put on 115 for the first wicket and really took to the Australian pace pair for the first—and only—time of the series. The MCG was as dead as a dodo and the quicker Thommo and Lillee bowled, the easier it seemed to play them. The wicket took all the life and bounce out of their attack and the ball seemed to come on nicely on that flattest of flat wickets. I suspected the England squad stored the information away and decided to slow the pitches at home to negate the pace threat. I put my suspicions to Thommo.

Yeah, I always reckoned they slowed down the tracks. I think the Poms doctored the wickets in 1975. Dennis Lillee and I were at our absolute peak. We would tear in and bowl flat out and the ball would bounce about knee-high. No matter what we did, the ball came on so sluggishly from the wicket. England in 1975 was really dry. I think there was a drought. The grounds were lightning fast. You only had to touch a ball and it sped to the boundary. The Poms, however, doctored the pitches for one reason only, to bugger us [Lillee and Thommo] up! No doubt about it.

There was only one match in the tour where we saw a tinge of green on the pitch in the semi-final of the World Cup, against England at Headingly, Leeds. England batted first and was bundled out for 93, Gary Gilmour bowling splendidly to take a World Cup record 6/14 off 12 overs. Max Walker grabbed 3/22, Dennis Lillee 1/26, and Thommo conceded just 17 off his 6 overs without taking a wicket. The wicket provided cut and bounce and allowed the ball to swing alarmingly. Gilmour took most advantage of the conditions, but so too did England bowlers John Snow (2/30), Chris Old (3/29) and Geoff Arnold (1/15). Thanks to a late stand by Doug Walters (20 not out) and Gilmour (28 not out), Australia limped home at 6/94 to make the final of the World Cup. The Leeds pitch was green and lively. All the others were 'doctored' to make them slow, with little bounce to curb the Thommo and Lillee threat.

The World Cup Final at Lord's proved to be one of the longest days the Australian team had ever experienced. We got to the ground at about 9 a.m. and didn't leave until well after 10 p.m. The West Indies won the toss and batted first, with Clive Lloyd hitting the ball with precision and power on the way to 102. He was well-backed by Rohan Kanhai (55) who provided the right amount of defence and attack and gave the more attacking Lloyd the strike at just the right moments. There were little cameos from Keith Boyce (34) and Bernard Julian (26 not out), but the openers Roy Fredericks (7) and Gordon Greenidge (13) and the prolific Alvin Kallicharran (12) failed to impress in the West Indies' total of 291 for the loss of 8 wickets. Thommo got 2/44 off his 12 overs, claiming the wickets of Greenidge and Boyce; Lillee conceded 55 runs for the wicket of Fredericks, and Walker was belted to the tune of 71 runs off his 12 overs.

Gary Gilmour, who said the best way to bowl to Clive Lloyd was 'with a helmet on', so many were smashed back past him on the drive, took 5/48 off his 12 overs.

Only fabulous fielding by Viv Richards, who threw down the wicket on a number of occasions, instigating 3 of the 5 run-outs, cost Australia the match. Allan Turner (40), Ian Chappell (62), Greg Chappell (15) and Max Walker (7) were all run out, before the last wicket stand between Dennis Lillee and Jeff Thomson. The pair came together at 233 and, with a hilarious mix of slogging and frantic singles, they rushed towards the Windies' total. Thommo recalls:

Dennis and I were playing the bowling quite easily, but then Dennis hit a ball high to a bloke at mid-off [Fredericks] *and the crowd— mostly West Indians—thought the game was over. They all rushed on to the field. Meanwhile Dennis and I started running because the bloke who caught it didn't hear the call of no-ball, he'd actually thrown the ball at the non-striker's end, the ball missed and we were running the overthrows. Then Dennis yelled out, 'Keep running, Thommo. We can win this . . .'*

Don't be bloody silly, FOT [Lillee], *you don't know who's got the ball. We could be run out!'*

The ball had run towards the Tavern in the direction of the Grace Gates, but in all the confusion and the masses of people, no-one knew where the ball was as Thommo and Lillee were rushing up and down the wicket. They must have completed at least half a dozen runs before umpire Tommy Spencer announced that they would award Australia only 2 runs. Thommo protested:

'Pig's arse, Tommy—we've been running up and down here all afternoon. Who are you kidding?' I really got stuck into him.

We were still 18 runs short of a win. Vanburn Holder came on. I couldn't find the ball against the background of the bricks on the pavilion. It was pretty late at night then. I missed a ball and started to run, but the keeper Deryck Murray gathered the ball and under-armed it back to the stumps to run me out. The game was lost.

Thommo was the fifth Australian batsman to be run out.

The West Indies won by 17 runs in a match that attracted 26,000 people to Lord's, producing £66,950, a record for a one-day match in England. Cricket's first World Cup final began at 11 a.m. and finished at 8.43 p.m. in fading light. Then there was the spectacle of Clive Lloyd holding the inaugural World Cup jubilantly high after the presentation by MCC President Prince Philip, the Duke of Edinburgh. For Thommo, the loss cut deeply:

The West Indians were due to tour Australia later that year and I vowed that I would make them pay for what happened at Lord's. They would never face faster bowling . . .

After the excitement of the first World Cup, the Australians had to re-group and prepare for a four-match Test series with England. In the leadup games, Thommo hit a brilliant 44 not out against Hampshire at Southampton, but he struggled with the ball and couldn't find much rhythm, taking 0/80 off 23 overs in the Hampshire first innings, during which Barry Richards hit a brilliant 96, and 0/63 off 10 overs in the second. It wasn't a great start to the first-class summer for Thommo. Then came the MCC match at Lord's and Thommo again struggled, taking 0/51 off 15 overs in the first innings and finally a wicket in the second, getting David Lloyd lbw to take 1/36 off 13 overs. Thommo didn't play the next match against Glamorgan, but played the First Test at Edgbaston.

England captain Mike Denness won the toss and put Australia into bat. Australia scored 359, with Rick McCosker (59), Alan Turner (37), Ian Chappell (52), Ross Edwards (56) and Rodney Marsh (61) leading the way, before Thommo came in to bat. He hit out brilliantly to score 49.

When I came to the wicket, Thommo was blazing and we put on 16 (of which Thommo scored 13) and he seemed certain to reach his maiden Test half-century. Then he drove lamely at Derek Underwood and holed out to Geoff Arnold at mid-off.

Then came the rain.

And the rain didn't only dampen English spirits and make the pitch unhelpful for the England batting line-up, it effectively meant the end for their skipper, Mike Denness. England collapsed for 101; Lillee 5/15 and Walker 5/48. Thommo bowled okay, conceding only 21 runs in 10 tight overs, but failed to take a wicket.

Batting a second time England managed 173, and this time Thommo bowled magnificently, taking 5/38 off 18 overs. Both Lillee and Walker took 2 wickets apiece and I got one, the last man, Underwood. Graham Gooch, playing his debut Test, was dismissed for a duck in each innings.

Thommo's 5-wicket haul after a bad run with the ball really fired him up. In the following county games, he took 4/54 off 16 overs and 3/21 off 14 overs in Australia's 28-run victory over Derbyshire at Chesterfield; before a further 3-wicket haul against Lancashire. The most satisfaction for Thommo in that bowling stint was when he clean-bowled Clive Lloyd for 33.

For the Second Test, England sacked their captain Denness and brought in Tony Greig to lead the side. They also brought in Northampton batsman David Steele, who wore glasses and had gone prematurely grey, not quite the image of a genuine red-blooded Test batsman hell-bent upon taking the fight to the world's most ferocious pace bowling pair.

England batted first and Dennis Lillee bowled brilliantly on that sluggish pitch to take the first 4 wickets: Barry Wood (6), John Edrich (9), Dennis Amiss (0) and Graham Gooch (6). England was a precarious 4/49 when Steele wandered onto the green sward of historic Lord's to join his captain, Greig. Thommo recalls:

> I saw this old-looking bloke with white hair approach the wicket and I said to him, 'Hey, what have we here, Groucho Marx or Father Christmas?'

Steele proceeded to play forward to all that Thommo and Lillee could throw at him. Gradually the England innings turned around, with Greig—

who was lucky to survive the first ball when he let it go from Max Walker and the ball took his glove for an obvious catch behind but the appeal was disallowed—scoring 96 and Steele getting bowled by Thomson, dragging a short ball onto his stumps, for a debut Test 50. Alan Knott hit 69 and Bob Woolmer, in his Test debut, scored 33 before the innings folded at 315. But Thommo had his doubts:

> *The more the innings went on, the more obvious it was that the pitch had been deliberately slowed by grounds staff. The outfield was lightning fast and the pitch slow and allowing no bounce at all. Dennis and I would let fly with balls of genuine pace and short of a good length and here we had this bloke Steele coming on to the front foot and the ball hardly bouncing knee-high.*

Lillee took 4/84 off 20 overs and Thommo 2/92 off 24. Some say it was David Steele who thwarted our pace attack: I say it was the Lord's groundsmen, part of a ploy to blunt our speed.

In his summary of the Australians in England 1975, Norman Preston wrote in the 1976 *Wisden Cricketers' Almanack*:

> . . . the fast bowlers laboured on very different surfaces than the rock-like ones of their own country. It was even suggested in some quarters that the groundsmen deliberately made soft pitches for the Australian matches, which was absurd. The same type of pitches prevailed almost everywhere for County Championship matches. There had been constant rain in Britain for almost twelve months.
>
> Not only had the water gone very deep down, but in the autumn and early spring much preparatory work on the grounds could not be done. So the batsmen who opposed the Australians were never subjected to the pace and bounce off the pitch, nor the hard knocks that were suffered by the England team in the Southern Hemisphere.[16]

The extraordinary aspect of Preston talking about all the rain England had experienced was that since the Australians arrived in England in June 1975, there was hardly a drop of rain; indeed we encountered drought conditions, with outfields parched and the wickets devoid of grass and as dead as a dead dingo's donger.

Earlier in *Wisden*, Preston wrote:

> At the beginning of August when England and Australia were engaged at Lord's in an intriguing contest it was hotter than in North Africa at 93 degrees Fahrenheit, the highest temperature in the London area since July, 1948. The Australians were also here, so perhaps there was some excuse for the streaker who filled up with Australian liquor, invaded the pitch while England were building up their second innings total of 436.[17]

The state of the wicket had the final say in the Third Test at Headingly, Leeds, when the game was abandoned after vandals had sabotaged the pitch in the early hours of Tuesday—the Fifth and scheduled final day of the Test. The perpetrators got under the covers at the pavilion end and dug out holes with knives near the popping crease, pouring a gallon or more of crude oil onto a spot where a good length ball would have pitched. England had scored 288, Australia replied with 135, then England was bowled out for 291, leaving the Australians needing 445 to win. The odds on an Australian win were 9–1, but at stumps on the fourth day Ian Chappell's men were 3/220 with Rick McCosker on 95 and Doug Walters 25.

Chappell believed Australia had a good chance of winning given the state of the benign pitch and the form of his batsmen. But the saboteurs had the last say.

In the final Test, Australia hit 532 for 9 wickets, declared, then rolled England for 191, with Thommo bowling skillfully, taking 4/50 off 22.1 overs, and Lillee 2/44 off 19 overs. Max Walker also grabbed 4/63 off 25 overs. Ah, back to the good old days, or so we thought. But Thommo believes:

> *We made a mistake of making too many runs. We sent them back in to follow on and they blocked the guts out of us. Up and down those bloody stairs every day. It was such a drag. From the Friday to the Wednesday we made the trek up the stairs out on the field. I'm not*

kidding, it was like a torture. Up and down the stairs, out and bowl, up and down the stairs, it was unbelievable. We bowled a million overs each, Dennis, myself, Max and Rowdy. Even the Chappells bowled and 'Freddie' Walters.

Bob Woolmer scored the slowest century—it took him six hours 36 minutes—against Australia in Test history. When I chatted with him after my 64th unsuccessful over, telling him to play a few shots and stop boring the shit out of all and sundry, Woolmer replied: 'Good Lord, man, I am trying to play strokes, but I simply can't get the ball through the field. But I am trying . . .'

Trying he was, and trying that match indeed had been.

In the England second innings of 538, Lillee took 4/91 off 52 overs; Thomson 1/63 off 30 overs; Walker 0/91 off 46 overs; I took 0/95 off 64 overs; Ian Chappell 0/52 off 17 overs; Greg Chappell 0/53 off 12 overs; Walters 4/34 off 10.5 overs, and Ross Edwards, playing in his final Test for Australia, 0/20 off 2 overs. It seemed very much like England was determined to curtail the effectiveness of our bowlers, especially Thomson and Lillee. And they devised a way—prepare slow, low wickets that would stop the threat in its tracks.

Norman Preston quoted a certain Dr R.W. Cockshut in the *Wisden* as saying:

'. . . we may expect in 1976 up to ten deaths and forty irreversible brain injuries caused by impact of cricket ball on skull'. Dr Cockshut hopes that the trouble will be dealt with at the source. He suggests that any ball which would hit a batsman standing up on any part of his anatomy on a line above the hips, should be called a bumper by the umpire and 10 runs added to the score. Bumpers would disappear overnight; the batsman could play in the certain knowledge that he would not be attacked by the lethal missile traveling at over 140 feet per second.[18]

Thankfully Dr Cockshut never got his way, although the English groundsmen did their job well in 1975. The Test match figures make interesting reading: Lillee took 21 wickets at 21.90; Thomson took

16 wickets at 28.56; Walker 14 wickets at 34.71; and I took 9 wickets at 42.88.

For England, Snow took 11 wickets at 32.37; Greig 8 wickets at 40.25; Old 7 wickets at 40.42; and Underwood 6 wickets at 44.33.

The great English sense of humour shone through and perhaps the best example of that cricketing summer came from the talented pen of Ian Wooldridge of the London *Daily Mail*. As a columnist Wooldridge had interviewed some of the world's great sporting figures including Muhummad Ali and that other renowned Ugandan boxer, Idi Amin. Wooldridge was taken by the Australian pace attack, Thommo in particular, so he created the character 'Terror Tomkins', ace Australian fast bowler, king of malapropism and his country's Pommie-hater-in-chief.

The cartoon caricature Wooldridge created was a person something between Thommo and Lillee, although his fictional 'letters to Mum' were so clearly Thommo. In one letter to his mother, 'Tomkins' wrote:

At London Airport they waved all the Abbos straight through immigration and made us get on the end of the queue about ten miles long. 'C'mon, let's pizzoff', said my oppo, Dennis, but I said, 'No, let's stay and kill a couple of their batsmen'. It just shows how the Establishment works in England, because by the time we got to Lord's they'd changed all the laws of cricket so that you couldn't bowl bouncers in the World Cup. They also tried to con us into playing two warm-up matches against some place called Gloucestershire. Well, we jumped at that because we thought that was right next door to Chelsea, where all the birds are. Not at all. We were thinking about Gloucester-road. Gloucestershire is bloody near Chicago. It's wild west country so we told them to stuff it and sorted out the local talent. You can't move for birds here. They've got this thing called the Permissible Society.[19]

Thommo survived Wooldridge's 'Terror Tomkins' column, a spate of no-ball problems, homesickness and being surrounded by pretty girls in the early part of the tour to play a key part in this Ashes-retaining side. But he was determined to give the West Indians 'what for' when they toured Australia later that year.

Clive Lloyd's men didn't know what feelings they had stirred in Thommo over winning the first World Cup at Lord's in 1975.

9 THOMMO IS A KNOCK-OUT

The umpire, Tom Brooks, came down the track to try and calm the
players down. Lennie and I were having a bit of a verbal stoush.
I knew how volatile Lennie could get, but Tom wasn't about to let us
be. 'Now listen here, umpire, you don't know the history between
us and you don't know Lennie. This is between me and Lennie—so stay
out of it.'

Despite missing the second innings of the Fifth Test in Adelaide and
the whole of the MCG Sixth Test, then bowling his heart out on the
unresponsive England wickets in 1975, Thommo still managed to take a
veritable truckload of English Test wickets within a twelve-month period.
He took 33 wickets at 17 Down Under in 1974–75, and 16 at 28 in England
1975. Nine Tests in all: 49 wickets at an average of 21.

Thommo was fit and rearing to go and his partner in speed, Dennis
Lillee, was bowling even better now than he had in England in 1972. Lillee
was no longer dependent upon all-out speed. He had learnt to mix his
pace better and use the leg and off-cutter to great effect. One of the dis-
appointments for England was Geoff Boycott's absence in both the Tests
Down Under and in England. It was amazing that Boycott ruled himself

out of the tour of Australia. Some suggested that he wasn't too keen to play to Thomson–Lillee pace combination; however, when he pulled out of the tour, Thomson was very much an unknown quantity to all but a few in Australia and Lillee was on the comeback trial, there being no guarantee that he would bowl as well in Test cricket as he once did before his back injury. But Thommo has his own theory:

> I think that when FOT [Dennis Lillee] and I came on the scene, Boycott went AWOL. I don't think for a moment that he was scared of being hit, but I do think he had a fear of failure, which is pretty hard to understand for a bloke of his ability.
>
> It was unfortunate that Boycott didn't tour, because I would have liked to have had a crack at him. He was a good player, no doubt, but by the time I got to bowl to him in a Test match, he was nowhere near the player he was a few years before.

It was extraordinary that the two heroes of Illingworth's successful Australian tour in 1970–71, Geoff Boycott and John Snow, missed the 1974–75 Australian tour. Boycott, of course, ruled himself out, but Snow was omitted. The moody Sussex fast bowler was accused of not trying in county games and he had an on-field altercation with Indian batsman Sunil Gavasker which went down like a lead balloon with the officials at Lord's. Many believed that once the strict disciplinarian Alec Bedser was named England tour manager, Snow didn't have a hope of getting a spot. Others maintained that England captain Mike Denness would not be able to manage Snow and have him bowl to the standard which he reached under a great captain such as Illingworth. Whatever the reasons, neither player made the tour and the England team was all the worse off because of that.

The 1975–76 Australia–West Indies series was billed as the 'World Championship' of cricket. Australia had a new captain, Greg Chappell. His brother, Ian, had made the Fourth Test at The Oval in August 1975 his last game as Test captain. Ian Chappell had led Australia 30 times for 15 wins, 5 losses and 10 draws. He was an outstanding captain, to rank alongside the likes of Australia's Richie Benaud and, later, Mark Taylor, and England's Ray Illingworth.

Predictably Greg Chappell took over from his brother as captain for the First Test at the Gabba. Doug Walters had suffered a dreadful knee injury in the SA–NSW Sheffield Shield match in Adelaide a few weeks before and was ruled out of the series. It was a blow because Walters had always played magnificently against the West Indians, averaging 92 runs per innings against them in just nine Tests.

The Fourth Test at The Oval in 1975 also marked Ross Edwards's final Test. Edwards retired after twenty Test matches, during which the self-effacing right-hand batsman and brilliant cover fieldsman scored a total of 1171 runs at an average of 40.37. He never considered himself a great player, but Edwards was very much a self-made cricketer—and if he wasn't a great player, he was a damned good one. Despite missing Walters through injury and the retired Edwards, Australia's stocks received a boost by the announcement that Ian Redpath, who was unavailable for the 1975 tour of England, was back to open the innings, probably with Alan Turner; while Gary Gilmour and Max Walker would fight it out for the third pace-bowling spot after Thommo and Lillee.

For the West Indies, fast bowler Michael Holding was making his Test debut. The Australian players had heard glowing reports of the young West Indian fast bowler. He was a former 440-yard runner, a man with superb style and rhythm. Holding had express pace and, we had heard, could bowl all day. What we didn't realise at that time was Holding had the longest approach to the wicket and the slowest amble back to his mark in world cricket. Watching Holding bowl was like watching paint dry, except that immediately after delivery it was as if a hand-grenade had been chucked into the tin of paint, for his deliveries fairly exploded off the wicket. Later in the series Rod Marsh made the observation, 'You could be in good form when you settled over your bat to face Holding and the by the time he got to his delivery stride you could be totally out of form.'

Thommo was keen to get stuck into the West Indian batsmen on his home turf. Many of the 1975 Australians believed the sluggishness of the English wickets negated the likes of Thommo and Lillee to such an extent that their effectiveness was pretty much tamed. The lack of bounce was the crucial missing ingredient. But we knew that the Australian wickets for the coming series against the Windies would provide plenty of pace and lots of bounce.

After Australia lost the World Cup, Thommo made a secret vow that he would make a big impact on the coming series against Clive Lloyd's team. The dead, 'doctored', unresponsive wickets he encountered in England helped fuel his determination to fire against the West Indians.

I think the whole England thing got up my nose. The homesickness, then the World Cup debacle at Lord's where we lost a match we probably should have won but for five run-outs. I was determined to let fly at these Windies blokes and show them that I was mighty quick. I was fit and fired up and ready to go.

Thommo played four Sheffield Shield matches in the lead-up to the series with the West Indies. Against NSW at the Gabba he took 2/69 and 3/59 in Queensland's 8-wicket victory, and against SA in Adelaide, a game Queensland lost by 9 wickets, Thommo took 4/60 and 1/19. Incidentally I got to bat early against Thommo in the SA first innings. Our regular opener, Ashley Woodcock, was inconvenienced, so Ian Chappell opened the SA innings and I went in at the fall of the first wicket. I got 34 and survived against Thommo by the usual ducking and diving and getting a single early in the over to watch the veritable carnage from the safety of the non-striker's end. It probably helped that I knew full well that Thommo never tried to knock a tail-ender's block off, although I was a stand-in number three. Thommo knew I couldn't handle the short ball very well; however, there was the ever-present danger of a Thommo delivery rearing from a good length and coming straight at 100 miles per hour [160 kph]. Rain washed out the first two days of Queensland's clash with Victoria at the MCG, but Thommo continued his consistently good form with 4/64 off 16 overs. Then it was off to play WA in Perth, always a tough match to win at the WACA ground. But win Queensland did, thanks to Thommo's blitz. He took 6/47 in the WA first innings and 4/73 in the second to help his team to a convincing 96-run victory.

In four Shield games Thommo had taken 24 wickets and he was indeed ready for the Test matches.

In the Brisbane First Test, Clive Lloyd won the toss and the West Indians batted first. The series began on an extraordinary note for Dennis Lillee's first ball saw Windies opener Gordon Greenidge pad up, the ball shot back off the seam and umpire Robin Bailhache slowly raised his index finger. What a start to a Test series!

One ball: West Indies 1/0.

That day, the Windies batting was swashbuckling and at times exhilarating, but mostly there were too many lazy and irresponsible shots. Roy Fredericks flayed the bowling to race to 46, Lawrence Rowe was run out for 28 and Viv Richards went for a duck. At lunch the West Indies was 6/120!

Poor batting, rather than great bowling, led to their downfall. Only Deryck Murray (66) looked at all convincing and the side managed a total of 214. To give you an idea of the way the West Indians played, Lillee took 3/84 off just 11 overs; Thommo took 1/69 off 10 overs; and Gilmour grabbed the spoils with 4/42 off 12 overs. While the runs came at a spectacular rate, so too the wickets. It seemed as though each Windies batsman came to the wicket, flayed the bowling for a while, then holed out, with either a slash caught in the slips or a wild hook caught on the boundary.

Australia replied with 366, Greg Chappell leading with a handsome 123. Turner (81), Redpath (39) and Ian Chappell (41) batted well before Rodney Marsh hit out for 48.

In their second innings the West Indies batted better with Lawrence Rowe (107) and Alvin Kallicharran (101) figuring in a splendid 198-run fourth wicket stand. But the rest, apart from Murray (55), fell away and Lloyd's men finished with 370, leaving Australia ample time to hit 219 runs for victory.

Ian Chappell (74 not out) gave Greg much of the strike to enable his younger brother to complete a hundred in each innings, some feat for a man leading his country for the first time. Greg Chappell was 109 not out at the end.

Three days after the Test ended, Thommo joined his Queensland team-mates for a Sheffield Shield match against NSW at the SCG. This was a very significant game for Thommo because his old mate, Punchbowl High School and Bankstown A-grade opening bowling partner, Len Pascoe, was making his Sheffield Shield debut for NSW.

Queensland batted first and despite the efforts of Greg Chappell (124), Phil Carlson (64), John MacLean (34), Thommo (42) and Malcolm Franke (36), Pascoe bowled splendidly and took 5/96 off 22.5 overs. Pascoe will never forget his first over to his former team-mate:

> Thommo played and missed the first ball, but the second one he snicked straight into the hands of Steve Rixon, our keeper. The ball went into the gloves and then out again. Thommo looked at Rixon and said, 'Hey mate, you fuckin' idiot. You don't know what's going to happen.'[1]

Thommo recalls that they weren't holding back:

> *The umpire, Tom Brooks, came down the track to try and calm the players down. Lennie and I were having a bit of a verbal stoush. I knew how volatile Lennie could get, but Tom wasn't about to let us be. 'Now listen here, umpire, you don't know the history between us and you don't know Lennie. This is between me and Lennie—so stay out of it.'*

Lennie thought his next ball should be a smart delivery:

> I bowled a slower ball—and Thommo hit it into the Ladies' Stand.[2]

When NSW batted, Thommo gave Lennie a slower ball, perhaps one of the rare slower balls he would deliver in any match, and Pascoe tried to 'clock' it, but only 'managed to hit the ball far enough to be caught at short midwicket'. NSW was dismissed for 260; Thomson took 5/84 off 16.2 overs.

Throughout their first-class career rivalry playing for opposing Sheffield Shield teams, Thommo baited his mate big time. He left a bowl of milk near the NSW dressing-room door, with a note attached: 'Well bowled, pussy-cat.' Pascoe says the bowl of milk was the forerunner to all manner of pranks Thommo perpetrated when the pair met in a Shield match:

> Another time he left me a bunch of flowers, with the note: 'Well bowled, Flower!'[3]

Batting a second time Queensland hit 5/276, with David Ogilvie (132 not out) and Ian Davis (61). Pascoe didn't fair as well as he did first up, this time having 67 runs taken from his 10 overs. At least Thommo didn't get him again when NSW batted. He fell to leg-spinner Malcolm Franke for a duck.

In the NSW second innings, Thommo got the key wickets of Peter Toohey (0) and Rick McCosker (18) in taking 2/75, and Queensland won outright easily by 172 runs.

The Second Test was held in Perth on the famously lightning-fast WACA ground wicket. It was destined for myself to be a hard-fought contest between Australia and the West Indies, but before the game got underway there was trouble.

On the eve of the Perth Test I had to go to the dentist to have a tooth removed. Unbeknown to me, an abscess had formed under the tooth and while the dentist explained that it had to be pulled out, he also explained that he had to do so without administering anaesthetic. The tooth broke off at the jaw line and it had to be dug out: no anaesthetic, lots of blood and plenty of pain. But the real agony was to come—bowling to the West Indians.

Thankfully we batted first. Ian Chappell (156) played a magnificent hand, one of his best in Test cricket, but had too few players batting in support and Australia scored a total of 329. Thommo and I were both bowled for a duck, courtesy of Michael Holding.

Then the West Indies batted, and all the Australian bowlers were thrashed unmercifully. Roy Fredericks smashed an unbelievable 169 off 145 balls with a six and 27 fours. Clive Lloyd scored 149, although Dennis Lillee dropped him, a skier, at mid-on before Lloyd had scored a single run; and Kallicharran (57) should have been stumped first ball by Rodney Marsh off my bowling. Cruel game, cricket. I finished with 0/103 off 26 overs and Thommo, who took the wickets of Lawrence Rowe (28), Viv Richards (12) and Michael Holding (0), finished with 3/128 off 17 overs. Lillee took 2/123 off 20 overs, Gilmour 2/103 off 14 overs, and Walker 2/99 off 17 overs.

Then Andy Roberts (7/53) in the second innings cut a swathe through the Australian batting line-up and we fell for just 169, giving the Windies an innings and 87 runs outright win. In three Test innings, Thommo had taken just 4/286—71.5 runs per wicket. It wasn't a great form guide to the Tests to come.

During the Perth Test, tragedy was to strike at the heart of Thommo's life. Martin Bedkober, a wicket-keeper-batsman who left his native Sydney to forge a new cricket career in Brisbane, was killed while batting in a grade match for Thommo's club Toombul. Bedkober was Thommo and Ian Davis's flatmate, and he was only 22.

Ian Davis, the NSW and Test batsman, who was also playing for Toombul, moved to Brisbane just before the start of the 1975–76 season. Davis says:

> I moved to Brisbane to play State cricket under Greg Chappell during the final Test in England in August, 1975. Errold La Frantz, who was on the cricket committee at Toombul, a former State selector and proprietor of a sports store, said there was an opportunity with Queensland.
>
> They had Majid Khan [the Pakistani Test batsman] playing for Queensland in 1974–75 and I thought it would be a good opportunity. I was transferred there with the Commonwealth Bank so, unlike many other cricketers, there was no problem with getting employment.[4]

Davis will never forget that fateful day when their mate was killed. He had encouraged Bedkober to go to Brisbane in the hope of getting a game for that State.

> Martin was a terrific wicket-keeper-batsman. He played for Petersham in Sydney and had represented the NSW Second XI. His batting was his strength, so he probably wouldn't have been picked for Queensland ahead of their keeper John MacLean, but he might have as a specialist batsman.
>
> I had just been dismissed and Martin was facing a medium-paced bowler. Apparently, it got up a bit off a length and he allowed it to strike him on the chest. Moments later Martin collapsed onto the pitch.

I went straight to the Royal Brisbane Hospital to be with him. In the hospital room, a doctor appeared from behind drapes and asked if there was anyone close to him here. I nodded. The doctor said softly, 'I am sorry. There was nothing we could do. It was a freak accident. The ball hit in a spot which caused a massive blood clot—no oxygen was getting through. I'm afraid we couldn't save the young man.'

I couldn't believe it. Martin, dead? He was a young, strong and fit bloke. How could this happen. Martin's death really knocked the stuffing out of me.[5]

It was at tea time on the second day, December 13, 1975 when Australian selector Sam Loxton came into the Australian dressing-room to relay the sad news of Martin's death to Thommo. Thommo remembers thinking:

Shit! Martin and Wizard [Ian Davis] *were playing together for Toombul against Sandgate–Redcliff. Martin was hit by a medium-pacer. I couldn't believe it. Martin was a good bloke and a really good player. A real tragedy.*

Thommo attended Martin's funeral in Sydney in the week between the Second and Third Test matches. He says that Martin's death 'really hit home' and while he never slowed his pace, it changed the way he thought about bowling.

During the Perth Test, a series of speed tests were carried out and Thommo's fastest ball was clocked at 99.7 miles per hour, or 160.398 kph. The top speeds recorded after Thomson were: Andy Roberts (West Indies) 93.6 mph (150.6 kph), Michael Holding (West Indies) 92.3 mph (148.51 kph), Dennis Lillee (Australia) 86.4 mph (139.017 kph), Keith Boyce (West Indies) 85.2 mph (137.086 kph) and Gary Gilmour (Australia) 83 mph (133.54 kph).

Thommo bowled his quickest ball at 99.7 mph (160.398 kph) to Roy Fredericks, giving the batsman 0.43 of a second to deal with it before it crashed into the bat. After hitting the pitch, the ball slowed considerably, as all deliveries do, and by the time Fredericks's bat came into contact with the ball, the speed was clocked at 81 mph (130.329 kph).

Western Australian University lecturer in bio-mechanics, Dr Brian Blanksby, with physical education senior lecturer Mr Tommy Penrose and WA coach Mr Daryl Foster, spent hours of painstaking study to analyse the data. The speed test study was carried out using two cameras synchronised to record ball speed on to the bat and the batsman's response. The bowlers were filmed mostly at 200 to 300 frames per second and sometimes up to 500 frames per second with the best precision equipment in the world.

Today's speed testing equipment may be superior to that of 1976, but I still wonder about speed tests that claim Brett Lee and Shohab Akthar have both registered speeds in excess of 160 kph. Those who played against Thommo at the peak of his pace powers believe he was much quicker than anyone else, including Lee and Akthar. One has only to observe the speeds shown on Channel Nine's cricket coverage to realise that technology can sometimes be misleading. Glenn McGrath might have the batsman hopping about, ducking and diving with his short-of-length deliveries, but when his average speed is shown on screen you find we are expected to believe that he isn't much faster than the average medium pacer, like New Zealand's Brian MacMillan. It all depends on the way the speed is recorded. A MacMillan full-toss might even be recorded as a faster ball than a McGrath bouncer. Why? Because the speed is recorded in a straight line, from delivery to the point where it passes the stumps. If McGrath's short ball goes from hand to the pitch, then on the up past the stumps, even though it leaves his hand much faster than any medium-pacer, it will take about the same length of time to get from his hand to the point in line with the stumps at the other end than your average, run-of-the mill medium pacer. So even the measurement of speed can be misleading.

Having won the Perth Test, the West Indians had locked the series at 1–all. Thommo's figures in the first two Tests belied his confidence.

I was bowling okay. My rhythm was fine and I reckoned the wickets would come.

Despite the typically sluggish MCG wicket in the Third Test, Thommo bowled like a tornado. He took 5/62 off just 11 overs, but a lot of those runs came off thick edges and slashes over the slips cordon. Lillee took 4/56 off 14 overs, which didn't leave a lot of the spoils for the other bowlers. Max Walker picked up the remaining wicket, clean-bowling Vanburn Holder for 24 to take 1/46 off 13 overs. The West Indians scored a moderate 234.

Thommo dismissed Perth Test hero Roy Fredericks (59), Gordon Greenidge (3), Lawrence Rowe (0), Alvin Kallicharran (20) and Clive Lloyd (2)—quite a haul. Rowe copped a Thommo special; the ball reared from a length at hurricane pace and the West Indian did well to get a touch, but the ball careered at breakneck speed on the 'up' to Ian Chappell at first slip. It was high and to Chappelli's left, but he took the ball as clean as a whistle. It was the best catch I'd seen by any first slip fieldsman, and I have seen the great Bobby Simpson, arguably the best first slipper of them all, take some fabulous catches in that position, so too Clive Lloyd and Mark Taylor. But this one was special because it was climbing at unbelievable pace. It was Ian Chappell's 100th Test match catch and, to me, the best of them all.

Australia scored 405 in reply, thanks mainly to a fine century by Ian Redpath (102), who wore the West Indies pacemen down by refusing to hook. The tall, angular Victorian laconically moved his head out of the way of all deliveries pitched short of a length and above shoulder high, and eventually the fast men realised that it was a waste of energy to bowl that length to Redpath. So they pitched the ball up and Redpath, a lovely cover driver, peppered the off-side boundary. Former Northcote, Victorian and later South Australian batsman Gary Gosier scored 109 in his Test debut. He too handled the short stuff well, often 'upper-cutting' the odd short ball outside the line of off stump and helping himself to a four over the slips cordon.

Clive Lloyd hit a fine 102 in the Windies second innings, but his was very much a lone hand. Lillee took 3/70 and Thommo 1/51, but their figures belie their impact on Lloyd's men. The West Indians hit out at everything and you got the distinct feeling that it was a matter of getting a few before they fell. The Windies totalled 312 in their second innings, and an 8-wicket victory for Australia restored the 'balance of power'.

Thommo had taken 6/113 off 20 overs for the match. He was expensive, but his pace was incredible and the Windies must have decided upon a collective policy of 'hit out before you get out'.

Just before the Fourth Test got underway in Sydney, Dennis Lillee was ruled unfit due to a chest infection. In came Gary Gilmour to join Max Walker and to open the attack with Thommo.

The Windies batted first and wicket-keeper Deryck Murray (32) was out to the best outfield catch I've ever seen. Fans will recall Glenn McGrath's catch at Adelaide Oval to dismiss Englishman Michael Vaughan, but Jeff Thomson's catch to dismiss Murray was out of this world. Max Walker bowled a big in-dipper and Murray scooped it high toward square leg. Thommo was fielding at deep, wide-mid. He ran towards the skied ball at full bore, just like the times he'd run down a wild pig in the Queensland outback. It seemed from my position in the gully and right behind the line of flight that the ball would land well in front of Thommo, however fast he was moving, and bounce over the fence for four. But no, Thommo somehow got within range and he dived head-long and took the ball in his clutching right hand just as he hit the turf.

Cricket writer Phil Tresidder wrote:

He [Thommo] sprinted 25 metres around the boundary to dive for a breath-taking catch from a Deryck Murray hook. Thomson's momentum sent him bowling along the turf but he came up clutching that ball and the 53,001 crowd roared applause for minutes.[6]

Some of the West Indian batsmen got starts, but the side only got 355, less than they really should have achieved. Thommo bowled 25 overs to take 3/117, but Walker got the lion's share, taking 4/70 off 21 overs. Greg Chappell also slipped in to take 2/10 off just 4.2 overs. I got 1/61, not helped by Cosier who dropped three straight-forward catches off me— Lawrence Rowe (twice) and Deryck Murray. Cosier was a rotund, tough and gritty batsmen and a good medium-paced bowler, but he had the reflexes of an elephant on rollerskates and if he had to move to get to the ball, he couldn't catch a cold.

But it was Thommo who caused havoc within the Windies camp. His sheer pace hurt his opponent both physically and psychologically.

Thommo struck Bernard Julien on the right thumb and subsequent X-rays revealed a fracture, and with the score at 3/166 a Thommo lifter hit Clive Lloyd on the jaw, forcing him to retire hurt. Lloyd resumed with the Windies score 5/233 and he went on to score a courageous 51, taking his team to 6/286 at stumps.

In his column in the *Sunday Telegraph*, Lloyd wrote:

It took me until yesterday afternoon to find what Jeff Thomson's knock-out delivery is all about. I almost went down for the count after taking one from Jeff fairly and squarely on the chin. I felt pretty groggy for a while and decided to quit the field because of the pain in my right ear. There was nothing I could do to avoid the blow—it just got up off a perfect length.[7]

In Australia's innings Greg Chappell was in superb batting form and his magnificent 182 not out took Australia to a commanding score of 405, just a 50-run lead, but to us that was a huge psychological advantage, especially if we could grab a couple of early wickets.

The West Indians had to negotiate a tricky 75 minutes of batting before stumps. The light was poor and rain threatened. Alvin Kallicharran opened the batting with Roy Fredericks because of the injury to Julien. Thommo bowled extremely fast, perhaps the quickest he had bowled all summer, and he soon had the visitors in trouble. In Thomson's 4th over he bowled a bouncer to Kallicharran, and the batsman attempted to hook, although it was part hook and part trying to evade the ball. He only managed to get a top edge and the ball flew high and wide of Max Walker, who ran the boundary line to played take the ball above his head—a fine catch. Gary Gilmour, who was bowling superbly in support of the fast man, dropped short to Fredericks and the little left-hander hooked high to Alan Turner at deep fine leg. Turner completed the catch and the Windies were a precarious 2/32.

With only 23 minutes of play remaining umpires Tom Brooks and Reg Ledwidge decided play should end for the day, although they said play would resume if the light improved. With just 10 minutes to go, back the players came and seven balls later Gilmour bowled Viv Richards a bouncer and the right-hander tried to pull the ball, but got it high on the splice and knocked it straight up in the air to backward square leg where Thommo cruised into position to take the catch. At stumps the West Indies were 3/33, and destined to lose the match.

As Lillee, out of the game with a chest infection looked on, Jeff Thomson bowled Australia into an unassailable position to win the Frank Worrell Trophy. I never believed it possible, but Thommo bowled even quicker in this innings than at any other time in the series. The pace he generated from the Randwick End was amazing and he sliced through the West Indians like a hot knife in a tub of butter. With Kallicharran an overnight scalp, Thommo added Lawrence Rowe (7), Clive Lloyd (19), Keith Boyce (0), Michael Holding (5) and Deryck Murray (50).

It was Murray who sparked the West Indian fight-back in their first innings and it was Murray again this time. He was like the England keeper Alan Knott in that he had plenty of grit and would dig in and play instinctively. But almost immediately after Murray had raised his bat to acknowledge his half-century, Thommo bowled him with a magnificent delivery. Murray was beaten by sheer pace. The ball knocked the off stump flying and it cartwheeled ominously towards a delighted Rodney Marsh behind the stumps.

Without Lillee, Thomson had bowled as fast as he had ever bowled; a blistering 15 overs of sustained pace to take 6/50. It was one of the most devastating spells of sheer pace any of us had seen and it was good to be on this man's side. Cricket writer Phil Wilkins summed it up well when he wrote:

> Thomson bowled for the first time in Sydney without his old sparring partner Dennis Lillee, who had a chest virus and could not be considered. If anything the responsibility made Thomson bowl better. After an erratic first morning, he worked out his length and line and gave the West Indies many torrid moments with his searing deliveries. No fast bowler in the world makes the ball rear as viciously off the seam from a good length or just short of a length as Thomson.[8]

The West Indians lost the Fourth Test match and only a few gallant individual efforts gave the West Indians hope for the final two matches, in Adelaide and Melbourne. As a collective, Clive Lloyd's men were down for the count.

Deryck Murray, who scored his 1000th run in this Test, became the first West Indian to make 100 dismissals and complete the wicket-keeper's 'double' when he caught Alan Turner off Holding in the Australian second innings.

Two days before the start of the Fifth Test match in Adelaide, news broke that Thommo had signed a ten-year contract with Radio 4IP in Brisbane, worth a staggering $633,000. In the *Melbourne Sun*, the headline read 'IT'S TYCOON THOMSON—$633,000 contract':

Test fast bowler Jeff Thomson yesterday made giant strides towards becoming Australia's first million dollar cricketer when he signed a 10-year contract worth $633,000.

He signed the contract with Brisbane radio station 4IP, which is promoting cricket in Queensland.

Thomson signed after 24 hours of negotiations with his manager, David Lord, 4IP board members and Queensland Cricket Association officials.

The 25-year-old bachelor-bowler said he would become a millionaire if his plans worked out over the next few years.

Station manager Mr Ken Mulcahy said yesterday that Thomson's contract was a package deal involving several big Brisbane companies, [but] he would not name them.

'The company will be paying the money to Jeff over 10 years and the companies who spend with 4IP can use him for personal appearances.

'I hope this contract does not create jealousy amongst the rest of his team-mates because my company is paying the money, not the QCA.'[9]

David Lord was over the moon about the Thommo contract:

That's the day I became his manager, the first manager of an elite sportsman in Australia. I arranged for Thommo to get this lucrative deal with Radio 41P, thanks mainly to great vision from the station manager, Ken Mulcahy. He was one of the first media executives to see the fantastic value of having a top sportsman as part of their stable.[10]

The widely reported $633,000 deal Lord negotiated for Thommo with Mulcahy was framed in such a way that Thommo would receive the bulk of the money at the end of the ten-year deal. Lord explains:

Still Thommo was on something like $40,000 a year, which was a helluva lot of money in those days. I never got a cent. That was 95 per cent my fault, I just wanted to help him. I later managed the likes of Viv Richards [West Indian batting great] and [Olympic swimming star] Stephen Holland.[11]

Ian 'Wizard' Davis recalls the day Thommo told him about the 4IP deal:

Thommo was all smiles. He went straight out and bought a boat, a Ferrari and a pick-up truck, then we sat down and had a whole lot of beers.

It was a great night. I was only up in Brisbane for a year, but I got to know Thommo really well. He's a fabulous bloke, a great man with a great heart; the most loyal bloke of them all.[12]

David Lord, however, didn't always see a clear pathway in his business dealings with the fast man:

You wouldn't call my relationship with Thommo a close liaison between client and manager. Thommo would rarely get in touch. He did so when something went wrong. For example, he had a beige-coloured Ferrari and was paying $600 a month to lease the car. He didn't like the colour of the car, so instead of replacing it, he simply went out and leased another Ferrari. I sorted that mess out for him.

There were other areas in his business dealing which needed sorting out, but in the main Thommo was terrific. I used to write stories for him under his name and he'd often say to me, 'Lordy, I love picking up the paper to see what I thought.'[13]

Lord wrote for the *Sydney Sun*, and he also covered cricket and rugby, working with Rex Mossop on Channel Seven's *Sports Action*. These days, despite a recent lengthy layoff with pneumonia, he continues to work for *Newsradio*, a 24-hour, seven days a week sports program on ABC.

Leading up to the 4IP deal, Thommo had been unemployed for more than six months over the past year, although most of that time was taken up playing cricket. Only a lucky few Test cricketers managed to marry full employment with a cricket career. Doug Walters was still with Rothman's, those in the banking industry such as Rick McCosker were looked after, but most players found having to eke out a living through Test cricket and at the same time take unpaid leave from work to be a constant frustration and huge financial struggle.

Then in January 1976, Thommo had become the highest paid team sportsman in Australia. When the news of his contract broke, it was said that a Sydney sports company had offered him a contract worth $30,000 a year to return to Sydney and play for NSW.

Greg Chappell, who was on a long-term contract with the QCA, said:

Jeff is worth every cent to Queensland. I would have been dis-appointed to see him go. Although Jeff received another offer from Sydney I believe in loyalty, but there is also the business side to think about. This contract is a great breakthrough for all Test cricketers in Australia because I can't see State associations paying out that sort of money to its own players. Station 4IP's decision will encourage others to get another player and use him. Maybe, one day, big companies could own all Test players in Australia.[14]

With Australia holding a commanding 3–1 lead in the series, the West Indians went into the Fourth and Fifth Tests fired up to save face. But the Australian onslaught continued, and they triumphed in both Tests, winning the series 5–1 and averaging their World Cup final loss in England.

A 6-wicket haul (4/68 and 2/66) against the West Indies in Adelaide, and a further four in Melbourne (0/51 and 4/80), gave Thommo a total of 29 wickets for the series. Dennis Lillee played one less Test than Thommo, missing the Sydney Fourth Test, and he took 2 less wickets. But it was the pace and fire of the two speedsters that ripped the heart out of the West Indian batting line-up. As with their impact on the Ashes series a year earlier, it was the Thommo and Lillee partnership which dominated proceedings.

Viv Richards batted well in his last four digs—30 and 101 in Adelaide and 50 and 98 in Melbourne—to give notice of what was to come from the man who would soon enough be called the 'master blaster'. But the West Indian captain Clive Lloyd was so incensed by the 5–1 humiliating drubbing from Australia that he devised a method of playing cricket that became a legendary success story. His men were beaten by two express bowlers, helped by a good, solid support team. What if a team launched an attack of four genuinely fast bowlers? This attack would be relentless and to make the whole thing work the team captain would have to ensure that there were a limited number of overs bowled in any one day's play.

This is how the plan eventually panned out.

The West Indian fast bowlers might go flat out for then first hour of a Test. That's 6 overs each—no more, no less, if you're taking the Lloyd plan to the letter. That allows the opening pair to give way to numbers three and four—say Curtly Ambrose and Malcolm Marshall. Andy Roberts and Joel Garner, the opening pair, are rested. Their 'rest' involves the second hour of the morning's play, plus the 40 minutes for lunch. After 100 minutes away from the bowling crease, Roberts and Garner reappear immediately after the lunch break. Most deliveries are just short of a length, rearing to strike the shoulder or throat, and anything pitched up is a yorker.

When the West Indians were beating everyone in the 1980s, they were using this bowling plan perfectly. They'd usually bowl around 72 overs a day. If the batting side scored at the rate of 1 run off every 2 balls, they would amass the princely total of 216. In Don Bradman's day it was nothing for a team to face a hundred 8-ball overs in a day's play; if batsmen scored at the rate of 1 run every 2 balls, their team would have a total of 400.

Little wonder when Bradman was asked by a group of England fast bowlers at his home in 1987 how he thought he'd fare against the West Indian attack, The Don said:

Well, I would score at the same rate as I used to in my prime, but we had more balls per day to play than nowadays. But I'll tell you something—I'd score a helluva lot more runs than the bloke who ran second to me.[15]

Unbeknown to Thomson and Lillee, it was their magnificent, aggressive attack on the West Indians in 1975–76 that had a profound effect on Clive Lloyd and was the inspiration for Lloyd's 'Body Line Revisited', which helped turn the West Indian team into a relentless machine.

For Thommo the Test season was over, but there was still a handful of domestic games to finish his summer of cricket. First Thommo played in a Gillette Cup one-day game at the Gabba; a day that he would remember forever. It wasn't the wickets, the runs or the result that is etched on his memory. For that hot February day in 1976, Thommo indeed met his match.

Cheryl Wilson was just 22. A stunning blonde with a bright smile, Cheryl was one of a few models working at the Gabba that day. She recalls:

I was one of the Gillette girls. Our job was to wander through the crowd giving out Gillette products. Then, at the end of the day's play, we presented the trophies.[16]

Did she take a shine to the big Queensland and Test fast bowler?

I don't know—maybe I did. Maybe it was the other way round. Anyway we started going out and by the end of the year we were married.[17]

All that remained for Thommo was a couple of Sheffield Shield matches to round off the cricket season. Rain, however, ruined both of Queensland's remaining matches—both at the Gabba. Against WA Thommo took 1/40 off 19 overs. Laird hit 119 in WA's only innings and heavy rain for days prevented any more play. Against SA, Queensland batted all first day and then it rained for three days, spoiling any chance Queensland had to wrest the Shield from the competition leaders. The South Australian players were pleased as punch to go away with a draw, ensuring they won the Sheffield Shield, quite an achievement after coming last the previous season.

For Thommo it was a frustrating end to the summer, but he had a lot going for him: he had met the girl of his dreams; he had landed a fantastic contract with 4IP; and he'd had a bumper summer of cricket which netted him 29 Test wickets.

Life was good.

10 JONAH ADELAIDE

Straight after lunch I was shitty as anything 'cos I hadn't got
him [Zaheer]. So I decided to stick it up him with a flyer in my first
over after the resumption of play.

While Greg and Ian Chappell, Dennis Lillee, Gary Gilmour, Martin
Kent and I joined a few Kiwis, Poms and one UK-based West Indian on a
goodwill International Wanderers tour of South Africa, Thommo stayed
home. He could do with a bit of rest after his hectic and highly successful
summer. There was his new job with radio 4IP to consider and lots of
special time to woo the beautiful model Cheryl Wilson.

Thommo was maturing. His carefree days of chasing girls were over,
and the casual attitude of turning up to State training in boardies and
thongs was long gone. At the time Greg Chappell was announced new
Australian captain after his brother Ian retired from the job, Thommo
was asked about captaincy.

Jeez, imagine being the captain, having a hard day in the field and
returning to the team hotel to get all those messages—all from blokes.
I wouldn't be happy about that. Captaincy is not my go.

The summer came around soon enough and by the time Queensland's first Sheffield Shield match, against NSW at the Gabba, arrived, Cheryl Wilson and Jeffrey Thomson were making wedding plans. A week after the couple announced their engagement in September 1976, Thommo was forced to field questions about another girl who featured in an advertisement with him. Thommo recalls:

Some of my cricketing mates might have thought I was caught up in some sort of love triangle.

The girl in question was a model who nuzzled up to him in a popular television commercial, promoting BRUT cosmetics for men. For a time the model had the tongues of Thommo's legend of fans wagging. Some thought the model was indeed Cheryl Wilson, but most probably assumed she was one of the names in a little black book of girl-friends. Thommo answered all the innuendo with his usual disarming honesty.

She [the model in the TV ad] *was a beaut-looking French bird, but I couldn't even remember her name. It was simply a job to me. I'd never seen that girl before and I never saw her again. Cheryl knew all about the commercial long before I made it.*

Cheryl and Jeff planned to wed on December 18 that year. It was to prove a busy time, full of early cricketing success and one particularly chal-lenging setback.

Queensland cricket had pulled off a major coup by recruiting champion batsman West Indian Viv Richards to replace Ian Davis, the opening batsman who decided to leave Brisbane after having played just one first-class summer with the northern State. Thommo, and all the players who bowled against Richards, recognised the man's immense talent. He always had so much time to play his shots against the fastest of bowlers, even Thommo, and he would prove a fabulous acquisition in Queensland's never-ending quest to win the Sheffield Shield.

Richards had only just got off an aircraft after a long flight from the Caribbean when he was thrust straight into his first match, Queensland versus an Invitation Eleven. This was a special one-day match to celebrate the Queensland Cricket Association centenary. Ian Chappell, Gary Cosier and I were among the invited players, so too Geoff Boycott.

Queensland batted first and Richards played a magnificent hand, hitting a thumping century out of his team's 283 for the loss of 7 wickets in 40 overs.

Thommo made early inroads with the ball and at one stage the Invitation Eleven was 3/15, but Doug Walters (89) helped the visitors eke out a respectable, if losing, score of 216. Thommo got Boycott early on, a lovely late in-swinger which touched the inside edge of Boycott's bat before taking out the Yorkshireman's middle stump. The fast man then produced his famous 'sandshoe crusher' to shatter Ian Chappell's stumps. Chappell made 22. To those who had seen a lot of Thommo at close quarters, he was bowling as fast and as hostile as he had ever bowled.

In the first Sheffield Shield match of the summer, Thommo took 3/58 and 4/52 in Queensland's 32-run demolition of Victoria. Greg Chappell hit 187, so the best bowler and the best batsman in the State team had led the way to victory.

A drawn match against WA at the Gabba saw the visitors hit 405 (Thommo 1/63) with opener Bruce Laird playing so well for 171. The faster you bowled to Laird, the better he played, Thommo soon found out.

A week later South Australia turned up to face the music at the Gabba. Having led SA to the Sheffield Shield the previous summer, captain Ian Chappell announced his retirement from first-class cricket. He left SA in favour of a club contract with North Melbourne. We had lost the heart of our batting line-up and the best leader Australian cricket had seen since Richie Benaud.

Geoff Dymock (5/24) and Phil Carlson (4/42) worked their medium-pacers to great effect and SA was bundled out for 97. I got 46 not out. Queensland scored a modest 238; Greg Chappell hitting 60 and Thommo, 32.

Then Thommo turned it on in the SA second innings. He took 5/32 off 9.3 overs. This was Thommo at his quickest. He trapped Rick Darling lbw for 25 and Darling collapsed in a heap on the pitch. That was the only time I have seen a man, hit flush on the front pad, be given out lbw and then get carried off. Pads in those days may not have been as comfortable or as protective as the streamlined versions of today, but you have to wonder about the force of J.R. Thomson when he hits a bloke on the pads and the batsmen needs a stretcher to be taken from the field.

Against NSW in Brisbane, Queensland struggled against some good bowling from Gary Gilmour (4/32) to reach 233. Viv Richards played pretty much a lone role to hit a classy 73 and then Thommo cut loose. He summoned all his amazing powers of blistering pace to carve through the NSW batting line-up like a razor-sharp knife, cutting one batsman after another off at the knees. They were mown down like clay targets by Thommo's deadly firepower. In just 9.7 overs, Thommo had ripped NSW out for 71, the State's lowest innings total against Queensland since the northerners entered the Sheffield Shield in 1926–27.

Writing in the *Sunday Telegraph*, Phil Tresidder, a man who saw Ray Lindwall and Keith Miller at their fiery best on the famous 1948 Australian tour of England, told his readers:

The slaughter lasted just 108 minutes with only three New South Welshmen—[Peter] Toohey (18), [Gary] Gilmour (11) and [David] Colley (11)—scrambling to double figures. The incredible Thomson spread sheer panic through the NSW ranks as he operated with frightening speed and bounce off a pitch lively after overnight sweat under plastic covers. NSW's 71-run disaster is the lowest-ever total in 50 years of Shield contest against Queensland.[1]

NSW fared much better when batting a second time. Gary Gilmour hit a wonderful century (115), but he raised more than the odd eyebrow among the world's batting fraternity when he said, 'I enjoy batting against Thomson':

'It's easier for left-handers because he slams the ball away from you whereas the right-hander is cramped for room.'

Keen judges enthused over Gilmour's 115, his third Shield century.

'The most controlled batting I have ever seen from Gilmour', said big Peter Burge.

And Ken 'Slasher' Mackay said: 'It was a real batsman's innings. He selected the right ball to hit and the right ball to defend.'[2]

Queensland won the match convincingly and Thommo, who took 5/79 off 21 overs in the NSW second innings, finished with 12/112 for the match.

Unbeknown to the NSW players, on the eve of the match Thommo was given a dressing-down by a Queensland cricket official for allegedly fooling about in the State nets.

> *NSW can blame a blast I received from Tom Vievers for the blitz I handed them. 'Big Tom', the former Test off-spinner, who was then QCA Secretary, gave me a heave-ho at the nets the day before the Shield match started.*

Vievers had found the need to tell Thommo to ease up from cracking too many sixes at net training because time was being wasted while players searched for the lost balls.

> *I had decided that I would bat properly, but I just couldn't resist belting Geoff Dymock 'out of the park' after Greg Chappell had said my record of not being bowled at the nets was about to end.*
>
> *Just as I sailed into Geoff, Tom came into the net area screaming at me, 'Okay, Thommo, that's you for the day'. The ball was still travelling into the distance as Tom spoke. So I ended up taking off the pads and bowling for the best part of two hours in mighty hot conditions and I was flat out all the way.*

Thommo did concede that the dressing-down and subsequent long spell in the nets did him a lot of good and he can point to his outstanding match figures as proof.

After the match Thommo grinned when he read of Gilmour having enjoyed batting against him and in his column for the *Sunday Telegraph*, he wrote:

. . . hopping into NSW gives me no end of pleasure. I have many angry memories of what NSW didn't do for me, and at a time when I really wanted a kick along. So now NSW can take a back seat and recognise that they aren't what they think they are.[3]

Australia was due to host three Test matches against Pakistan. The Pakistanis boasted a top-line batting line-up, said to be the best in the world, headed by Majid Khan, the gifted Zaheer Abbas, Mushtaq Mohammad, Asif Iqbal and a promising young right-hander, Javed Miandad.

On their previous tour of Australia in 1972–73, Pakistan were whitewashed in the three-Test series. Thommo has bad memories of his Test debut in Melbourne where he conceded more than 100 runs off his 17 overs in the Pakistan first innings—with a broken bone in his left foot—and in the wake of that match became lost to the first-class game for many months.

Thommo knew the history; he had the frustration of being dropped from Tests, then the indignity of not getting back in the NSW team. Naturally, Thommo was keen to prove himself against the highly-rated Pakistan team.

But first the sound of wedding bells.

Exactly one month before the wedding Thommo's fiancée was quoted at length by Paul Wicks of the *Daily Telegraph* in an article with the headline 'She'll be full-time Mrs Thommo':

When Queensland Mannequin of the Year, Cheryl Wilson, walks down the aisle on December 18, she won't become Mrs Jeff Thomson . . . instead it'll be Mrs Jeffrey Thomson.

Cheryl and her Thommo, the world's fastest man in Test cricket, will marry on December 18, in the Anglican Holy Trinity Church, Fortitude Valley.

'Jeffrey doesn't like being called Jeff. He likes me to call him Jeffrey', the future Mrs Thommo said today.

'Anyway I always call him Jeffrey', said the tall, leggy 22-year-old blonde model.

Cheryl said that marriage would probably mean the end of her successful modelling career.

'Jeffrey (he's 26) doesn't like me modelling all the time. He's jealous. I guess I'd be a little disappointed about giving it up. I'd still like to do it on a part-time basis.'

But as Thommo will be on the move playing first-class cricket and working around Queensland for 4IP—Cheryl could be pressed for modelling time in Brisbane. She intends going away with him whenever possible.

Cheryl said that Jeffrey's views on her modelling probably stemmed from the fact that he was very old fashioned.

'He's a square, but I love him.'

What does she find most appealling about one of the last remaining top Australian cricket bachelors?

'He has lovely blue eyes, lovely big hands. And he makes the most fantastic chips. He's a good cook.'

And his favourite dish?

'Steak and chips, of course. Jeffrey doesn't eat cakes or biscuits.'[4]

Thommo's Queensland and Test captain Greg Chappell was the fast bowler's best man and his only attendant at the wedding.

Cheryl looked stunning in her white chiffon and lace gown, and Thommo scrubbed up a treat in velvet.

As the best man kissed the bride, Thommo said with a grin, 'Me skipper's outdone me already'.

Then he embraced Cheryl and added, 'Now I might get a bowl'.

Life was good for Jeffrey Robert Thomson. He had found the love of his life. And in remembering his wedding day, he said that his roving days were over:

You get jack of running about all the time, especially when there is a loving and caring girl waiting for you at home. Seriously, I am a one-girl man.

On December 18, 2007, Cheryl and Jeffrey Thomson celebrated their 30th wedding anniversary.

The First Test began in Adelaide just six days after Thommo's wedding. The match was billed as the 'Honeymoon Test for Thommo'.

Dick Tucker, the bald-headed journalist of Sydney's *Daily Mirror*, the man we all called the 'Toffee Apple', wrote that Thommo was 'in hiding with his new bride on the eve of the Test'.

Thommo told Tucker:

I'm on my honeymoon and it's my own business. As far as I know I'm not upsetting anyone.[5]

In those less-than-enlightened times when our Test men were treated like serfs by the ACB gentry, the Board condescended to allow a Test player to live with his wife during a Test match. But the Board always insisted that no wife of any player could ever stay with her husband at the team hotel.

Just over a session into the first day's play and Test cricket's latest married couple had their honeymoon turn upside-down. That fine, hot Adelaide morning of December 24 found Thommo at the top of his fast bowling form. Here was a chance to really show the Pakistanis the great bowler he had become.

I reckon I was getting quicker in every match I bowled. It may have seemed that I bowled faster against the Poms in 1974–75 than against the Windies the following summer, but I think that is perception. It may have seemed quicker against England, because of the way their players ducked and dived and fended off the flyers. The Poms were always looking to defend, to survive, whereas the West Indians, better back-foot players, attacked the bowling. I knew I had to bowl well against the Windies after what happened against them in the 1975 World Cup at Lord's. I knew I had to be on my mettle and I was ready for them. Similarly I was ready for Pakistan.

Pakistan won the toss and batted on what appeared to be a flat, hard Adelaide Oval pitch. Openers Majid Khan and Mudussar Nazar walked out to face the demon pair, Jeff Thomson and Dennis Lillee. Thommo recalls:

I was bowling a million miles an hour that game. Bacchus [Rodney Marsh] and the slips were standing miles back. You ask the blokes who were there, I was as quick if not quicker that morning than at any other time in my career. The Pakistani batsmen were shitting themselves.

He didn't hit the stumps in that first session, but he bowled very fast indeed. Up until quite recently Thommo did not realise why his Queensland and Test keepers and slips fielders ducked for cover after he had clean-bowled a batsman.

After I hit the stumps, the keeper and the blokes at slip would duck and it looked pretty funny from where I had finished in my follow-through. I didn't know why until they told me that when I clean-bowled a bloke, the bails used to fly almost all the way to the boundary. Imagine a bail, gyrating madly as it flew towards you at real speed—there was always the chance to cop a whack in the eye.

Thommo made the early break, having Majid Khan—the man who hit 158 in Pakistan's first innings in Jeff's debut Test—caught at slip by Rick McCosker for 15. Minutes later he dismissed the Pakistani captain, Mustaq Mohammad (18), again producing a catch for McCosker. At lunch Thommo, the pick of the bowlers in the Australian attack, had 2/34 off 8 very fast overs. He also worried the life out of the classy Zaheer Abbas, who twice fended off rearing deliveries from Thommo, but on both occasions the popped half-chances went in the direction of the slow-moving Alan Turner at short mid-wicket. Thommo was not a big fan of Turner as a batsman, let alone his fielding:

Straight after lunch I was shitty as anything 'cos I hadn't got him [Zaheer]. So I decided to stick it up him with a flyer in my first over after the resumption of play. The ball got on to him, a bit quicker than he thought, and he sort of fended it with an angled bat and the ball ballooned. I quickly looked over and there was Fitter'un [Turner] and I thought 'Shit, not you again, you spastic. I'll get it myself!'

It is an unwritten law in cricket that if a ball is hit in the air and the bowler is within easy reach then any other fieldsman allows him to go for the ball without interference. An exception is when a ball is skied and it is a mere formality for the man with the gloves—the wicket-keeper—to move forward and take the catch.

Thommo was in a perfect position to take what would have been a very straight-forward bowled-and-caught chance. The supreme athlete that he was allowed him to get into position smoothly and easily in plenty of time. The ball had popped up in the air about midway down the pitch and slightly to the on-side.

> *Out of the corner of my eye I saw Turner rush towards me, stumble and suddenly he was airborne and he hit me, his whole body weight slammed down on my right arm. The pressure on my arm must have been great for the collision ripped away muscle, ligaments and tissue. I later found out the ligaments had torn from the shoulder and were sort of hanging about two inches down the arm. At the time I didn't feel a lot of pain, until I tried to use the arm to get up off the ground. I thought, 'Shit, my arm won't move'. I remember seeing Turner lying on the ground. He looked as dead as a maggot. I felt pretty ordinary and I was cursing and was very pissed off with Turner.*

Umpire Max O'Connell, who was standing in the Test with Robin Bailhache, said the snapping of muscle and ligaments in the fast bowler's arm an instant after the Thommo–Turner collision sounded life a rifle shot.

> *I tried to get my arm over in a bowling motion, but the arm was torn away. If the collarbone had been broken, it would have been easy but the ligaments were torn away. My arm was just hanging off the shoulder. We got into the dressing-room and a bloke had to cut my shirt off.*

Keen to get up off the massage table and back out on to the field, Thommo said to the Australian physiotherapist that he should be bowling, but his pleas went unheeded and a doctor was called. The doctor took a long look at the injured shoulder and then spoke of urgent surgery and mused over where he would put the pins. But Thommo didn't want to hear the diagnosis:

> 'Get me a doctor to put this thing back in and I'll go back to the action', I found myself saying. 'And, anyhow, who are you?'
> 'I am the doctor and I will be the surgeon operating on your shoulder.'

Dr Adrian Munyard was to operate on Thommo, although the South Australian Cricket Association doctor, Donald Beard, organised the surgery. Dr Beard would have performed the operation; however, on this particular Christmas Eve, he was busy saving lives among a string of car-accident victims. Meanwhile, Thommo still refused to accept the extent of his injury.

> Cheryl came with me to the hospital. We waited for about an hour before I went into the operating theatre and the blokes around the table were joking and carrying on. I said a few words to the doctor: 'Listen, you blokes, you'd better fix this thing up properly because I'm going back to the motel tomorrow, so get that for a start. The boys are having a party and I want to be there. Fix me up and I'm leaving in the morning, OK?'

Merry Christmas, Mr Thomson.

Thommo had never experienced being operated on before and he awoke in the recovery room feeling slightly odd.

> I struggled to open my eyes. My eyelids felt like lead weights, they were so heavy and I could hear noises, the nurse was checking on me. I said to her, 'When are you going to take me in and do me?'
> 'You're done', she said. 'Have a look.'

Thommo had a look. He was a mass of bandages. He found he was slurring his speech due to the anaesthetic and he was having trouble making himself understood. Thommo wanted to get back to the team motel for the Christmas party. But the nurse told him firmly that the cricket field might well be his area of authority, 'but I'm in charge here, Mr Thomson'.

In the surreal world of that hospital recovery ward lay the world's fastest and most hostile fast bowler, having crashed out of a crucial Test match due to an accident of the most senseless kind.

Back in the ward I was falling in and out of consciousness, but the aching in my shoulder, from my head right down my neck and all round the shoulder, where the muscles were torn, was something else. The pain was incredible. I was on morphine, a shot every couple of hours. I had pillows stacked behind me, propping me up. I must have looked like a mummy, swathed in bandages. Whenever the nurse came into the room to give me another needle, I'd be saying, 'Look, I'm leaving here in the morning. I want to get out!'

Early the following day, must have been about six o'clock—after the pain had prevented me from getting any sleep—I thought, 'The only way I'm going to get out of this joint is to pretend that I'm okay'. So I struggled out of bed when no-one was about. I'm not kidding, I went arse over head. My legs were like jelly. The sling around my neck had begun to cut into the flesh and my injured arm felt incredibly heavy. So there I am walking about the room, trying to look as if I am okay to leave the hospital.

Even through the intense pain, Thommo maintained his sense of humour and would crack jokes between shots of morphine. When Cheryl—who couldn't believe their honeymoon had ended this way— made one of her many visits to see her husband, Thommo would yell, 'Where's the double bed?'

Despite the fact that he was hardly able to stand, Thommo some-how convinced the doctor that he was right to leave. He caught a cab to the team motel on Christmas Day. Thommo wasn't about to miss the party.

By the time I got to the motel, my arm was aching. A doctor had to come out to see me at regular intervals. Sometimes he'd be late and when the effect of the morphine wore off, the pain was unbearable. As it turned out the players had their Christmas party, but I didn't make it. When the painkillers wore off, I was smashing glasses and bottles. The pain was so great I nearly flaked out. Once when the doctor was an hour late, I began throwing glasses at the wall. Poor Cheryl just sat there through it. I couldn't do anything about it and neither could she.

After a couple of days Thommo was considered fit enough to fly home. Back in Brisbane he was installed in a room with a TV so he could watch the cricket, and he spent his time taking painkillers and thinking of better things to come. At least the Australian team without Thommo was doing okay.

The Adelaide Test was drawn, Australia won the Second Test in Melbourne by a massive 348 runs, Thommo's fast-bowling mate Dennis Lillee taking a match haul of 10/135, but the pain of loss returned at the SCG in the Third Test where Pakistan, thanks to Imran Khan taking 6/102 and 6/63 of sustained pace, won by eight wickets. With Thommo tied to a hospital bed, the series was levelled 1–all.

As soon as he was weaned off the morphine, the pain began to subside and Thommo immediately started his own exercise program.

I began to exercise with an enlarged squash ball, just squeezing it. Dr Tom Dooley gave me a course of exercises. Apart from Dr Munyard, the surgeon, and Doc Beard, the SACA doctor who organised everything, I owe most to Dr Dooley, who really helped me get back to cricket.

Dr Dooley had an involvement with the QCA and the Valley football club in Brisbane and he orchestrated the planned set of exercises for Thommo, step by step, and eventually Thommo's arm got stronger.

Some people said I would never play again, but I was determined to get back to my full playing strength. I was never going to quit.

Writing in the *Sun*, former Australian champion fast bowler Ray Lindwall let the cricket world know that he thought:

The loss of Thommo meant the loss of venom from the Australian attack. He'd be missed more than Dennis Lillee. His shock value, ability to bowl that 'killer' ball only just short of a length to rear up at the batsman was amazing. I reckon plenty of Test batsmen around the world had a much happier Christmas when they heard of Thommo's accident.[6]

The accident was front-page news throughout the land—a national sports disaster. Newspaper editorials are usually reserved for great world events, but on December 28, 1976, the *Sydney Morning Herald*'s editorial was devoted to Jeffrey Thomson in the wake of his horrific accident in the Adelaide Test match:

THOMMO SHOULDERS ARMS

No one who follows test cricket can do other than sympathise with Jeff Thomson in the regrettable accident which put him out of the current series with Pakistan. As Greg Chappell has said, a bowler of his devastating speed and ability comes along only once every 20 or 30 years, and Australia, with Lillee, palpably below his best, will miss him sorely in the encounters with Pakistan and New Zealand, and very possibly in the tour of England next year.

It is particularly unfortunate that he will not be able to take part in what promises to be a great occasion—the Centenary Test against England in Melbourne.

Before the freakish accident which put him out of the first test against Pakistan he had been bowling extremely well, with the old pace and hostility but with greater accuracy than in past seasons. In fact, 1976–77 promised to be a vintage season for him.

He had prepared for it very carefully, and had reaped the benefit of his thoroughness with some outstanding successes in the early Sheffield Shield games. In the Adelaide Test he was clearly moving into top gear, being superbly fit and with his infectious enthusiasm giving a keen edge to his mature fast bowling. It will be a thousand pities if his serious shoulder injury writes finis to an already distinguished Test career.

In spite of encouraging medical opinion, his chances of a complete recovery and a return to his position of dominance among the world's express bowler brigade do not appear bright. It is easy to be wise after the event, but the unfortunate accident was surely avoidable—a sharp word from either the captain or wicketkeeper would have warned both Thomson and Turner of the danger of a collision. But that is just another of the myriad might-have-beens of cricket.[7]

More than twenty years later during a Test match in Kandy against Sri Lanka, Steve Waugh and Jason Gillespie collided after both men set off for a skied shot from Jayawardene. The ball flew high in the air and Waugh set off from square leg and Gillespie ran from deep square, on the fence. Both were looking at the ball and completely oblivious to the other man. They hit at some speed, Waugh's face striking Gillespie's shoulder and Gillespie's legs being taken from beneath him as Waugh collapsed. Gillespie suffered a broken right tibia and Waugh sustained a broken nose. Both men recovered fully, although Gillespie was out of Test cricket for months.

Back in December 1976, Thommo's manager David Lord announced that the accident would not jeopardise his $633,000 contract with 4IP. Events moved swiftly. Thommo continued to work hard on his fitness. He gradually recovered full strength, having from day one after the accident set his sights on making the 1977 tour of England.

Unbeknown to the QCA or Radio 4IP, Thommo was among the 30 Australians who signed up for World Series Cricket. Thommo had missed the short tour of New Zealand in February 1977 and he would miss the much-celebrated Centenary Test match against England at the MCG. In fact Thommo did not play a first-class match again until he turned out for the Australians against Kent on May 4, 1977. He passed muster on fitness, the Test selectors having great faith in Thommo's ability to get fully fit and they unanimously picked him for the 1977 England tour. Dennis Lillee had withdrawn from the tour, making Thommo's selection all the more vital.

Meanwhile, Thommo trained and fished and swam and spent lots of quality time with Cheryl. Life was good again.

11 1977: ENGLAND TOUR IN TATTERS

I pulled out of World Series Cricket during the Test match at Trent
Bridge because . . . Radio 4IP told me that I had to . . . David Lord . . . had
a lot to say about it at the time, but my pulling out of Packer cricket
had nothing whatsoever to do with David Lord. It really shits me
people think he organised it all.

To speed his recovery time it was essential that Thommo have a steel pin
inserted in his shoulder. All his doctors and medical advisers told him
that while the pin was in his shoulder he would not be able to lift his
arm above the horizontal. But no-one in the medical fraternity figured on
Thommo's amazing recouperative powers, his strength and his will to get
back to full fitness.

*Even with the pin in my shoulder I could swing my arm over. I worked
all the exercises with the pin in. It amazed them until eventually the
physiotherapist told me to stop or I'd snap the pin. I worked really
hard, even harder than I needed to work, but I made sure I did all
the exercises and got myself right. Dennis Lillee had gone through the*

*same thing with his damaged back. You have to work hard to get back
to full fitness. It's the only way.*

*The doctors took the pin out early. The doc cut the shoulder exactly
where it had been initially cut, through the scar tissue, and I meant to
get the pin off him as I intended to make a necklace out of it to wear
when I was bowling, but I forgot.*

*But I saved the shirt. You could see where the shirt had been cut
off my shoulder. I later had the shirt stitched up and wore it again.
I bowled in it and wouldn't have chucked it out for quids. Accidents
don't worry me. I am not superstitious.*

After all the trouble Thommo seemed to have in Adelaide after his
collision with Turner, it wouldn't be surprising if a little bit of superstition
had crept into the Jeff Thomson psyche. It was not uncommon for Australian
cricketers over the years to be extraordinarily superstitious. According to
his old mate Clem Hill, Victor Trumper trembled at the sight of a man in
the cloth wearing a 'dog collar'. Many players don their favourite shirts
and socks. In fact one Australian captain used to wear the same pair of
socks for the duration of the match. He didn't have to pack them up at
the end of the game: they 'walked' their own way to the next venue. The
champion England wicket-keeper Alan Knott, arguably the best gloveman
in Test history, used to wear a handkerchief in his left pocket and as he
squatted to prepare for each ball Knott touched the hanky for 'good luck'.
Clever medium-fast bowler Alan Connolly always carried a part of Hugh
Trumble's Test team boater hat band in his pocket when he played.

Australian cricket's unlucky number is 87, a myth started by Keith
Miller when he saw Harry 'the Bull' Alexander clean-bowl Bradman at
the MCG in the 1930s. The number 87 subsequently became the devil's
number—thirteen from a hundred. Years later Miller checked up the
score Bradman got that day and discovered that Bradman actually made
89, not 87, but the dreaded number 87 remained in our cricket folklore.
Bradman once said to me:

Fridays, black cats, walking on cracks in the pavement and the
number 87 means nothing. I deal in realism and the facts. Superstition is meaningless.[1]

So while superstition seemed to go with the territory for most Test cricketers, not so Donald George Bradman, nor Jeffrey Robert Thomson.

Only weeks after the Adelaide Oval accident, the Australian selectors were keen for Thommo to undergo a fitness test as soon as he was ready, for the tour of England loomed.

> *I decided to go flat out in the Brisbane fitness trial. There was a funny sort of pins-and-needles feeling in my arm, but that didn't deter me. I bowled really quick and the arm didn't hurt at all—just the normal stiffness you experience in your first stint in the nets after having not bowled for a while. I sprayed them about and I think I was erratic because my breathing wasn't right, but I bowled quick enough and they said I could tour.*

Missing the New Zealand tour was no big deal for Thommo. In fact he was quoted as saying he'd rather have played Sheffield Shield cricket for Queensland instead of touring New Zealand in the build-up to the England tour. He also missed the Centenary Test match, the game in which Dennis Lillee, who visited his fast bowling mate in hospital only hours after the accident, bowled so well, taking 6/26 and 5/139, to help Greg Chappell's men to a 45-run victory—exactly the same winning margin achieved by Charles Bannerman's Australians in the very first Test match at the MCG in March 1877. For the Australian team of 1977, the victory margin meant the Poms had not improved one bit in 100 years.

The Melbourne Centenary Test was a brilliantly organised match and old Test players from England and Australia turned up in their droves—one last hurrah—but Thommo didn't go. A man of action doesn't merely sit and watch.

But unbeknown to the Establishment, while the Centenary Test was played out there were dozens of clandestine meetings as Kerry Packer's World Series Cricket agents were busily signing up the cream of the world's cricketers for their proposed revolution.

As soon as Packer learnt that Thommo had been passed fit for the 1977 England tour, the WSC agents contacted him. At the same time, the 1977 Australian touring team bound for England was announced: Greg Chappell, (Queensland) (capt); Ray Bright (Victoria); Gary Cosier (South Australia); Ian Davis (NSW); Geoff Dymock (Queensland); David Hookes (South Australia); Rick McCosker (NSW); Mick Malone (Western Australia); Rodney Marsh (Western Australia); Kerry O'Keeffe (NSW); Len Pascoe (NSW); Ritchie Robinson (Victoria); Craig Serjeant (Western Australia); Jeff Thomson (Queensland); Max Walker (Victoria); Doug Walters (NSW).

Thommo was delighted to see his old sparring partner and mate Len Pascoe selected and when Austin Robertson, the WSC agent and Dennis Lillee's manager, contacted him about signing for the revolution, Thommo didn't forget Lennie. Lennie recalls:

> Thommo rang me just before the tour, urging me to sign up with WSC. Austin Robertson was at Thommo's place getting him to sign and Thommo said, 'C'mon Lennie, sign up with me. We'll be playing with and against the best of the best.'[2]

A fit Jeff Thomson was always going to be a key figure for Ian Chappell to target when he started to assemble his list of players for the WSC revolution. And while Thommo signed with WSC for $35,000 per annum for three years, he could not have foreseen what was to happen to his immediate cricket career because of his commitment to Brisbane-based Radio 4IP.

With news of the WSC revolution about to create havoc in world cricket, the 1977 Australian tour of England was never going to run smoothly. A big blow to team morale was the loss of Dennis Lillee, who announced that he was not making the tour. But in the overall scheme of things concern over Lillee's withdrawal was but a drop in the ocean, compared to the tidal-wave of condemnation that would be unleashed upon the 'rebels' by the cricket Establishment and a hostile press.

Rain hampered the Australians' progress in the early matches against the counties. Thommo played in the first game, against Kent at Canterbury, and bowled 3 overs for 7 runs, no wickets. It must have been a huge relief for him to look over at short mid-wicket and see a face other than NSW opening batsman Alan Turner, the man with whom he collided in Adelaide five months before. Turner didn't make the cut for the touring squad. Rain also ruined the match against Sussex, Thommo not batting or bowling in a game where Australia batted, scoring 1/111, before the heavens opened and the ground was flooded for the duration.

On May 9 the news broke of the Kerry Packer World Series Cricket revolution. The Australian team was only weeks away from the start of an Ashes series with many of the players having signed up for the revolutionists and others not. Tension was inevitable among a close-knit group of sportsmen living and working together for months on end. Within days of the WSC Revolution becoming known, the English Establishment moved quickly to dismiss Tony Greig from the Test captaincy. He was replaced by Mike Brearley as leader, but he retained his place in the team, along with other WSC signees Bob Woolmer, Alan Knott, Dennis Amiss and Derek Underwood. The Australians were left pretty much in the dark. Team manager Norm McMahon and his deputy Len Maddocks made it clear that they did not approve of the WSC 'defectors' and the atmosphere within the touring party was, to put it mildly, tense.

Against Somerset at Bath, Greg Chappell hit a brilliant 113 and Thommo got his first decent stint at the bowling crease, taking 0/60 off 16 overs. He bowled 15 no-balls, which was a concern, but in the second Somerset innings Thommo got a wicket (Brian Rose caught behind), taking 1/57 off 12 overs. Somerset beat the tourists, and Thommo's match figures of 1/117 off 28 overs didn't thrill him.

Greg Chappell had been concerned about Thommo's no-ball problem. It happened in 1975 and it was happening again. Greg had a good look at what Thommo was doing in the nets. He noted that the fast man was over-stepping the front line all the time at training.

> I asked Greg, 'Which foot am I taking off with, mate?'
> And he said, 'Your left foot . . . try the other one.'

And so ended the no-ball troubles.

In late May, around the time Thommo took 2/50 and 3/50 against the MCC at Lord's—delivering not one no-ball in the entire match—Packer flew to London to show support for the WSC players in the Test team. Packer set up camp in the Dorchester Hotel and he was there for the First Test at Lord's, dubbed the Jubilee Test to celebrate 25 years of the reign of Queen Elizabeth II.

This was Len Pascoe's debut Test and the two former Punchbowl High School opening bowlers took the new ball together in a famous Test match at Lord's, the home of cricket.

England batted first and Thommo, bowling off a longer approach, where he appeared to run in a bit faster than he did before his collision with Turner, bowled with pace and fire to take 4/41 off 20.5 overs.

I did change my approach, if not my action, after the collision in Adelaide. I ran in a lot further, but, looking back on it, I reckon I didn't have the same load-up before delivery. I found that after the accident I didn't get the ball to rear as much off a good length. I was still bowling pretty quickly, but had to drop a lot shorter in length to get the ball whizzing about their ears.

It might not have been vintage Thommo, but he bowled fast and accurately and he had the Poms hopping about, defending as if their very lives depended upon it. It was a fabulous performance in the wake of his injury.

Pascoe took 2/53 so the Punchbowl High 'old boys' took the lion's share of the wickets between them to steamroll England for a modest 216. Pascoe, however, went into the game under a cloud, for former England Test captain Ted Dexter had branded him a 'chucker'. Lennie says:

It was great to play my first Test opening the bowling with Jeff. But I had a few problems with some people other than the bats-men I was about to face. I was being called a chucker and there was the headline, 'PASCOE'S A CHUCKER' on the back page of a newspaper.[3]

Australia got an 80-run lead thanks to a solid 81 from Greg Chappell and a fine debut 66 by Craig Serjeant. Batting again England scored 305, thanks mainly to that 'crashing bore' of a batsman Bob Woolmer, who batted solidly for 120. Thommo again bowled well taking 4/86 off 24.4 overs and Pascoe supported him well with 3/96 off 26 overs. Australia struggled in its second innings and was 6/114 when the game finished, with England having much the better of a draw. Poor Dennis Amiss, Dennis Lillee's 'bunny' of 1974–75, was bowled in both innings by Thommo for 4 and 0. The boys from Bankstown took 13 of the 20 England wickets to fall. Some 101,050 people attended the game which brought in a record £220,384 gate receipts.

England won the second Test at Old Trafford easily, thanks to a first innings 437, of which Woolmer hit 137, Derek Randall 79 and Tony Greig 76. Thommo again bowled solidly, taking 3/73 off 38 overs. But England had gained a lead of 140 over Australia's 297, of which Doug Walters hit 88, his highest-Test score in four tours of England. Batting a second time Australia fell to the medium-paced cutters of Derek Underwood, who took 6/66 off 32.5 overs. Only Greg Chappell stood out with the bat, hitting a majestic 112 in his team's paltry 218. England then had the formality of hitting 82 runs for victory.

On the morning of July 28, 1977, Thommo stunned the cricket world— and many of his touring team-mates—by announcing that he was 'pulling out of his World Series contract'. For a parochial cricket crowd at Trent Bridge, Thommo's timing could not have been more perfect because there was an undercurrent of fear among cricket lovers who were asking 'What would WSC do to our great game?' When Thommo walked out to bat after the team adjournment, he received a standing ovation. There were claims that his manager David Lord had persuaded Thommo to stay with the Establishment, but Thommo firmly denies this was so.

> I pulled out of WSC during the Test match at Trent Bridge because my employer, Radio 4IP, told me that I had to withdraw or else. David Lord, who had set himself up as my 'manager', had a lot to say about it at the time, but my pulling out of Packer cricket had nothing whatsoever to do with David Lord. It really shits me that people think that he organised it all. 'Lordy' had nothing to do with

my pulling out. It was strictly between World Series Cricket, Radio 4IP and me.

Brisbane-based lawyer Frank Gardiner, acting on behalf of Radio 4IP, had flown to England to tell Thommo that he had to pull out of WSC because of his contractual arrangements with the radio station. A large part of his agreement with Radio 4IP was based on Thommo playing cricket for Queensland and as WSC players would be banned from playing any form of the game under the control of the Australian Cricket Board—club and Sheffield Shield cricket—he was legally bound to withdraw from WSC.

Gardiner and Lord also brought grim news that creditors were chasing a substantial amount of money from Thommo over an Allsports sporting goods firm that he, with money earned from Radio 4IP, had helped set up for his brother Greg and a friend. David Lord has always been critical of Thommo's business acumen; however, he maintains that he always sorted it out for his famous, fast-bowling 'client', saying:

Thommo's brother [Greg] was a bricklayer without any experience in business which made it pretty hard to make the sporting goods stores work. From the outset Allsports was doomed to failure.[4]

Buoyed by Thommo's WSC withdrawal, Lord approached Len Pascoe to try and persuade him to opt out of his Packer deal, but this Bankstown boy wasn't going to budge. Although he later said, 'Jeez, my mate talks me into joining the Packer troupe, and then he goes and pulls out'.[5] Lennie knew Thommo withdrew under sufferance; forced to cut and run by the threat of legal action by his employer.

West Indian Alvin Kallicharran was targetted by Lord and, much to the chagrin of Packer, he subsequently pulled out of his WSC contract and was seconded to play for Queensland, along with a Radio 4IP deal. Lord claimed that he persuaded both Thommo and Kallicharran to rip up their WSC contracts. Lord recalls that at the time he said:

This will be the beginning of an exodus from the Packer circus. The players themselves have just followed each other like sheep without thinking about it. But suddenly they have had an attack of brains.[6]

Peter McFarlane, the Melbourne-based pressman who broke the story on World Series Cricket, a world scoop, said Packer 'not only looked like a hammerhead shark but acted like one'.[7]

But the greatest predator was the press, which acted like a white pointer among a school of seals, gobbling up juicy quotes from both sides. Privately Packer was not so concerned about Thommo for he understood the fast bowler's predicament; however, he didn't allow his private thoughts on that score to hit the press. Kerry Packer was a tough businessman and an unrelenting opponent to the Establishment, but he unreservedly believed in honouring a contract. He proved that in 1978 when he insisted that the WSC players be paid 'according to the contract' for the six-week tour of the Caribbean. Privately Packer admired Thommo for sticking to his guns.

On the surface Packer was livid because two men pulling out could well cause other players to opt out. Packer met with the WSC men on the England tour and gave them the rounds of the table. Anyone who dared to try and follow the exits of Thommo and Kallicharran would be hounded by his legal team and brought to account in court. There would be no mercy shown and no exceptions to his tough stand.

The Australian Establishment obviously had their eyes on turning the young players, such as David Hookes, around. In fact, Hookes was a little undecided. It was okay for the likes of Ian and Greg Chappell, Dennis Lillee and Doug Walters to sign with WSC to secure their financial future. They had played lots of Test cricket. They had made their mark, all of them legends of the game and would remain so whatever happened with World Series Cricket. What of the youngsters? In fact when Hookes arrived back in Adelaide from the England tour, Test selector and SA top administrator Phil Ridings offered Hookes a package, which was about double the size of his WSC contract, to defect. He was teetering on the precipice, likely to fall the way of the Establishment offer, when he flew to see Packer, with a financial adviser in tow. Hookes said:

I had my resignation speech memorised to the letter, and when we turned up Packer stood there with a huge grin. He was very welcoming, but he also insisted, before I could utter a word, that there was no way I could pull out of my WSC contract. 'If you do happen to pull out, you will pay me 90 per cent of your salary for the rest of your life.' He pointed out that my name and image had been used in advance promotional material, so 'I will sue you to the hilt for damages.' I knew then that I'd be playing alongside Chappell and Lillee.[8]

Under pressure from member countries, especially England and Australia, the International Cricket Conference announced in July 1977 that WSC players would be banned from all first-class and Test matches if they did not tear up their contracts by October 1, 1977. After legal hitches trying to restrain WSC from promoting its product in Australia and the threat of bans on his players, Kerry Packer took the cricket Establishment on in a High Court challenge.

The case rolled on for weeks. Ex-England captain Ray Illingworth, Cricketers' Association secretary Jack Bannister and Worcestershire secretary Mike Vockins gave a total of 137 hours of evidence. The Australian Cricket Board's treasurer Ray Steele, a respected lawyer and great friend of all Test cricketers, told the court:

I have it on good opinion that the only way to get out of a Packer contract is by becoming pregnant.[9]

Packer was working on a budget of $12 million for the first two seasons of WSC. That revelation stunned the court. His detractors called WSC the 'Packer Circus', but Packer knew the majority of clowns were intimately involved with the various Test-cricket playing nations around the world.

In July 1977, England's Test and County Cricket Board (TCCB) directors Doug Insole and Donald Carr told the ICC that enforcement of a ban on the WSC contracted players would, according to Queen's Counsel advice, be extremely difficult.

While Packer won his High Court battle for the rights of his players, the Establishment slapped bans on the players. Banned from first-class and Test cricket, the players in Australia were not even allowed to play club cricket, or train on the ground of a club that had affiliation to the State association. State players were urged to completely disassociate themselves from WSC players and not to talk to them.

Just who were the clowns?

England won the 1977 Ashes series in England by a commanding 3–nil, but Thommo bowled well in a side that lost so convincingly and took 23 wickets at an average of 25.3. But it was not a happy tour. The team was a team divided by the WSC revolution. Players went their separate ways.

Back in Australia the Great Divide that was the summer of 1977–78 was about to get underway and the glossy Australian Cricket Board season program was adorned by the magnificent action image of Jeff Thomson; ironically countered by the World Series Cricket summer program featuring Dennis Lillee. The ACB had as its catch-cry, 'Here come the Indians'.

While WSC began in Melbourne before a sparse crowd at Waverley, Australia under new captain Bob Simpson, hauled out of retirement after a decade of not having played Test cricket, took on India in Brisbane. Some 30 players, the cream of the nation, had 'defected' to Packer, so the Test eleven saw a flood of new faces.

Making their debuts were WA's medium-pacer Wayne Clarke, Victorian opening batsman Paul Hibbert, WA leg-spinner Tony Mann, Queensland batsman David Ogilvie, NSW wicket-keeper Steve Rixon and NSW batsman Peter Toohey. A few among the new faces can thank their lucky stars for WSC for they would never have played at the highest level had Kerry Packer not been forced to set up a rival competition in his clever strategy to win exclusive rights for the televising of all top cricket in Australia. Thommo was part of an Australian attack which also comprised Clarke, Victoria's Alan Hurst, medium-pacer Gary Cosier, Mann and Bob Simpson, probably a bit better than a mere part-time leg-spinner.

Simpson won the toss and Australia batted, but were routed for 166, of which debutant Toohey scored a dashing 82. Left-arm spinner Bishen Bedi took 5/55. Thommo swung lustily and was bowled by Chandrasekhar for 3.

Thommo bowled well and it was largely due to his pace and fire that India could manage just 153 in their first innings. Clarke took 4/46, but it was Thommo who set the Indians back on their heels after opener Dilip Vengsarkar hit his wicket was trying to avoid a nasty rearing delivery, and then Ashok Mankad was caught behind by Rixon for a duck.

Batting again Simpson's team did better, scoring 327; the captain leading the way with a patient 89, supported by Ogilvie (46) and Toohey (57), after a bad start where Hibbert fell for 2 and Cosier for a duck. Craig Serjeant bagged a pair. Alan Hurst, one of the worst number elevens imaginable, joined Thommo at the wicket with the score 9/277 and the pair slogged and snicked their way to an extraordinary last wicket stand of 50. Thommo (41) was left lamenting how many more he could have got when Hurst was run out for 26.

The Indians had to score 341 to win and they nearly got there. Thommo again bowled with great pace to take 4/76 off 19.7 overs. He broke the heart of the Indian batting, taking out Amarnath (47), Viswanath (35) and Patel (3). Clarke backed Thommo brilliantly, taking 4/101 off 26 overs and Hurst picked up 2/50 off 15 overs.

Immediately after the First Test victory. Queensland beat NSW outright at the SCG, with fine bowling by Thommo (2/71 and 5/70) and a century by Alvin Kallicharran, the West Indian who opted out of his WSC contract.

Australia won a high-scoring game in the Second Test at the WACA in Perth, Thommo getting 4/101 off 24 overs in India's first innings of 402. Newcomer and left-arm medium-pacer Sam Gannon took 3/84 off 16.6 overs and Clarke grabbed 2/95 off 17 overs. For India, Chauhan (88) and Amaranath (90) did best. Then came a fabulous knock from Bobby Simpson, hitting 176 in Australia's reply of 394. In the Indian second innings Sunil Gavaskar scored a classy 127 and Amaranth 100. Thommo followed his first-innings 4-wicket haul with 2/65 off 21.5 overs.

Australia needed 339 to win, and night-watchman Tony Mann hit his maiden Test century (105), an innings that paved the way for a narrow 2-wicket victory. Bedi took 5 wickets in each innings, a great performance on the Perth wicket, ever a hard and fast pitch with steepling bounce, a pace-bowler's delight.

In Melbourne, the Third Test became a saga of the spinners with Chandrasekhar taking 6/52 and 6/52 to turn the match into an Indian victory by a massive 222 runs. Thommo got 3/78 off 16 overs in India's first innings, Clarke taking 4 in each innings, but the Indian spinners had the last laugh. Chandrasekhar had support from Bedi who took 2/71 and 4/48, the pair getting a total of 18 of the Australian 20 wickets to fall.

The Fourth Test at the spin-friendly Sydney Cricket Ground was a fascinating tussle. The wicket turned square and was in direct contrast to the lightning-fast wicket at the nearby Sydney Showgrounds three weeks earlier where Australia took on West Indies in a WSC Supertest which was more like a gladiatorial battle than a cricket match. Batsman were ducking and diving against the pace of Michael Holding, Joel Garner, Andy Roberts and Wayne Daniel.

While at the Showgrounds the pace was relentless, the SCG was a spinner's paradise, although all the great spin came from the Indians. After Australia was spun out for 131 (Bedi 3/49, Chandrashekhar 4/30 and Prasanna 1/14), India scored 396, while Tony Mann conceded 101 runs off 20 overs without taking a solitary wicket. On that sluggish and turning SCG wicket, Thommo bowled his heart out to take 4/83 off 27 overs.

In the Australian second innings, despite good knocks from Cosier (68) and Toohey (85), they could amass only 263 and India won by an innings and 2 runs. Prasanna was the pick of the bowlers with 4/51 off 29 overs, supported by Bedi and Chandrasekhar, who grabbed 2 wickets apiece.

Simpson's Test side were nursing mental scars in the wake of a match campaign gone horribly wrong. The Indians had fought back brilliantly to level the series 2–all, leading into the crucial Adelaide Fifth Test. After four Tests Thommo had taken 20 wickets for 504 runs, an average of 25.2.

So here he was again in Adelaide, the Jonah Adelaide, where Thommo damaged his shoulder playing tennis at Yalumba Winery in the Barossa Valley, and where he collided with Alan Turner in the Test against Pakistan at the Adelaide Oval. Surely the cricket gods had decreed that Thomson had suffered enough in Adelaide.

After two successive losses it was inevitable the selectors' axe would fall and Australia made four changes to their side, bringing in Victorian pace bowler Ian Callen, SA opening batsman Rick Darling, WA opening batsman Graeme Wood and WA off-spinner Bruce Yardley. Test selector

Phil Ridings, having seen the explosive pace of Thommo and Dennis Lillee, told me a few years later that WA's Sam Gannon was 'in danger of hitting himself in the back of the head with the ball in his follow-through';[10] derogatory words to tell what he thought of that bowler's ability to run in faster than he bowled.

Australia batted first on a hard and flat Adelaide Oval wicket. Centuries to Graham Yallop, a tall and neat left-hander who always made merry on a batsman's paradise, and Bob Simpson, with good support from Darling (65) and Toohey (60), helped Australia to a score of 505.

After three days came the rest day and Thommo was looking forward to a relaxing time with Cheryl at lunch with the SACA doctor, Dr Donald Beard, his wife, Margaret and their two sons—both tall like their father and fast-medium bowlers—and a couple of Indian players. What Thommo didn't know was that Sir Donald and Lady Jessie Bradman would also be joining them.

12 MIRACLE ON BEULAH ROAD

> At the sight of the two fast bowlers Bradman's eyes lit up and
> you could see he was thinking, 'Who are you two clowns? Do you
> think you are going to get me out? I've news for you.' . . . He did not
> play a false shot in twenty minutes of the most amazing batting
> I have ever seen.

Miracles do happen.

At midday on January 30, 1978, when Mr and Mrs Jeffrey Thomson arrived by taxi at 134 Beulah Road, Norwood, a leafy suburb some two Keith Miller hooks and a Thommo tee-shot from the Adelaide CBD, they knew they were in for a treat: grand company, good food, fine wine and plenty of ice-cold XXXX beer. But they couldn't have envisaged the events were about to unfold.

The Thomsons were guests of Dr Donald Beard and his wife, Margaret, cricket fans both and people with kind hearts and generous spirits. Dr Beard was the South Australian Cricket Association medical officer for more than 40 years. An eminent surgeon, the Doc also served as an army medic in field hospitals in the Korea and Vietnam conflicts. A man of distinction, tall with flowing grey hair, luxuriant moustache and laughing eyes, the Doc has been both friend and doctor to myriad State and Test cricketers. It was the Doc and Margaret's pleasure to invite players from both Test sides to lunch at their home on this rest day of the Adelaide Test match. For Thommo, the occasion was an even greater privilege as Sir Donald and Lady Jessie Bradman were among the guests that day.

There was joyous, animated discussion throughout the meal. Bradman was especially happy. Australia's Test series against India was a resounding success. The series was locked 2–all, with Adelaide hosting the series decider. A close Test series was something the Establishment wanted more than anything else as it fought with World Series Cricket for the hearts and minds of cricket fans.

Many of the 'Supertests' had been financial flops; games played on 'drop-in' wickets and mostly before meagre crowds. Thommo, however, had enjoyed a consistent bowling summer as the ACB's star attraction and in Cheryl's company, along with good friends, he couldn't have been happier.

I was sitting alongside Sir Donald and Cheryl was next to Lady Jessie. There were a couple of the Indian players there. Bishen Bedi was one and Vishy [Gunduppa Vishwanath] was also present. We finished eating. And there I was drinking a cold XXXX beer.

Bradman was sitting in his slacks, shirt and tie. He looked pretty fit for a bloke of his age. The Doc's two sons then announced that they were about to go outside and have a hit in the nets. The Doc had a grass tennis court and a turf cricket pitch in his spacious backyard. I watched the boys get up from the table and one of them laughingly asked, 'Would you like to come and have a bat against us, Sir Donald?'

All eyes turned to Bradman and without hesitation he replied, 'Yes, lads. I'd love to have a hit.'

The guests fell silent.

Any cricketer, any fan, would give much to get a glimpse of Don Bradman batting, the king of all batsmen: 6996 Test runs at an average of 99.94. And Bradman simply did not give impromptu batting performances.

I was unbelievably fortunate to witness one such performance. It was 1967 and Sir Donald had come into the South Australian dressing-room, as was his habit those days during matches at Adelaide Oval at a time when he was an SA and Test selector. He would drop in before play on each morning of a Sheffield Shield match, have a cup of tea and chat to people nearby. He was always polite, cheery and positive. On this particular day, Sir Donald finished his cup of tea and was about to walk out of the dressing-room door when he stopped. Greg Chappell was holding a bat and Bradman said: 'I'd change my grip if I were you, son.'

When a cricketing god speaks, even the grass bows. Greg was very much his own man, but he was also a person who never allowed an opportunity to pass by. And a gem of batting advice from Bradman seemed too good an opportunity. At that stage in his career, Greg was mainly an on-side player. Then came the magic moment. Bradman picked up a bat and he played a shadow drive.

Wow.

It wasn't quite life-defining but from a cricketing point of view, it was a stunning and precious moment. Bradman's action was such that he had swung the bat at great speed: the bat was a blur, like a propeller blade at full tilt.

Incredible.

Then The Don played another shadow cover drive. Again there was a blur as he swung the bat. Pure magic.

Bradman was once a scratch golfer and in golf they talk incessantly of 'club head speed'. Bradman had 'club head speed' in spades, so too did Adam Gilchrist of the modern era. Ex-Queensland and Test opening batsmen Bill Brown once said there was something very different about Bradman's batting; something he never found in any other batsman. The stand out feature? 'Bat-speed', Bill said.[1]

At the Doc's house, those Beard boys couldn't believe their luck, having lunch with Don Bradman, cricket's greatest batsman, and Jeff Thomson, the world's fastest bowler. Their joy increased when Thommo stood up, still clutching his can of XXXX, and announced:

If Don Bradman's batting . . . Jeff Thomson is bowling!

Bradman walked briskly out the door and headed towards the net. Thommo followed. He had a cricket ball in one hand and a can of XXXX in the other. He had to move smartly to catch up with Bradman, who was striding forward confidently; every inch the Roman Centurian with the scent of victory in his nostrils. As Bradman neared the backyard pitch, Thommo recalls that The Don confessed:

> 'Gee, Jeff. I don't know why I am doing this—I haven't batted for twenty years.'
>
> He smiled and he had a gleam in his eye. There was total certainty in the way he carried himself. Instinctively I knew that this was going to be some event. I was still hanging on to the can of beer and the ball when Bradman faced his first ball.
>
> The wicket was covered in a thick mat of grass: green and hard. It looked as if it would bounce and seam. It was 'made' for any fast bowler and these two tear-away quick bowlers were eager to make an impression on Bradman and the small group watching. I just bowled a few leggies at gentle pace.

Mind you, Thommo's idea of 'gentle pace' came at you around the speed of Dennis Lillee. He couldn't bowl a slow ball if he tried.

> But the way Bradman was shaping I decided to sit back and watch. I didn't realise at the time that I was about to see one of the greatest events of my cricketing life.
>
> There was this little old guy in horn-rimmed glasses facing fast bowlers on a green pitch in an Adelaide backyard on the rest day of a Test match. He wasn't wearing any protection: no pads, box or gloves. He was just standing there with a borrowed bat. I couldn't keep my eyes off Bradman. He was beaming. I'm sure those two young fast bowlers were thinking, 'How good is this? We've got Bradman and Thomson playing in our backyard net.'
>
> I guess then I decided not to keep bowling—even my leg-breaks or anything at all—because I could just see the headlines if I had come in at him off my long run: 'THOMMO KILLS BRADMAN IN BACKYARD TEST.' It really couldn't get any better than what I was seeing, so I sat back with my beer and enjoyed seeing Don Bradman

in full flight. I thought to myself, 'How good is this? It just doesn't get any better.'

Every Australian kid to play the game knows the Bradman batting record. It is so stupendous even the Australian Broadcasting Corporation (ABC) paid tribute to the man by ensuring that its head office post box number—9994—remains to this day, a silent salute to the man's remarkable batting average of 99.94. There have been other batsmen to score more runs than Bradman. Allan Border, for instance, hit nearly twice the number of Test runs as the Don, but no-one would seriously consider Border, a fine Test match batsman, was a better player than Bradman.

Bill Ferguson was the man they called 'Mr Cricket' (long before Mike Hussey was given the tag). Fergie was baggage-man-scorer to every Australian touring side to England from 1905 until 1956 and he made this observation of Bradman's batting genius in a book he wrote in 1957:

Don was a phenomenon with the bat. When he was in the mood— and that was nearly all the time—he would pulverise the bowlers, indulging in what I make no apology for describing as a picturesque massacre.

Like the ranks of Tuscany, who could scarce forebear to cheer Don Bradman's pitiless punishment—brought forth, so often, applause from those he punished. He told me: 'Plenty of batsmen watch the bowler's fingers hoping to detect what sort of ball he is going to deliver, but that's no good to me. Let me see the ball coming, and I'll decide the best place to hit it.'[2]

After Thommo watched Bradman play on Doc Beard's Adelaide backyard pitch, he could easily relate to Bill Ferguson's description of Bradman:

At the sight of the two fast bowlers Bradman's eyes lit up and you could see he was thinking, 'Who are you two clowns? Do you think you are going to get me out? I've news for you.' He assumed an air of supreme confidence. Now as he hoed into those two young fast men with relish, it was as if Bradman was wearing a suit of armour; he was invincible, merciless. That little guy in glasses was suddenly transformed into Don Bradman, the human thrashing machine, belting every ball with power and precision. He did not play a false shot in twenty minutes of the most amazing batting I have ever seen. If anyone shit-bags this bloke's batting, I'll tell them the truth.

Bradman was then 70 years old, yet he belted hell out of every ball. There wasn't a false stroke. Not one defensive shot and I likened the batting show to what we see of Bradman on the old film. The old black and white films of Bradman have him blasting every ball, not one false shot and certainly no defensive shots. I thought those old films were edited—you know, the editor cuts out all the shit shots. Now I know different.

How good must Bradman have been in his heyday? I reckon any player from then or later on, blokes like Viv Richards and Ian or Greg Chappell, or any star from today, Brian Lara or Ricky Ponting, absolutely anyone, other than Bradman, would have struggled against those two young quicks on that green pitch. It was seaming all over the place and those youngsters were operating at around Glenn McGrath's pace.

If it was you or me, we'd be thinking of how we might get hit, but not Bradman. How do you reckon any other bloke of 70 years of age would fare in similar circumstances? I don't care if they were former Test batsmen, they wouldn't have hit a ball—not one ball.

Having witnessed the miracle on Beulah Road the guests were left pinching themselves. For they were a privileged few. That a man, as great as Bradman undoubtedly was, could at the age of 70 bat in such a manner defied imagination. Thommo became an instant disciple of Bradman's batsmanship. He was rapt.

The rest day over, Thommo turned his mind from Bradman's remarkable batting on that green pitch at Doc Beard's place to business at hand.

Australia had amassed a huge first innings total (505) and when Thommo took the new ball he bowled with gusto and, as usual, genuine pace. Thommo let a full toss slip and Gavaskar dispatched the ball to the cover boundary. The score moved to 23, then Thommo got a ball to rear like a striking cobra and Gavasker could only fend it to Peter Toohey in the gully. Mohinder Armanath was scooped up at slip by Gary Cosier and he had to go, although not everyone on the ground thought it was a clean catch. Thommo had 2/12.

Halfway through his fourth over, Thommo suddenly pulled up in his run-up, clutching his leg. He had pulled a hamstring muscle. He was forced to leave the field and while he batted in the Australian second innings, scoring 3, he didn't bowl again in that Fifth Test match. Thommo's absence from the bowling seriously hampered Australia's efforts to win, although Bob Simpson did give his remaining bowlers a reasonable target, setting the Indians 494 runs for victory. Without Thommo, Australia's attack looked pedestrian and India almost reached what would have been a world record victory target. However, India was finally all out for 445 giving Australia a comfortable 49-run buffer.

As for Thommo, the Adelaide Oval jinx remained.

He finished on top of the Australian Test bowling averages with 22 wickets at 23.45; only Wayne Clarke, with 28 wickets, having claimed more victims in the series.

For Thommo and the other ACB players, the coming tour of the West Indies should have been a highlight of the cricket calendar. But the controversy of the WSC revolution, in its ongoing battle with the Establishment, continued to cloud the game.

On July 26, 1977, world cricket's controlling body, the International Cricket Conference (ICC) decreed that any player contracted to Kerry Packer's World Series Cricket as of October 1, 1977, would be ineligible to play in any Test match without the express consent of the Conference. In the wake of a British High Court ruling on November 25, 1977, the ICC resolution was withdrawn for the High Court ruled that it represented a unreasonable restraint of trade. The England and Australian Establishment lawyers racked their brains and they finally discovered a method to remain recalcitrant towards any notion of compromise.

They successfully circumvented the implications of the British High Court decision by obliging players to choose between World Series Cricket and Establishment cricket. Packer's Australian signees were told that they would be considered for representative teams if they could give an undertaking to be available for all scheduled Sheffield Shield and Test matches. It would, of course, have been impossible for the WSC players to be available for all such matches, so it was a victory for the Establishment over the rebels.

Thommo was less than happy. He was—because of his contract with Radio 4IP—forced to make himself available for all Sheffield Shield matches and the Test team. Yet he yearned to be with his mates—Dennis Lillee, Lennie Pascoe and company—all of whom were with WSC.

Meanwhile, the West Indian captain Clive Lloyd was still smarting over Australia's 5–1 victory against his team Down Under in 1975–76. Lloyd began his four-pronged fast bowling attack in the 1976 series against England in the Old Country. If Thomson and Lillee could cut through his strong West Indian batting line-up, what damage could four genuinely quick fast bowlers do against any team? After drawing the first two Tests in England, the West Indians won the final three Tests to rout the home side. Viv Richards emerged from that tour as one of the great batsmen in Test history, revealing his undoubted class and power with 829 runs in the series.

Although Lloyd didn't quite have the perfect pace attack, for Michael Holding, Andy Roberts and Wayne Daniel were supported by medium-fast merchant Vanburn Holder, his strategy was largely responsible for the West Indies domination. The Windies beat India 2–1, England 3–nil and then Pakistan 2–1 in the space of 12 months leading up to the Australians' 1978 tour of the Caribbean. Lloyd's pace attack was described by England fast bowler Bob Willis as 'the most sustained barrage of intimidation [on the Test cricket arena] that I have seen',[3] and his tactics brought accusations of 'barbarism' from Indian opener Sunil Gavaskar. In the fourth and final Test of the series against India, captain Bishen Bedi declared his innings closed with the score at 97. Only five men had been dismissed, but there were several players nursing bruised or broken hands. Four men—Gaekwad, Patel, Bedi and Chandrasekhar—were declared 'absent hurt' and Bedi declared in protest of the West Indians' intimidatory attack.

Thommo had to be available for the 1978 Australian tour of the West Indies. He was unimpressed at the prospect and as the tour dragged on in controversy, Thommo became more and more homesick. He spent something in the order of $2300 in overseas phone calls to Cheryl.

I didn't want to tour the West Indies because I wanted to play World Series Cricket. That much-publicised $63,000 a year [for ten years] was a much-inflated figure. The actual cash I would have received was more in the region of $28,000. But the money I lost after my busted shoulder against Pakistan led to conflict. I put myself out to play for the Board [ACB]. When I didn't feel like going on the tour of the West Indies, Radio 4IP came in again and said, 'You'll have to go or your contract's not on'. No option—again. Against my will, I had to go on this tour. Under the circumstances, how can they expect you to play well?

Little wonder Thommo pulled out of his 4IP contract as soon as he could do so.

Thommo was duly picked in the Australian squad for the Caribbean and Bob Simpson successfully lobbied for Thommo to be his Test vice-captain. The squad was: R.B. Simpson (42, NSW), captain; J.R. Thomson (27, Qld), vice-captain; I.W. Callen (22, Vic); W.M. Clarke (24, WA); G.J. Cosier (24, Qld); W.M. Darling (20, SA); J.D. Higgs (27, Vic); K.J. Hughes (23, WA); T.J. Laughlin (27, Vic); S.J. Rixon (24, NSW); C.S. Serjeant (26, WA); P.M. Toohey (23, NSW); G.M. Wood (21, WA); G.N. Yallop (25, Vic); B. Yardley (30, WA). A.D. Olgilvie (26, Qld) was flown to the Caribbean three weeks into the tour to replace Kim Hughes who went down with appendicitis.

Thommo was 'really proud' to get the vice-captaincy.

It was a terrific honour. But it wasn't a great side. All my mates were in WSC and they were about to again play for the best against the best in the coming Australian summer.

Thommo was so rapt in being named Australian vice-captain of the touring party that he rushed out and a bought a tie to complement his stylish, powder-blue suit. He astonished team-mates by wearing his new outfit to team practices. Imagine the faces of those who could never forget the Bankstown duo, Thomson and Pascoe, who used to turn up to the State nets in their board shorts and thongs and terrorise their NSW squad team-mates. However, Thommo had to shelve plans to wear his powder-blue suit, for the ACB decreed players wear team-issued grey slacks and the Australian team blazer wherever and whenever they travelled as a group. Thommo wasn't happy.

> *I bought the fucking blue suit to wear in the West Indies, but the bloody Board wouldn't let me wear it. I had to wear that bloody stupid schoolboy's uniform all the time!*

But the series had bigger issues clouding proceedings; far bigger than Thommo's powder-blue suit. The West Indian Board of Control had reluctantly gone along with the original ICC resolution on World Series Cricket, but they did not wish to stand in the way of professional sportsmen earning a living. The West Indian Board announced that their players would be penalised only if WSC commitments made them unavailable to play for the West Indies. As the first WSC tournament finished in early February and the next was not due to start until November, the Windies Board was then able to pick the best Test team possible for the series against Simpson's side. And the best possible side meant the inclusion of all the champions among the Packer contingent, including the likes of Gordon Greenidge, Desmond Haynes, Viv Richards, Clive Lloyd, Deryck Murray, Andy Roberts, Colin Croft and Joel Garner. It was a case of the No. 1 West Indian team versus the Australian Third Eleven.

The mismatch was clearly evident in Australia's first Test at Queen's Park Oval, Port-of-Spain. Batting first Australia was bowled out for a paltry 90; Croft getting 4/15, Roberts 2/25, and Garner 3/35. Then the Windies hit 405. Alvin Kallicharran, the stylish, pint-sized left-hander, who raised the ire of Kerry Packer by pulling out of his WSC contract, hit a brilliant 127 and he was well supported by Clive Lloyd (86), Test debutant Desmond Haynes (61) and Gordon Greenidge (45). Thommo grabbed two prized scalps—he trapped Viv Richards lbw for 39 and he also clean-bowled Lloyd on his way to 3/84 off 21 overs. But Thommo didn't get another crack at the West Indies because Simpson's men fell

for a modest 209 in their second innings—Andy Roberts taking 5/56—
and Australia lost the match by an innings and 106 runs.

The second Test match at Kensington Oval in Bridgetown, Barbados,
had the crowd abuzz. Again Australia struggled with the bat, falling
for 250. Bruce Yardley slapped and slashed for 74, Graeme Wood hit a
solid 69 and Graham Yallop fought for his 47, but the rest struggled.
Thommo was suffering from homesickness. He missed the climate
and wide open spaces and the beaches of Queensland and, most of all,
he missed Cheryl. Getting hit in the ribs by an Andy Roberts short
ball didn't improve his sense of wellbeing, nor was he or the rest of
the players greatly impressed by Graeme Wood copping a nasty blow
to the hand. Perhaps it was a combination of events, maybe no more
than Thommo deciding to prove to the cricket world that he could be
just as fast as ever, but whatever the reason, Jeff Thomson was about
to provide the Barbados crowd with the most amazing spell of fast
bowling they had seen.

On this day Thommo was fired up, big time. And the wiseacres at
Kensington Oval, good judges of cricket, intently watched Thomson's
explosive performance. Men who had seen the likes of Wes Hall and
Charlie Griffith at their fastest, as well as Michael Holding, Andy Roberts
and Joel Garner, were moved to say that no fast man in history was quicker
than Jeffrey Robert Thomson. Thommo turned on the pace; the fastest
and most furious spell of bowling he had delivered in big cricket since the
shoulder injury he sustained in Adelaide.

*After the collision in Adelaide and subsequent shoulder injury I
wasn't consistently as quick. After a major injury—and that was my
only one—I found there seemed to be a bit of a mindset. I tended to
do things to compensate for my shoulder. I ran in faster and took a
longer approach. I found I couldn't load up as well as before and that
hampered my ability to get the ball up around the batsman's ears from
a fairly full length. It wasn't just my pace. I think my ability to get the
ball to bounce off a good length was my greatest asset. But on this day
in Barbados I just loped in like my old self and bowled as quick as I
had ever bowled.*

The crowd fell silent as Thommo's first ball thudded with a resounding thwack into Steve Rixon's gloves. Gordon Greenidge was facing and Thommo's third ball cracked him across the knuckles and the ball ballooned gently to Craig Serjeant in the gully. Bloody beauty, one for none. Or so it seemed. There was a unanimous appeal by the Australians, but what was so obvious to all the players and the wiseacres in the Kensington Oval stands would not wash with umpire Steve Parris, who stood impassively, unmoved. Greenidge ruefully removed his gloves and rubbed his right shoulder. Thommo thought that to be an Academy-Award-winning performance by the West Indian opener.

> *His hand must have been hurting a helluva lot, so it was a good piece of acting on Gordon's part. That really steamed me up, an obvious out given not out and then out comes the physio with ice and the magic spray for the Greenidge hand that held the glove that produced the easy catch.*
>
> *Gordon* [Greenidge] *just stood there after the 'catch' was taken cleanly and I said to him, 'You're fucking joking!' I was really pissed off that he wasn't given out and that he made no move to walk off, given that it was an obvious dismissal. I loped in like I used to approach the wicket and let fly. I hit a few blokes some near-crippling blows. The ball was coming out a treat. I got Greenidge cheaply, and in walked Viv* [Richards].
>
> *I like Viv. We got on well and I got to know him pretty well when we played together for Queensland. In he came chewing his gum, looking as confident as ever. I said to Viv, 'G'day Smokin''* [a nickname for Richards, after Smokin' Joe Frazier, the champion US heavyweight boxer], *and I thought over what sort of delivery to give him first up. You pitch the ball up to Viv and he's likely to smack it. So I decided to bounce him. Yeah, he won't smack my bouncer. So I bounced him and Viv took the bait. He hit the ball off the splice and it ballooned in the direction of mid-wicket. And there is Roo* [Bruce Yardley] *bumbling in like Alan Turner, running up and down on the spot. Roo got to the ball but dropped what was an easy chance. I stood and glared at him, 'What do you think's going on? This bloke is the best batsman in the world—you cunt.' Viv just stood and laughed aloud. He was laughing and chewing his cud.*

But Thommo was in no mood to laugh. He stormed back to his bowling mark. What ball to bowl this time?

> *So I decided to bowl another bouncer. I came in purposely and gave*
> *him another one, a second successive bouncer. But Viv seemed to be*
> *reading my mind. He was in position swiftly and he hit it as only Viv*
> *Richards could hit it.*
>
>   *The ball careered low and fast over square leg and hit the tin roof*
> *of the little building just over the boundary fence at square leg. I had*
> *barely finished my follow-through when the ball hit the roof with a*
> *loud bang and clatter. It was a fabulous shot; went off like rifle fire.*
> *I said to him, 'Shit, Viv, that's fucking bullshit!' Viv knew that he had*
> *played a lucky hook, the ball hit right in the middle of his bat and he*
> *got away with it. He looked at me and shrugged and we both laughed.*
> *He wasn't laughing next ball when I smashed him on the hand and*
> *then I gave him another bouncer.*

Richards was living dangerously. He played an audacious back-foot drive which cleared mid-off, then Thommo gave him an extra-quick bouncer. Viv got into position to hook, but the ball came on too fast and he got it mostly off the splice of the bat. Earlier Richards was dropped by substitute fieldsman Trevor Laughlin off the luckless Thommo, so the fast bowler was relieved to see Richards mishit lob over Laughlin's head and balloon towards Wayne Clarke who was moving in from deep fine leg. Clarke made a last-ditch, desperate dive and he somehow got his hands under the ball, grimly holding on to it as he hit the ground.

The last ball of the day saw Kallicharran get an inside edge off Thommo, the ball looping towards a grateful Bruce Yardley at backward square leg and he accepted the easy chance.

Thommo's amazing pace that day was a revelation for the young Australian players in the team. They had seen Thommo at his top either at the ground during recent home series, or on television, but to see him in full-flight at close range in the heat of a Test match battle was something else. Batsman Gary Cosier, who hit a debut hundred against Clive Lloyd's men at the MCG in 1975–76 said:

I've been lucky enough to see some fast bowling in my time, but Thommo that day was incredible. There was no way that Viv was going to stick around.[4]

Former NSW and Test batsman John Benaud was at the ground that day and he marvelled at the way Thommo revisited his great pace. Benaud was Thommo's first State captain and he was the man who advised Thommo to go 'out and have a drink' to relax before his Sheffield Shield debut at the Gabba in 1972.

Talk to Ian Chappell and former Sri Lankan batsman Duleep Mendis about the knowledgeable crowd at Kensington Oval, Barbados, and they will unequivocally tell you that the fastest of all the fast bowlers seen on this ground is none other than J.R. Thomson.

Having bowled brilliantly Thommo left the field that evening a satisfied fast bowler. He had bowled at his fiercest, proving to himself and all the others that he still retained the flame and the mantle as the fastest bowler to draw breath. More satisfying, perhaps, was his contest with Viv Richards, the mercurial one. Thommo not only beat him morally, but he claimed his prized wicket.

My rhythm was terrific. Something within me told me to lope in as I used to and it worked perfectly.

Next day Thommo bowled only 3 overs before he left the field with a leg strain. While he was receiving treatment in the Australian dressing-room, the Windies batsmen made merry. Desmond Haynes got to 66 and the little wicket-keeper Deryck Murray compiled a typically neat and gritty 60. Thommo returned in time to wrap up the West Indian innings, finishing with 6/77 off 13 explosive overs.

Despite Thommo's heroics, the West Indians won the match easily, by 9 wickets. Thommo bowled only 6 overs in the Windies second innings of 1/141 and Yardley was belted for 55 runs off just 10.5 overs. Gordon Greenidge (80 not out) and Desmond Haynes (55) did it easily.

But even though the West Indians won the first two Test matches convincingly, all was not well within Clive Lloyd's camp. The West Indies

Board had wanted to avoid a showdown with the Packer players. However, those who signed with WSC were disenchanted with the selectors axing Deryck Murray and bringing in Viv Richards as his replacement as team vice-captain. The word was that Murray was getting on in years and Viv was the man in line to take over from Lloyd.

Moreover the Board wanted to know how many among the players would be available to tour Sri Lanka and India. Anticipating the obvious need to blood new players, the Board set a deadline of March 23, 1978—a window of time between the Second and Third Tests against Simpson's Australians—for the West Indies WSC players to declare their intentions: they had to choose to go with Packer or make the Test tours of Sri Lanka and India.

Lloyd's WSC contingent wanted more time and they asked for an extension of the deadline so that the West Indies could field their best side for the whole of the series against Bob Simpson's team. Not surprisingly, the Board refused to extend the deadline beyond March 23. They were waving a red flag at the bull.

Kerry Packer made a rushed visit to Barbados to join discussions and he stated his case on television. But all was to no avail for the WSC cause and relations were further cooled between the players and the Board when it was revealed that three young players—Richard Austin, Colin Croft and Desmond Haynes—had signed with World Series Cricket. The Board claimed that the trio signed with WSC after they had assured the Windies management that they would not do so.

Tension turned to crisis when the West Indian team was announced for the Third Test. Austin, Haynes and Murray were omitted. Clive Lloyd, who was not satisfied with the Board's explanation that other young players had to be tried, resigned in protest over what he called 'gross victimisation'. A few hours later the remaining WSC West Indian players in the team—Colin Croft, Joel Garner, Gordon Greenidge, Viv Richards and Andy Roberts—declared themselves unavailable.

Without their stars the West Indians fielded a third-rate outfit for Bourda. Although the Australians reckoned they had every chance to win the match without the galaxy of champions they confronted in the first two Tests, Thommo was less than impressed.

I wanted to play for the best against the best West Indian team and I guess the announcement of all those players walking out of the Windies team affected my motivation for the rest of that tour. Being with the best against the best: that's what I wanted.

But for Bob Simpson here was the chance to win a Test against the West Indians. With Thommo getting 4/57 off 16.2 overs and Wayne Clarke taking 4/64 off 24 overs, the West Indians were rolled for 205. Australia replied with 286. The Windies fought back magnificently, hitting a second innings 439. Thommo bowled without luck, taking 1/83. Thanks to centuries by Graeme Wood (126) and Craig Serjeant (124), Australia got the required runs (362) for victory.

Stung by defeat, the West Indies won the Fourth Test at Queen's Park Oval, Port-of-Spain, by 198 runs and the Fifth Test at Sabina Park, Kingston, was a draw. There were times when Thommo excelled and looked a level above the exceptional pace of even the best of the Windies attack when they fielded their best eleven. His explosive spell at Kensington Oval left no-one in doubt as to who was the fastest bowler in Test history, but Thommo's fire flickered as the tour wore on.

All my mates—FOT [Dennis Lillee], Lennie, Tangles [Max Walker] and Solo [Mick Malone]—were gearing up for WSC to play the best of the best and here I was opening the bowling with Trevor Laughlin [the Victorian medium-slow bowler], whose pace was barely of the medium variety.

The Australians should have won the Fifth Test at Kingston, for at one stage in their second innings the Windies had slumped to 5/88 in their quest to score 369 runs for victory on the final day. With 38 balls left to bowl and 1 wicket to fall, Australia was on the verge of victory. Vanburn Holder was the 9th West Indian wicket to fall. Holder (6) was given out caught behind by Steve Rixon off the bowling of Victorian leg-spinner Jim Higgs and it was 9/258.

Holder hesitated at the crease and he seemed reluctant to move off towards the pavilion. He appeared dissatisfied with the umpire's decision and the crowd sensed great loss. Within seconds, thousands of jeering spectators became a seething mass of discontent. Hundreds of fans began throwing bottles and stones on to the field. And as the mob invaded the Test arena, the players ran for their lives. Australian radio legend, Alan McGilvray, covering the Tests for the ABC, as he had since 1934, told me later:

> You know how much I love this game, but to think that so honourable a pursuit as cricket could suffer such madness makes my blood boil.[5]

Riot police, equipped with shields and brandishing automatic weapons, eventually restored order, but before doing so they fired warning shots into the air to dispel the madding crowd.

Hopes of a resumption of play were forsaken. Lengthy discussions took place between officials of both teams. West Indian Board representatives Alan Rae and Gerry Alexander decided that the match be extended into a sixth day to make up for the time lost in the riot. Unfortunately, the umpires were neither consulted nor informed of the decision. Umpire Ralph Gosein, when summoned from his hotel the next morning, refused to continue. He said there was no provision for extra time in the conditions of play for the tour. Stand-by umpire John Gayle supported Gosein's view and the match was abandoned as a draw. West Indian-based journalist Tony Cozier wrote in *Wisden* that the tour had been 'bedevilled throughout by rancour and controversy'.[6]

In the desperate atmosphere of the riot, Thommo swapped his baggy-green Test cap for a couple of athletics medals, won by a policeman he befriended in Jamaica.

> *During the riot I looked for my copper mate. This bloke was built like Silvester Clarke* [the giant West Indian fast bowler of the 1980s]. *My mate knew Jamaica and during my stay there he told me where I could go and be safe and where I should not go in town. He knew the place like the back of his hand. He'd been shot a few times in street scraps, but he'd come through it all.*

*I thought he was a good friend to have in a war. I gave him my
baggy-green and he gave me some of the medals he'd won for Jamaica.
He was a discus and javelin champion.*

That was the second and last time Thommo had swapped a baggy-
green Test cap. He swapped one for a bobby's helmet during the equally
controversial Australian tour of England in 1977.

13 BACK WITH MATES

There's a few clowns around in the newspaper world. They'd do anything
for sensationalism, but they find out that in the long run that by writing
bullshit . . . they bugger themselves up . . . In the end you don't trust
any of them.

Back in Australia, Thommo had some big decisions to make. He talked
with his life-long mate, Lennie Pascoe, and told Lennie that he wanted to
have another crack at World Series Cricket.

*When I got back from the tour, I went to see Frank Gardiner. Frank
was sort of my manager and had been for more than a year, since
England 1977 when I was forced to pull out of the first WSC contract.
I told Frank that I had had enough and that I wanted to go to World
Series. Station 2SM had taken over Radio 4IP and formed a company,
but the company wasn't registered at the time, so the new contract
wasn't valid. Frank found that out by searching. So we said, 'See ya
later boys!' It was a lucky break. I was free.*

*The first thing I did was to get in touch with Lennie Pascoe. I rang
him from my parents' house in Bankstown and Lennie rang WSC and*

they soon rang me back. They wanted to come out and see me that same
afternoon. I said that I had things to do so three of them—Andrew
Caro, Austin Robertson and a WSC solicitor—turned up next day.

The Thommo saga had been one of the WSC lowlights because he was
seen as a real coup for Packer, given his sensational partnership with
Dennis Lillee. When Thommo pulled out of WSC in England in 1977,
Kerry Packer had been persuaded by John Cornell not to hound Thommo
through the courts because there was some sympathy for him.

Packer was a man of his word and he would have admired Thommo
for his sticking to his contract with Radio 4IP, which meant he had to be
available for Sheffield Shield matches with Queensland and to play Test
cricket for Australia. Thommo has always been a fiercely loyal person and
Packer identified with that loyalty.

But the fast man had financial problems. His backing of Allsports
stores—with cash he made from 4IP—backfired and he had become a
discharged bankrupt. For all his help in Thommo's early career, David
Lord was highly critical of what he called Thommo's 'recklessness' in
allowing his brother Greg, a bricklayer, and a friend Ashley Colbert, to
run the Allsports shops. When liquidators were appointed, creditors
were chasing $30,000. At the time Thommo, then West Indian Alvin
Kallicharran, pulled out of their WSC contracts, Lord claimed that their
withdrawal would spark the 'beginning of an enormous exodus from the
Packer circus'. How wrong could Lord be; Thommo was now clamouring
to get back to playing for 'the best against the best'.

The financial problems wouldn't go away. Due to a surge in his
income in 1977–78, after a virtually cricket-less year in 1976–77 because
of the shoulder injury he sustained in the First Test against Pakistan
at Adelaide Oval, Thommo was hit with a $24,000 provisional taxa-
tion bill.

While Thommo wanted to play with his mates at World Series Cricket—
he'd much rather open the attack with Dennis Lillee than the dribbly slows
of Trevor Laughlin as he did in that final Test in the West Indies—the ACB
seemed hell-bent upon preventing Thommo moving camps.

During the WSC flare-up, the various cricket boards around the
world were signing their players up for future tours; insurance, it seemed,

against their defecting to 'the enemy'. Three days after the 1977–78 Test series against India had finished, Thommo was contracted by the ACB for the 1978–79 Ashes series with England. Thommo was metaphorically hamstrung. There was no way he could play WSC.

Or was there a way?

Allen, Allen & Hemsley lawyer Jim Thynne hit upon the idea of having Thommo write a letter of resignation to the ACB. If a jaded Thommo officially retired, the Board would have no option but to release him from any contracts and he would be free to play for WSC. A letter was forwarded to the ACB on August 9. ACB Chairman Bob Parish had been hearing a variety of Jeff Thomson retirement rumours since June. And all rumours to that effect were denied. Parish consulted his lawyers.

Around the time Thommo sent the ACB his retirement letter, the Board received a similar one from Bob Simpson, who announced his retirement from Test and State cricket. The Board immediately accepted Simpson's letter of resignation.

Six weeks after the ACB had received Thommo's letter of resignation, his lawyer-cum-manager Frank Gardiner called a press conference in Brisbane where he told a gathering of journalists that Thommo wished to play for Queensland and his club, Toombul. He wanted to be 'released' from playing Test matches. A week later Thommo, staying at Lennie Pascoe's Bankstown home, signed with World Series Cricket.

The ACB were not amused.

On Sunday, September 25, 1978, Thommo paired with Dennis Lillee, playing for Ian Chappell's team, with other WSC players, at Drummoyne Oval in the annual charity fundraiser for the NSW Spastic Centre.

The ACB reacted swiftly, hauling Thommo before the NSW Equity Court. Thommo was never the ideal witness. He forgot details of letters and telephone calls. He simply didn't think these things important. After all, he didn't expect to be having to think about names and dates and places and be grilled by lawyers for hours on end. All Thommo wanted to do was to play cricket with his mates. Asked if he would sign a letter written for him without reading it, he told the court:

I have written very few letters on my behalf in my time.

Asked if he had lied to ACB chairman Bob Parish, he said:

> *At the time I had a million people bothering me. I'm not sure what I said to be absolutely correct because I was sick and tired of every Joe Blow ringing me up.*

The lawyer then asked Thommo if Mr Parish was 'every Joe Blow'. To which Thommo replied:

> *No, guess not.*

Asked if he had lied to journalists (and the name of journalist Simunovich cropped up) Thommo said, 'He rings me up every blasted day, just about. Him and all the rest—they get on my goat most times. I would have told him anything to get rid of him.'

By this time Thommo was heartily sick of being hounded.

> *The phone was sometimes ringing all bloody day. I was asked if it was true that I told one journalist one thing, and another something different. Well, why should I tell a reporter what I am doing? What business is it of his? I told reporters anything to get rid of them. I'd made a gentleman's agreement that I wasn't going to tell anyone anything anyway. Why should I break my promise? There's a few clowns around in the newspaper world. They'd do anything for sensationalism, but they find out that in the long run that by writing bullshit instead of doing the right thing by us, they bugger themselves up. I don't know why they do it. They make it hard for the other blokes. In the end you don't trust any of them. At one stage I wouldn't speak on the phone to anyone. I didn't care who rang me. I just told them I had nothing to say, and to go to buggery and then I hung up.*

Thommo's honesty might not have served him well in court, for he virtually admitted telling untruths to journalists to get them off his back. But when it comes to honesty, no-one could ever doubt Thommo. Greg Chappell knows Thommo as well as anyone who played with him and he came to greatly admire the fast man's honesty:

He has stayed true to himself and Thommo is very honest. Once during a Sheffield Shield match in Perth, I had occasion to speak to Thommo for he was bowling all over the place. When I questioned him, he said, 'Shit Greg, you wouldn't think the sixteen beers I drank last night had anything to do with my form out here today?'

In my experience, Thommo's honesty ranks with that of the likes of Ian Chappell and Doug Walters.[1]

That summer of 1978–79 Thomson played just one match for Queensland, a one-day game against South Australia at the Gabba on October 28, and he came up with a 'Man of the Match' 6/18 off 10 blistering-fast overs. But the court case was ripping him apart mentally. With little cricket and having to front up for a constant grilling, Thommo had had enough. He was grilled relentlessly for 12 hours and in the end, on November 3, 1978, Justice Kearney ruled that the fast bowler's World Series Cricket contract was null and void.

The same night the NSW Equity Court ruled against Thommo, he drove to the Gold Coast to collect Cheryl. He was driving at his normal, flat-to-the-floor speed when a traffic cop stopped him and issued him a $20 ticket. At least Cheryl had some good news. She won the annual Concourse d'Elegance for fashion models with cars.

Not much cricket seemed in store for Jeffrey Robert Thomson for the rest of that 1978-79 summer. Thommo spent time with Cheryl. He went fishing and pig hunting and attended a number of WSC matches. His dislike for the ACB increased because they had purposely kept him out of big cricket with their vindictive handling of his Board contract and his being hauled before the courts.

While Thommo spent a summer without bowling a ball—apart from his stirring 6/18 in the one-dayer against SA—Australia's veritable Third Eleven was belted by Mike Brearley's England team. Led by the lacklustre Victorian batsman Graham Yallop, Australia was totally outclassed.

There was some consolation for Thommo as John MacLean, his Queensland keeper, was given four Test matches. MacLean was a tough campaigner, who really could have done a similar job as Rodney Marsh at the top level had he been given like opportunities. Yallop wasn't a strong captain and he had continual run-ins with his fast bowler Rodney Hogg, who bowled superbly, especially against England opener Geoff Boycott.

Late in the summer, too late for Thommo to play Sheffield Shield for Queensland, the ACB released him from his contract with the Board. It was the sort of schoolboy, tit-for-tat stuff that the Board had always done with the players. But Thommo was relieved.

At least I was now free to be back with my mates; blokes who could bat, blokes who could bowl, blokes who could bloody catch the ball.

ACB Chairman Bob Parish looked like the smiling assassin as he faced the cameras and spoke of the Board's 'goodwill gesture' in releasing Thommo. In reality, the Board was in trouble. The Packer challenge was hitting Australian cricket hard. The Queensland Cricket Association was struggling financially, as was NSWCA. There was a school of thought which believed if the Board could just hang in there, sign up all the up-and-coming players, WSC would die because their players could not go on forever and if they had no youngsters coming, the future was bleak indeed. However, Packer had the resources to squeeze the life out of the Establishment within a few years. The smart ones on the Board saw the inevitability of a compromise. Thommo's release from his Board contract was the beginning of the end for the big cricket war. The Establishment knew that they had better extend an olive branch to WSC soon, or the game could end up in Packer's 'meat mangler'.

According to all press reports, Thommo was back with WSC. Because the ACB had magnaminously released him from their iron-clad hold, he was free to go with the Packer troupe, but had he tied up all the loose ends?

No.

A few weeks before the World Series Cricket Australians, led by Ian Chappell, left our shores to take on the might of the WSC West Indians, Austin 'Ocker' Robertson rang Chappelli. Chappell recalls Robertson saying:

'C'mon Chappelli, we've got to go out to Thommo's place in Bankstown and get him signed up.'

'Ocker, I'm busy, you can do that stuff.'

'No, mate. This is important, we have to do it now—we don't want anything to fall over at the last minute.'[2]

Chappelli and Robertson dutifully trooped out to Thommo's place and they waited all day for the WSC 'new chum' to arrive.

He did not appear.

There they were exchanging pleasantries with Thommo's mum and dad, Don and Doreen Thomson. As the afternoon wore on Chappelli couldn't help but notice a pianola standing proudly against a wall of the lounge room. Next to the pianola were stacks of those familiar perforated rolls. Chappelli then realised why Thommo knew all the words of the songs in the singalongs during those long hours on the road in the team coach in England.

> Dad always brought his mates home to our place after cricket on a Saturday night. Some of the blokes could sing and they would gather 'round the pianola, drink piss and sing. I pedalled like mad and I reckon I got pretty fit pedalling that pianola. And I got to know all the words. The words were on the left of the roll and the perforations to the right of the words. I got to know all the words off by heart and knew all the old favourites.

Next time Chappelli saw Thommo, he said:

> 'Jesus Thommo, you're an irresponsible bastard. We were at your place all day.'
> Thommo just said, 'Yeah I know. Sorry mate. You are right, I am irresponsible.'
> 'Christ, you didn't even turn up.'
> 'My solicitor told me not to show.'
> 'Well, Thommo, you could have at least given me a phone call.'
> 'Sorry mate.'[3]

Just a day before the WSC Australians were due to fly to the Caribbean, Chappelli was called in to Australian Consolidated Press (ACP) headquarters in Sydney. Along with ACP boss Kerry Packer, Austin Robertson, WSC executive Lynton Taylor and Allen, Allen & Hemsley's John Kitto awaited him.

'Happy with the side, Chappelli', Packer said straight up, ignoring any formality.

'Yeah, Kerry. Everything's okay, although a couple of the blokes aren't too pleased that the fixed sum for the coming eight-week tour [$16,000] turned out less than the daily rate stipulated under the WSC contract', Chappelli said.

Packer asked Lynton Taylor if the players were being paid according to their contracts.

Taylor replied, 'No, Kerry, but I can assure you that the matter is okay.'

Packer said with concerned tone, 'Lynton, aren't we paying according to the contract?'

'No, Kerry.'

'Well, Lynton, pay 'em according to the contract.'

Packer asked Taylor how much more money would be required to pay the players according to the letter of the contract.

Taylor got out a small computer and after a few minutes he came up with the figure. 'Kerry, it comes to $340,000.'

'Well, Lynton, pay 'em.'

Ian Chappell then chimed in, saying that the players were happy. 'You won't be making any money out of this tour. The players are happy. They know they're making a lot more money on this tour than they could in jobs back home, so all is fine.'

'Listen son', Packer eye-balled Chappelli, '$340,000 is about what I pay for a B-grade movie on my TV station. That amount—$340,000—is not going to break me. What will break me is not sticking to the word of my contract. Lynton, pay 'em!'[4]

Kerry Packer's actions in this matter gave us an insight into the mind of Australia's richest man. He wielded great power, but he was also a man of tremendous loyalty and he knew all about fair play. Packer ensured that each player would receive something in the order of $32,000 for the eight-week tour of the West Indies, instead of the initial $16,000. And that sort of money in 1978 was big biscuits.

Packer then talked to Chappelli about the Australians' firepower.

'You'll have Lillee and Thomson and Pascoe to put to the Windies—Thommo's signed, hasn't he?'

Ian Chappell gave Packer a detailed picture of what transpired at the Thomson family home.

'He's in, Kerry. There isn't a problem.'

Packer turned to Robertson: 'Is Thommo signed?'

Robertson said, 'Well, Kerry, Thommo's agreed to play.'

'Is he fucking signed?'

'The last time I saw him, Lynton was going to see him and get the contract all fixed up', Robertson said.

Packer turned to Lynton Taylor and said with a hint of anger, 'Is Thomson fucking signed?'

Taylor said in his smooth style, 'Oh, well, you know, when I spoke to Thommo he'd verbally agreed to play WSC. He's been booked on the plane . . .'

'Has he actually signed the fucking contract?'

'Well', said Taylor, a little less confidently, 'we had the contract. It's all drawn up. I left it with [John] Kitto.'

Packer leaned back in his chair, feet on the table and he asked with frustration: 'Has Jeff Thomson signed the fucking contract?'

Then John Kitto came in with, 'Well, I'm not actually dealing with that. Jim Thynne's dealing with Thommo . . .'

Packer pushed one of a number of buttons at his desk. A woman's voice came on-line.

'Where's Thynne?'

'Oh, he's on holiday, Mr Packer.'

'Where is he on holiday?'

'Somewhere on the Gold Coast.'

'Well, we'll fuck that holiday up!'[5]

Every person around the Packer table that afternoon learnt a very valuable lesson about Kerry Packer. When he wanted something done, he wanted it done pronto. And he wanted it done properly.

Thommo was signed up well before Ian Chappell's Australian's were aboard the Jumbo jet to take them off to the Caribbean, much to the relief of Robertson, Kitto, Chappelli and poor Jim Thynne, whose Gold Coast holiday was indeed 'fucked up'.

The drama of recent days never really dawned on Thommo. He was out of his ACB contract and he had signed the dotted line with WSC. Packer got his way and the Australians had the team to mount a serious challenge on Clive Lloyd's rampaging West Indians. For Thommo, it felt like a new beginning.

> *Boy, did I enjoy this series. I was with a good, committed team. FOT [Dennis Lillee], Solo [Mick Malone], Lennie [Pascoe] and myself would give it to the Windies. It was all-out war. And we wanted to beat them on their home soil. It would have been a tremendous achievement given the way the West Indians had begun to steamroll all opposition.*
>
> *We lost the first Supertest by a fair margin and things were grim, but the group really did believe in their ability. I always thought that we'd bounce back.*

Thommo took 1/46 off 14 overs and 2/67 off 22 overs. Here it was February, 1979, his first big match since he played in the Fifth Test against the West Indies in April 1978. Dennis Lillee bowled impressively to grab a match haul of 8/168 off 43.2 overs, but the match belonged to Clive Lloyd, who mauled the Australians with a match winning second innings of 197. Then came an embarrassing Australian batting collapse. Ian Chappell was as distraught as he was livid. When cricket writer Phil Wilkins of *The Australian* approached Chappelli, sitting alone poolside at the team hotel, he copped a curt, 'Fuck off, prick', and he wisely beat a hasty retreat.

Just before the Second Supertest in Bridgetown, some of the players joined ex-West Indian fast bowler Richard Edwards on a fishing trip. The players returned home empty-handed and with stories of those that 'got away', but the street-smart Bankstown boys, Thommo and Pascoe, came to the rescue. They had taken what they considered a 'necessary precaution' and scoured the local fish markets. The fast bowling duo then turned on a splendid barbecue for all of the touring party.

At Sabina Park Chappelli noticed that Lennie Pascoe wasn't going full tilt at training. Pascoe was chatting with a group of Jamaicans and at a cocktail party Chappelli turned on him: 'So, Lennie, who booked your tour then, Jetset or Qantas? You're obviously here for a holiday.'

'What do you fucking mean?' Lennie replied angrily.

'Well, everyone's bowling their guts out and you're down at fine leg talking to the locals. There's a third pace spot in this side and I haven't decided who's going to fill it.'

Chappelli noted Pascoe had become sullen and withdrawn, so he decided to lighten the exchange.

'C'mon, Lennie, where's your sense of humour?'

Lennie grabbed Chappelli by the collar and dragged him upwards.

'I haven't got a sense of humour.'

Bruce Laird became the self-appointed mediator and the tough, little opening batsman tried to separate the pair. An ugly incident was defused and Lennie let go of his captain, who landed back on terra firma.

'See', said Lennie with a false laugh, 'I *have* a sense of humour.'[6]

Chappelli and Pascoe were destined to have a showdown. It would come sooner than either might have thought. Lennie ducked a non-compulsory training session at Kensington Oval and Chappelli ordered that Pascoe appear in the nets. The team bus had driven off and Thommo was delegated to find Lennie and get him to the ground. Ian Chappell had already left for the ground when Greg Chappell wandered out of the team hotel and he saw Jeff Thomson standing by some bushes near the hotel entrance.

'G'day, Two-Up', Greg said. 'Haven't seen your mad mate about have you? Chappelli wants him down in the nets.'

'Okay, mate. I'll tell him', Thommo replied.

Thommo, of course, knew exactly where Lennie was—hiding not two metres from where Thommo and Greg chatted. Lennie had seen Chappell come from the foyer and he ducked into hiding and asked Thommo to cover for him.

By Greg's tone, Lennie realised that Chappelli was running out of patience with him. He also wanted to join Thommo and Lillee in the Supertest side. So he decided to get down to Kensington Oval.

Chappelli seemingly virtually ignored Lennie when the big fast bowler turned up at the nets. He noted that Pascoe was just rolling his arm over from a couple of paces, just going through the motions, so he entered the Pascoe net, ensuring that he left his helmet behind. Chappelli wanted to provoke Lennie into some action. He wanted Lennie to try and knock his block off. It might well turn Pascoe's tour around. Lennie took the bait and for the next twenty minutes he bowled flat out at the skipper, many balls humming about his ears. Lennie bowled some fireballs from 18 metres and a spectator at the back of the net yelled out, 'Hey skipper, I tink dis Lennie want to kill you, man'.

Phil Wilkins writing in the Australian said Chappelli gave the 'finest exhibition of net batting' he'd seen. Chappelli had hooked and driven, ducked and weaved, while Lennie got up such a head of steam those watching thought the fast bowler's head might blow off. At the end of that remarkable session, Chappelli said, 'Thanks, Lennie. Best workout I've had for a long time.'

'Thought you'd fucking say that . . .' was Lennie's reply.

That night Ian Chappell picked Pascoe for the Second Supertest. And Pascoe took 2/74 and 3/20. He made crucial inroads by dismissing Roy Fredericks and Gordon Greenidge with the new ball. Thommo took 3/56 off 13 overs and 1/53 off 14 overs in the game and Lillee got match figures of 3/95 off 23 overs.

This was the toughest cricket of my career. Talk about a war on the cricket field. There were no beg-your-pardons, no quarter asked or given. We had a lot to prove.

After the humiliating first Supertest loss. Chappelli had asked for his team to re-group and at least play well enough to gain respect from the West Indians. According to Thommo, 'All the guys responded. Greg [Chappell] batted well and "Super" [Martin Kent] really came of age on this tour.' A riot in Bridgetown foiled Australia's chances of a win. For Thommo, it wasn't the first time a riot had stopped play.

Every time we got into a winning position there was a riot, which effectively had the match abandoned and prevented the West Indies from losing. I saw it all before on Simmo's tour, when we had only one wicket to get to win the Fifth Test at Sabina Park. Now it happened again. Same place, different time.

Australia had two spinners on tour—Victorian left-arm orthodox bowler Ray Bright and NSW leg-spinner Kerry O'Keeffe—who made the touring party on the strength of the side needing two specialist spinners for Trinidad. On training runs Mick Malone had the annoying habit of yelling 'Look out!' when his jogging team-mates left the pavement and started across the road. After a while the blokes reckoned he 'cried wolf' so many times that they would make their own decisions on whether to cross the road or not. But on one occasion, as Malone and O'Keeffe ran the pavement in Trinidad, Mick yelled 'Look out!' and O'Keeffe kept going. The leg-spinner was thrown on to the bonnet of a car and deposited rather heavily on the pavement. Mick insisted O'Keeffe 'run it out', but his leg was broken in three places and he could look forward to a plane trip home, his leg in plaster from hip to toe.

Thommo proved his mettle, taking 5/78 off 20 overs in the Third Supertest at Queen's Park Oval, Trinidad. The wicket is traditionally a haven for spinners, but although it was a slow track and afforded turn, Ray Bright got just 2 wickets for 96 off 44 overs, while Thommo, Lillee and Pascoe got 14 wickets between them and Ian Chappell's leg-spin accounted for 3/35 off 10 overs in the Windies second innings. At last, a win. And significantly Thommo's only bag of 5 wickets coincided with an Australian victory.

The Australians were in buoyant mood when they arrived in George-town, Guyana, for the Fourth Supertest. Thommo took 4/85 and was in fine form, but heavy rain and another bout of crowd trouble spoiled the game. The ground was saturated, but spectators were allowed in. While sun bathed the field and the wicket was relatively dry, the bowlers' approaches were sodden and both captains, Ian Chappell and Clive Lloyd, feared that to play would prove a danger to their fast bowlers.

Umpires Douglas Sang Hue and Ralph Gosein agreed with Chappelli and Lloyd that conditions meant that play was impossible. However, it was also agreed that a 4 p.m. start should be attempted because officials had opened the gates, allowed the people in, and there should be some cricket to avoid a potential riot.

Then came a ground announcement by Vic Insanally, WSC West Indies public relations manager, that play would commence at 3 p.m. That was one hour before the agreed time. Chappelli was so incensed that he fronted Insanally and ended up giving the official a backhander to the stomach, an act which saw him charged for assault and fined US$44.

However, even with the announcement, the crowd had already begun to take things into their own hands. The spectators had been sitting about in the sun all day. There was nothing else to do but drink rum and watch the ground staff sit about in idle fashion while all manner of officials and players wandered about, looking at the wicket and checking their footwear for mud and water. The steel band continued to play, but the scene was set for a riot. The great West Indian fast bowler Wes Hall said to WSC's Bruce McDonald, 'It's gonna blow, man. It's gonna blow!'

And blow it did. The mob surged forward. They overturned tables and chairs, pushed fences over, threw bottles indiscriminately, smashed and grabbed—a mob hell-bent upon destruction.

Martin Kent recalls:

We were shitting ourselves. We expected the police to arrive, restore order and tell us to calm down, things are okay. But no, this armed sergeant dived into our change room for his own safety. He was visibly shaking.[7]

Thommo had already shut, barred and bolted the door.

Chappelli remembers asking the team physiotherapist, Dave 'Doc' McErlane—who had been on many a Test campaign and once punched a Gestapo officer in the face (and lived to tell the tale) when taken POW in France during World War II—'You're the only bloke among us who has been in a war. What do we do if they get in here?' The Doc replied:

Grab all the chairs and tilt them upwards—one leg high, another low: one to the eyes, one to the balls.[8]

Austin Robertson and Wes Hall didn't make it to the safety of their dressing-room, they huddled behind a wall, both shaking in fear.

Lennie Pascoe described the scene in the Australian dressing room:

When the chairs and bottles came raining down, Thommo and I put on our helmets. Each of us grabbed a bat and we had our cricket coffins as shields. The head of security looked at the two biggest blokes—Thommo and me—and within seconds this bloke was standing between us. Who's supposed to protecting who? Other security staff were at the team fridge hoeing into the chicken and washing it down with beer. They weren't about to die on an empty stomach.

Mick Malone gulped down one beer and he went from a meek, mild bloke to Arnold Schwarzenegger, wanting to take on the world. He's ordered the security blokes stuffing themselves at the fridge to 'Get out there and save us'. Greg Chappell checked out the lid of a bench top. Perhaps a place to hide? Max Walker was running about taking photographs like he's some photographer for the *Women's Weekly*. David Hookes threatened to sue Tangles [Walker] if a magazine publishes a photograph of him which makes him look scared and all the while FOT [Lillee] was dashing about clapping a pair of sandals behind our ears, the sound simulates gunfire. Bruce 'Stumpy' Laird couldn't stop giggling and I said to Thommo, 'Mate, what are we going to do?'

'Lennie, I have a plan. It's so obvious. When they break down the door, we start smashing things up. They'll think that we are part of their gang, so we'll be fine.'

'Yeah, Thommo, good plan, good plan . . .'[9]

For Thommo, the riots may have interrupted an unforgettably tough series, but at least he was back with his mates, and playing with the best.

The riot stuffed our chances of winning. So we drew the series against the toughest outfit going. Because we were so far ahead in a couple of games and only drew the games because of the riots, the WSC Australians came away winners. In effect we beat the West Indies on their own shit-heap. We were the better side overall. Great credit to all the blokes. It was easily the toughest cricket I ever played and the best series I was lucky enough to be involved in.

14 'I WAS THE SCAPEGOAT'

> Poor old Graeme Wood . . . I bowled a quick one and Woody didn't
> react at all . . . and the ball crashed into his jaw . . . I've hit a lot of
> blokes and some, like Woody, seemed to lose the ball, they froze,
> like a rabbit in a spotlight.

Thommo and Lennie never got to 'smash things' as per their survival plan as the riot lasted less than two hours. Riot police arrived with rifles and tear gas to disperse the crowd. A team of armed security men in an escort van joined the team buses at a secure exit on the far side of the ground. However, the Australian team bus was being driven by a Pakistani and he careered ahead of the armed escort on its way back to the Pegasus Hotel, without any misadventure, thankfully.

Just days after the end of Australia's World Series tour of the West Indies, a deal was struck between Kerry Packer's PBL Sports Pty Ltd and the Australian Cricket Board. WSC and the ACB had signed an agreement to join hands and that signed document was lodged with the Trade Practice Commissioner on May 30, 1979. Meantime Kim Hughes's Australian squad was in England, about to play in the 1979 World Cup. Hughes was buoyed about the team's prospects, but many members of the squad must have thought that their tenure as an Australian player would be short-lived, for some 25 WSC Australians would return to the Sheffield Shield competition.

Thommo was unimpressed with the way the WSC and ACB officials suddenly changed their attitude:

> *I was livid seeing* [Bob] *Parish with his arm around a WSC official when it was Parish and the Board who put me out of the game for all of the Australian 1978–79 summer. That I was allowed to go to the Caribbean with WSC smacked of a looming deal between the warring parties, not any goodwill towards me on behalf of the Board.*

Hughes's team in England struggled and they flew back to Australia in time to watch the World Cup final between the West Indies and India on television. A few weeks later Hughes's men embarked on a ten-week tour of India. Few people cared about that tour for all the 'action' was happening back home. Some of the players in Hughes's team wouldn't have a hope of playing Test cricket when the stars returned. In fact, a number of his men upon return faced a rude shock. Andrew Hilditch, who was the Test vice-captain to Hughes in India, found himself out of the NSW Sheffield Shield team. Other players such as WA wicket-keeper Kevin Wright was axed in favour of the returning Rod Marsh. Even Graeme Wood, who had signed a lucrative five-year deal with WSC, but because of the settlement between the warring factions never actually played one WSC match, had mixed feelings. Wood had a truckload of money but he had been axed from that first WA State match of 1979–80.

Thommo was selected in the first Test. Ian Chappell had withdrawn from the captaincy race after he had a slight altercation with an umpire in Tasmania and Greg Chappell was reinstated as Test captain, with Hughes as his deputy for the first Test against Clive Lloyd's West Indians in Brisbane. The Australian team was: Rick McCosker, Bruce Laird, Allan Border, Greg Chappell, Kim Hughes, David Hookes, Rod Marsh, Ray Bright, Dennis Lillee, Rodney Hogg and Jeff Thomson.

The old firm—Thommo and Lillee—was back in business. And they took the majority of the West Indian wickets—Lillee 4/104 off 29.1 overs and Thommo 3/90 off 25 overs. Rodney Hogg took the new ball and Thommo was relegated to first change. Hogg failed to take a wicket, conceding 55 runs off 25 overs. Viv Richards hit a glorious 140 and the West Indians reached 441 in their first dig, a good reply to Australia's 268.

Batting again Australia prospered, declaring at 6/448, with Greg Chappell hitting 124 and Kim Hughes scoring an unbeaten 130. There was no time to force a result and the West Indies was 3/40 in its second innings; Thommo (1/3 off 3 overs) and Hogg (2/11 off 5 overs) opened the bowling.

Thommo played the Second Test against England in Perth. He bowled well, but again was denied the new ball. He took 2/70 off 21 overs and 1/30 off 11 overs in an Australian victory over the old enemy by 138 runs. Then Thommo was axed for the rest of the Test summer.

> *There's no doubt in my mind that I was the scapegoat over what happened with me at the Board. Taking the Board to court wouldn't have sat very well with them and they must have been itching to get back at me.*

Of course, it was always the case before WSC that if anyone spoke out of turn or complained, they were axed. Bill Lawry took the brunt of the Board's wrath in the wake of the Australian team refusing to play a Fifth Test in South Africa in 1970. A slight stutter in form and the axe fell. Lawry not only lost the captaincy, he was dropped from the side ... forever. In that Perth Test Thommo's Queensland team-mate Geoff Dymock bowled superbly into the breeze at the WACA Ground, taking 6/34 in the England second innings. Thommo bowled well enough in the Sheffield Shield matches too, winning consistent hauls of wickets for Queensland, but he found himself on the outer.

Yet, despite all the negatives, Thommo was selected in the 1980 Australian tour of England. Greg Chappell's men would play a handful of first-class matches, a couple of one-day slogs and the Centenary Test match. Everyone, of course, was interested in playing in the Test match. The first Test in England was played at The Oval in 1880; however, the wiseacres at Lord's decided that the Centenary game should be played at headquarters. When the Australian team was read out, I was astounded. There I was in the eleven and Thommo was out. We were playing two spinners. Dennis Lillee was in the side, as was Lennie Pascoe, who was pretty miffed:

> I fully expected to be 12th man in this game. I thought Thommo
> missed the first Centenary match at the MCG, so this one would

surely have the great Lillee–Thomson combination back together. So I got the shock of my life when Thommo missed out—he was made 12th man.

He was coming down the stairs from the Australian dressing-room at Lord's and I said to Thommo, 'Mate, I've just heard the news. It's wrong. I don't believe in it—I'm pulling out. I've suddenly pulled a hamstring coming up these stairs.'

Thommo said to me, 'You do that, Lennie, and I've pulled a hamstring as well.'

So when I went out to play, I was playing for Thommo and myself. And I took five wickets.[1]

The 1980 Australian tour of England was conceived to accommodate the Centenary Test which was a drawn game. It was the only Test between Australia and England that English summer.

Thommo played the whole of 1980–81 for Queensland without playing a Test match. The New Zealanders and the Indians toured and Thommo didn't get a look in. During the summer, he accepted an offer to play for Middlesex in English county cricket.

It was a terrific experience. Cheryl and I had a flat near St Paul's Cathedral and there were lots of drinks and parties with some of the blokes from Australia living and playing cricket in London. Many a time blokes such as Greg Ritchie, Carl Rackemann, Wayne Phillips and Sam Parkinson would turn up at our flat and we'd drink, piss and laugh for hours.

Thommo's first game for Middlesex was against Essex at Lord's. Thommo hit 35 in his team's first innings of 153, and then he took 4/66 off 16 overs. Rain ensured a draw.

Middlesex then won the encounter against Yorkshire at Headingly, Leeds. Thommo took 3/39 in the Yorkshire first innings and Dennis Lillee bowled beautifully, taking 5/41 off 11 overs. West Indian Wayne Daniel did the damage in the second, and Middlesex won by 81 runs. Thommo enjoyed the encounter against the 1981 Australians. He dismissed Graham Yallop and Allan Border in taking 2/35 off 15 overs.

In the second innings he clean-bowled John Dyson for 49, to take 1/30 off 11 overs. But he didn't enjoy hitting an Australian opener flush on the jaw.

> *Poor old Graeme Wood. He seemed to freeze. I bowled a quick one and Woody didn't react at all. He just stood there and the ball crashed into his jaw. He fell in a heap. I've hit a lot of blokes and some, like Woody, seemed to lose the ball, they froze, like a rabbit in a spotlight.*

Thommo played his last match for Middlesex in mid-June, 1981. He had broken down and didn't play again that English summer.

> *I pulled up with what I thought to be a groin strain and ended up having a hernia operation. And that was the end of my county summer. I was determined to get myself right for the coming Australian season.*

While Thommo played only a handful of matches that English summer, he made a lasting impression on a team-mate, Mike Selvey, who in 1981 was a fast-medium bowler who often bowled in tandem with Thommo and later became a noted journalist. And in July 12, 2007, Selvey enlightened his readers of *The Guardian*:

> I still cherish the memory of an hour's cricket for Middlesex at Lord's in 1981 towards the end of a day against Somerset when Jeff Thomson, bowling, he told me years later, as fast as he ever bowled on a slow pitch, slugged it out with Viv Richards, batting as only a genius can—hook from his eyebrows, sway as another bouncer almost removed his head, back-foot drive, ferocious riposte from Thommo, punch and breathless counter-punch. It was glorious, cricket from a different planet to which I inhabited, put into even more stark relief by the academic battle at the other end between Peter Roebuck and my own less physically challenging stuff. Roebuck says he was staunchly protecting Viv.[2]

A moderate start to the 1981–82 summer saw Thommo take 3/76 and 1/47 for Queensland against Victoria at the Gabba; 0/53 versus NSW at

Newcastle; and 3/76 against the Pakistanis at the Gabba. Two Pakistanis—Javed Miandad (138) and Zaheer Abbas (84)—batted beautifully.

Jeff Thomson found himself in the Test team for the First Test against Pakistan in Perth. Australia, thanks to a splendid 4-wicket haul from speedster Imran Khan, was bundled out for 180. Then Pakistan fell like a pack of cards for 62: Dennis Lillee took 5/18, Terry Alderman 2/36, and Thommo took 1/4 off 2 overs. Australia ultimately won the match by 286 runs, but Thommo bowled only sparingly, taking 1/36 off 12 overs in the Pakistan second innings.

Because Lillee and Terry Alderman had bowled so brilliantly in England on the 1981 Ashes tour, they took the new ball and Thommo found himself back in the side, but bowling first-change. Australia won the series 2–1, but Pakistan's Imran Khan inspired a dramatic Third Test victory for the visitors.

The West Indians dominated the Tests against Australia, winning the series 2–nil. Thommo, while he didn't do anything startling with the ball for the remainder of that summer, did enjoy bowling with Lennie Pascoe in the second innings of the Test against the Windies in Adelaide.

Dennis Lillee broke down after 4.5 overs in the first innings. Thommo took 4/112 off 29 overs, getting Gordon Greenidge, Desmond Haynes and Clive Lloyd among his victims. Thommo and Pascoe shared all 5 of the West Indian wickets to fall in the second innings (Pascoe 3/84 and Thommo 2/62) as the Windies cruised to a 5-wicket win. At least the Jonah Adelaide didn't show and Thommo got through the Test match week in Adelaide unscathed.

Thommo toured New Zealand in the late summer of 1981–82 and took 4/51 off 21 overs in the Third Test match. He helped Australia forge a comeback victory in the series, after losing the Second Test match at Eden Park, Auckland, by 5 wickets. But the game gave him the chance to watch the batting mastery of Greg Chappell in full flow. It was a performance he'll always remember.

That's the time I realised how great a batsman was Greg Chappell. He toyed with their attack and even came down the track to talk to me, saying how he was going to blast Richard Hadlee here and Lance

Cairns there. We came together at the fall of the seventh wicket [256]
and when I left 79 minutes later, we had put on 84 runs.

But it wasn't the number of runs, it was Greg's intent and his
execution. He said he'd hit one over mid-wicket and he did it. Then
he talked about a cut, then a drive, a hit down the ground. It was an
incredible display of batting.

Chappell scored 176 in 266 minutes with 23 fours and 2 sixes. Thommo,
playing the support role to perfection, hit 25 in 79 minutes. He faced
43 balls and he hit 1 four. It was during the Chappell.innings that Thommo
became convinced that it was Greg and not Viv Richards who should wear
the mantle as his pick for the best batsman of his time.

The Three-Test 1982 series in Pakistan didn't enthuse any of the Australian
fast bowlers, including Thommo, for the pitches were bone-dry and
devoid of any grass cover. They were perfect for the leg-spin sensation
Abdul Qadir, whose spin cut a swathe through the Australian batting at
Karachi, Faislabad and Lahore, with Pakistan winning all three Tests.
Thommo's thunderbolts were dulled in the conditions. Another tilt at
the old 'enemy' loomed with England due to tour Down Under in the
summer of 1982–83.

Another crack at the Poms did enthuse Thommo. His Ashes summer
began in the Second Test at the Gabba. Thommo got 0/43 off 8 overs,
while Geoff Lawson took 6/47 off 18.3 overs. England made only 219, and
Australia replied with 341, Keppler Wessels scoring a gutsy 162.

England fared better a second time, hitting 309, but Lawson, who
completed a great double with 5/87 off 35.5 overs, became Thommo's
partner in speed, while the fast man himself chimed in with 5/73 off
31 overs. Australia won by 7 wickets and they won the next one at Adelaide
by a whopping 8 wickets.

The Boxing Day Test loomed, and Allan Border, who had scored just
81 runs in his past five innings, was under enormous pressure. But if
Border felt the pressure, he didn't show it. Thommo took 3/51 and 2/41
in the game, but it was his skill as a batsman which was so badly needed.
Australian hopes depended entirely upon the out-of-form Border and

the tailender, Thommo. All other performances in the match took on an air of insignificance as Thommo wandered out onto the vast MCG arena. The crowd clapped in quiet and decent appreciation of a man about to fail.

There was hardly a word between them. They knew the enormity of the task. Australia was 9/218, chasing 292 runs for victory. Border was having an horrendous Ashes summer with the bat, and this wicket was none too easy to bat on. The track was displaying its usual Melbourne petulance; disarmingly easy one ball, then a low ball or one that flew a bit higher the next. Uneven bounce is always a concern to any batsman. For Thommo, this innings would become one of the most memorable in Test cricket.

> *I liked to get on with it and give the ball a thump, but I knew that I needed to hang about. Survive. I had to stay with AB [Border]. If I stayed with him, he could win the match for us. We decided to take all the runs, singles included, every time, not just at the end of an over to give AB the strike. The victory target was a long, long way off, so we had to take every run and that meant my being exposed to the danger end a fair bit.*

Allan Border was always splendid when he batted with the tail. He took the runs as they came, just as Doug Walters did, and that seemed to give the tail-enders confidence. They were empowered. Australia required 74 runs when Thommo joined Border. By stumps on the fourth day, the pair had whittled the target down by exactly half—37 runs needed.

In those days the Australian team stayed at the Hilton Hotel, just a couple of Wes Hall approaches from the entrance to the members stand at the MCG. Thommo will long remember that final morning.

> *We walked out from the Hilton that last morning. I suppose we were both a little nervous, yet by the time we got to the dressing-room, the other guys were all chatting and packing their bags. They almost ignored us. There was no official practice, although when AB and I went out for a knock-up on the side of the oval, we were amazed to see that thousands of people had gathered.*

In their wisdom the Melbourne Cricket Club declared free admission for the last day. One wicket to fall and 37 runs needed was the equation. Border recalls that:

> There was something in the air that day. The crowd gathered in their thousands and they were buoyant, as if they expected that something out of the ordinary was about to happen.[3]

By the time Thommo and Border walked on to the field the crowd had reached about 10,000. Within a few minutes it had swollen to 18,000.

> *The ovation we got was amazing, like a football crowd and the grand final. I said to AB, 'If it's good enough for these people to turn up in support of us, let's give 'em their money's worth, let's go down fighting.'*

The MCG crowd got good value for turning up. At nine down and with plenty of runs to get, the game could have been over first ball of the day. But the pair held firm.

England captain Bob Willis was roundly criticised for setting a negative field the previous evening. Willis set the fieldsmen deep for Border, and the nuggetty left-hander collected ones and twos. While he kept the strike as much as possible to 'protect' Thommo, he began to become increasingly confident of Thommo's ability to hang on. But on the final day, the pressure was immense. Border was proud of Thommo's resolve:

> They brought the field in for Thommo. Three slips, gully and a couple of close fieldsmen set for the short ball. It was one of the very few times I had seen Thommo restrain himself with the bat. He was terrific, thoroughly responsible. Thommo had to face the new ball first up and he played out the over easily. The next 90 minutes produced some of the best, tension-filled cricket of my career.

Thomson, the batsman, had the MCG crowd enthralled.

I was concentrating like hell and whenever I played a ball safely the crowd went wild. As the runs gradually came more easily, the crowd sensed, as we did, that Australia had every chance of stealing the match.

The fans clapped Thommo's block shots and whenever he got a run, they brought the house down. When Border scored there was loud applause, but nowhere near the ovation Thommo got when he got a run. Twos and threes were greeted with mass elation and a lot of noise.

As Border and Thommo inched their way towards the victory target, the Englishmen started to chat heatedly among themselves. Each run by Australia tested the England players. Victory was now not quite as close to them. They sensed that the game was slipping away.

The strain was getting to us too. We started to yell at each other, especially when there was a poor shot up the other end or a ridiculous call for a run that was just not on.

Thommo and Border had negotiated 17 overs. Everything the likes of Bob Willis, Ian Botham, Ed Cowans, Derek Pringle and Geoff Miller could throw at them was stoutly resisted. The match had come down to the wire. With Australia needing 4 runs for a win and 3 to tie the game, Willis turned to the 'miracle maker' of Leeds in 1981, Ian Botham. The MCG electronic scoreboard was being used for the first time and the operator was getting into the act, flashing up the numbers of runs required and replaying every incident. Botham came in, that familiar bouncy approach and he dropped short outside Thommo's off stump. It was a gift. Thommo flashed at it and got a touch, the ball flying swiftly to Chris Tavare at second slip. Tavare dropped the ball, but the ball popped over his shoulder and behind him, where the ever-alert Geoff Miller completed the catch to give England a 3-run victory.

Although the Australians were disappointed, they realised they'd witnessed something special. At that moment of loss, Border thought:

We've lost the game after all of that effort.

Poor Thommo, he made 21 runs out of out 70-run partnership. He was magnificent. Knowing him as I do he would be thinking that he let his country down. No way, Thommo was an Australia hero in defeat.[4]

The Fifth Test in Sydney was drawn despite Thommo taking a match haul of 7/80 off 26.5 overs. Although he was in good form, Thommo then found himself on the outer in terms of Test selection:

> *I was made the scapegoat for the World Series stuff, taking the Board to court and all that. I kept heading the Sheffield Shield table in tally of wickets and still they would not pick me. I was pissed off, but I guess because they rejected me I wanted to go on, to show the pricks.*

In his last match for NSW Thommo blitzed Queensland in 1974 and single-handedly he prevented the northerners from winning their first Sheffield Shield. Next summer for Queensland he destroyed the Victorian batting line-up to give WA the Shield. Thommo desperately wanted a Queensland Sheffield Shield. The 1984–85 final was played at the SCG. How good would that have been for Thommo—to wrest the Shield away from NSW and into the hands of his adopted State.

Thanks to a fine century from Trevor Hohns (102), Queensland scored 374. Thommo took 3/83 off 27.3 overs to help dismiss NSW for 318, and give his team a handy 56-run lead. NSW import Imran Khan took 5/34 to restrict Queensland and, batting a second time, they could manage only 163. They didn't have enough runs for Thommo to realise his dream. But he wasn't about to give up. Carl Rackemann bowled his heart out, taking 6/54 off 30 overs, and Thommo took 3/81 off 29 overs. NSW needed only 223 runs to win and they got there . . . by 1 run.

In October 1984, Thommo was offered $200,000 to play for the rebel Australians in South Africa. However, Thommo didn't trust the South African negotiators; he had been bitten before and he was definitely twice shy:

> *I don't trust those arrogant bastards. They're always promising a lot of money. But there's never any guarantee they'll ever pay up. I was never all that keen to go on that tour anyway. I'd rather try and play for Australia the right way.*

In the end Thommo opted out, though he wished the other players well, blokes like Carl Rackemann, 'if they can make a quid out of it'. The Kim Hughes-led Australian rebels did make a sizeable amount, the average player getting $200,000 per season and not having to pay one cent in taxation. It was a loophole that the Australian Prime Minister Bob Hawke quickly fixed.

As for Thommo he got a belated call to play for Australia on the 1985 tour of England. He was only a few wickets off his Test 200. This was the chance to reach that Test wickets tally. Thommo struggled in the Headingly first Test taking 2/166 off 34 overs. He missed the Second, Third and Fourth Tests, and came back for the Fifth Test at The Oval. He took 1/101 off 19 overs; his 1 wicket was Graham Gooch, also his 200th wicket in Test cricket.

Thommo decided to play the 1985–86 Australian Sheffield Shield summer. A Sheffield Shield would be a superb victory for him.

In 51 Tests Thommo had taken 200 wickets. After his indifferent form in England in 1985, Thommo didn't expect to play much Test cricket again. After all, he realised that his selection for England came only after a number of fast bowlers had signed on for the South African rebels and were unavailable to play for the official team.

I 'spose I had just about had enough cricket. Cheryl and I had a young family, I loved Queensland, the weather, and I wasn't greatly taken with all the travelling associated with cricket. But I did want to play one more summer for Queensland. I dearly wanted to be part of bringing the Sheffield Shield home to Brisbane for the first time. Whatever happened 1985–86 was going to be my last season playing first-class cricket.

Queensland made the Sheffield Shield final, again against NSW in Sydney. This was Thommo's third final and it was to be his last first-class match, his 187th.

We'd stuffed the other two finals. All we had to do was to play our natural game and take it up to them. NSW were the favourites. They

won the Sheffield Shield in 1985 by one lousy wicket. I really wanted
that Shield, more than anything in cricket. A Sheffield Shield victory
would have been the perfect way to go out of big cricket. It was a big
game for me.

Queensland batted first and scored 9/436 before declaring. Keppler
Wessels led the way with 166 and Glenn Trimble (son of Sam) hit 112.

Because of the ludicrous situation of the home team final, the side
on top at the end of the minor round plays the game on their own track
and if they only have to play a draw, occupation of the crease becomes
paramount. They bat slowly. The idea is to get the home curator to produce the flattest, slowest pitch imaginable. Perhaps they even got advice
from the England curators who 'doctored' the wickets in 1975.

Thommo took 3/91 off 20 overs. It was tough going. It may have been
a record too with Harry Frei bowling 15 no-balls, as against Thommo's
mere 8. Frei bowled a marathon 37 overs for 2/87 and Dirk Tazlaar took 3/48
off 22 overs. Queensland scored 133 for the loss of 7 wickets and declared,
then NSW held out for a draw. A draw meant NSW had won the Shield.

It was a great disappointment, a draw, which meant we didn't win the
Shield and it was all over for me. I didn't want one of those bloody 'tah tah'
announcements over the loud speaker as I went off or a mob of journalists
meeting my plane back in Brisbane. I had about all I could take.

But the crowd knew. They yelled for Thommo. Instead he reached for
another cold XXXX. Cheryl watched that last day and admits she had a
cry. The cricket thing was all over.

Thommo just wanted to go to bed, but Harry Frei wouldn't be deterred.
He belted on Thommo's door until the fast bowler emerged. One last big
drink with the boys. Thommo got to bed as the sun came up. He fell into
the seat on the plane trip to Brisbane and when he saw Cheryl with their
young son Matthew the tears welled. But after all the heartache of the
Shield final, they were tears of joy.

Thommo was home.

15 THOMMO'S MANY TALENTS

> I've always been a person who says what I think. It gets me into trouble
> sometimes, but you'll never die wondering with me.

Jeffrey Robert Thomson was speed crazy in more ways than one. I cannot
think of another bowler to approach the sort of speed Thommo attained
in those two halcyon seasons between 1974–76. To me he was the fastest
bowler to draw breath. But speed came to Thommo in a number of forms.
He seemed fascinated with it.

In England in 1975 I sat in the back of one of the team's four V12
Jaguars, with Thommo hurtling along the M1 expressway. At the speed
we were doing, Thommo could have been at Le Mons. Visibility was poor
due to constant heavy rain and the road was, in parts, awash; however,
that only inspired our driver to test the manoeuvrability of the machine.
As we sped and aquaplaned along the expressway, the urgency of sirens
and the sight of flashing blue lights had Thommo finally easing to a halt
on a shoulder of the road. His fast bowling mate, Dennis Lillee, was in the
front seat and it was FOT who kept urging Thommo to step up the pace.

The policeman was at first a model of officiousness, and he had his
notebook and pen at the ready. Then he recognised the famous pair in

the front seat and smiled. After a mild lecture on the hazards of driving fast on the M1, the police officer skipped back to his car and emerged with a colleague. It turned out that both police officers loved cricket and here were their bowling heroes sitting together in a Jaguar V12. There wasn't even the hint of a fine, despite Thommo having been clocked at 146 mph (235 kph). 'And the speed you were going, Mr Thomson, happens to be 76 mph OVER the speed limit', one of the policemen said.

Later Thommo said that if he stuck to the 70 mph speed limit, he would crash, 'because I'd go to sleep with boredom driving at that pace'.

Many of the players who experienced being a passenger in a car driven by Thommo turned up with similar tales and on every occasion Thommo got off with a few autographs and a promise to drive safely in future.

After helping to blitz the West Indians at the Gabba in November 1975, Thommo invited a few players to try out their waterskiing skills at the Surfer's Paradise Water Ski Gardens. Dennis Lillee, Gary Gilmour, Rod Marsh, Alan Turner and Ian Chappell took up Thommo's invitation and all might now agree that they consider themselves lucky to have survived the ordeal. Thommo drove the souped-up speed boat and he took off flat to the boards every time. Bacchus nearly crashed into a water wall, and Chappelli and FOT nearly drowned.

Agility and speed was required, too, in jumping off a vehicle hurtling through the bush after razorback boar, as Thommo often did.

Speed was the key. You'd dive and grab the pig's back legs, then knees in his back and a knife thrust behind the shoulder blade. Done swiftly the boar died instantly.

Greg Chappell, Thommo's Queensland and Australian captain, knew his fast bowler well. He played with and against Thommo and he was his best man when Thommo married the love of his life, Cheryl Wilson. Greg says:

Thommo was the fastest athlete over the first 30 metres I have seen. He was explosive. Thommo could run and jump and he had the strongest throwing arm I've seen, including all the world-class baseballers.

Once in Sydney Thommo threw a ball in from the boundary and Bacchus took it above his head. It was still on the up. Then he fetched a ball and was about to throw from about 60 yards [55 metres] and Bacchus yelled, 'No, no, Thommo—don't!'

Forget Daly Thompson, Thommo could have been an Olympic gold-medal winning decathlete.[1]

Greg Chappell was once at a function with West Indian fast bowler Michael Holding. Holding was the man they called 'Whispering Death'. He cruised in from a long way, seemingly pushed off the boundary fence and his lightning-fast deliveries were either at your throat or at your toe. There were a number of luminaries in the room, and Holding said to Chappell:

'Greg, you look around the room. The other quick bowlers in the West Indies, Andy [Roberts], Joel [Garner], Colin [Croft] and Curtly [Ambrose]—I was a fair bit quicker than all of them, but Thommo was at least a yard quicker than me.'[2]

Former NSW opener Warren Saunders, a champion exponent of the hook shot, was once late on a Thomson bouncer. After recovering in hospital, Saunders rang State selector Neil Harvey and said, 'Ninna, you've got to pick this bloke, he's the fastest bowler I've ever faced.'[3]

Younger brother of Richie, John Benaud, recently wrote a delightful piece on Thommo, which I have reproduced (in part) here:

My favourite Thommo moment was in the Barbados Test of 1977–78 when I saw him tear into Gordon Greenidge, Des Haynes, Viv Richards, Alvin Kallicharran and Clive Lloyd.

If those elite batsmen were not intimidated by his pace and aggression, then body language is a flawed yardstick, Thommo took 6/77 off 13 overs in one innings. Think of that—a wicket every two overs. We like our favourites alone on a pedestal. Wishful thinking abounds in Australia that Shaun Tait is 'another Thommo', but Tait lacks that sliding foot-cross which enabled Thommo to maintain height at delivery and generate his extreme pace and lethal bounce.

The good news for Thommo fans and batsmen . . . I've never seen a
bowling machine with a larrikin streak.[4]

Thommo's brother Raymond loves telling the story about Jeff's amazing throwing the day the kids in the Bankstown area turned up to one of
Wes Hall's coaching classes. The great West Indian fast bowler was teaching
the youngsters about how to return a ball and he told them to throw the
ball as hard as they could hurl it. Wes shook his head and broke into a big
grin when Thommo, then aged 14, threw the ball further than him.

Thommo's Queensland wicket-keeper John MacLean said Thommo
was always quicker than Dennis Lillee at his fastest:

If the guys today are bowling 100 mph [161 kph], Thommo was
definitely a lot quicker than that. And when selector Peter Burge
wanted to leave Thommo out of the State side because he was
erratic in the trial match, GC [Greg Chappell] insisted he play.
I think that was a bit of self-preservation for Greg. He didn't want
Thommo rushing back to Sydney.

One day Thommo said to Phil Carlson at mid-off, 'How are they
coming out?'

Phil replied, 'Bloody quick, Thommo. Bloody quick.'[5]

Ian Chappell recognised that Thommo was the veritable 'unhookable
one' in a match at Adelaide Oval in 1972–73:

I went to hook him in that NSW–SA Sheffield Shield match and
the ball got on to me too quickly and I was struck on the gloves.
I discovered that day that this bloke was one fast bowler that
couldn't be hooked.[6]

Being hooked was something Thommo didn't relish and he reckoned if he
could generate enough pace and bounce, he would become a pretty tough
proposition for even the great hookers in the game.

I made a sort of promise to myself that I wouldn't ever get hooked.
I guess I mean hooked with authority, not a top-edge hook that goes

over the fence more from the pace of the ball I am bowling, not a good shot. Those shots, top-edged attempted hooks that go for four or six, are really moral victories for the bowler. The only time a bloke hooked me with authority was Viv [Richards] that time I got stuck into them in Barbados in 1977–78. I reckon he was in position waiting to hook it. And boy did he smash the ball.

Years after they had both hung up their boots, Ian Chappell and Jeff Thomson had a chance meeting at Singapore's Changi Airport. They met at the lift and spent time in the airport lounge. Chappelli recalls he asked:

'Thommo, what do you reckon made you quick and able to get bounce from a fairly full length?'
   'Ah, mate, I braced my front leg and I came over that braced front leg, over like a catapult.'[7]

Thommo believes that his load-up and braced front leg was the catalyst for his great speed and bounce.

I reckon it was all in the load-up. I'd just lope in and go whang, but after the shoulder injury, when I stuffed around with a longer run, I lost rhythm and the load-up was never as good. Then in Barbados that time I went back to my old way and bowled as fast as ever I bowled. I was able to get steep bounce from a good length because of my load-up and getting very tall through the crease, bowling over my braced front leg.

As Warren Saunders once said to Ian Chappell, 'I know he just runs in and goes whang, But he goes whang pretty bloody fast.'[8]
   England's fast bowler Frank Tyson had speed approaching Thommo's pace. They called him 'Typhoon' and Tyson blitzed Australia in Sydney and Melbourne in the 1954–55 Ashes series. I saw the match at Sydney, where Tyson bowled like the wind and Australia's Neil Harvey hooked and cut like no left-hander I've seen, scoring 92 not out in a losing match. I was aged nine and before Thommo happened along in the summer of

1972–73, I couldn't believe that anyone could have bowled faster than Frank Tyson. The balding England fast bowler has been a long-time writer on the game and at the end of the brilliant Thommo Ashes summer of 1974–75, Tyson made these observations:

Thomson owes little of his super speed to his run-up. He lopes rather than runs some fifteen yards before moving into his own peculiar version of the delivery stride. His final pace is in the Bill Bowes, Neil Hawke mould, with the right foot moving behind the left in a reverse chassis step. The leading left arm shoots convulsively skywards and his powerful shoulders adopt a perfectly closed position, pointing in a straight line from fine leg to mid-off. His front leg stiffens and extends with all the energy of a goose-stepping Pomeranian Grenadier, whilst his bowling arm sweeps in a violent semi-circle from its concealed position behind his back. Speed is expressed by the strength of Thomson's shoulder movement. The bowling arm moves so quickly at the beginning of its swing that even the slow-motion camera can capture no more than a white blur. Thomson bowls like the former javelin thrower that he is, moving briefly to the point and delivering with all the strength at his disposal. A dual strange facet about Thomson's surprising bowling was the way in which he seemed to bowl faster into the breeze than Lillee did with it, and the manner in which he appeared to bowl better and faster with the old ball than he did with the new. He bowls with brimstone in his heart but lives with an olive branch in his hand. One gains the impression that he is the Happy Warrior, the fast bowler that is content doing his appointed task.[9]

Some time back the Australian bowling coach Troy Cooley spoke about identifying fast bowling talent and how the Australian Centre of Excellence would target tall youngsters of a minimum 6 foot 2 inches. If that means shorter fast bowlers would not get a look in, it was best that the likes of Ray Lindwall (5 foot 11 inches) and Jeffrey Thomson (6 foot 1 inch) weren't playing in this era. The great West Indian Malcolm Marshall was also less than 6 feet tall, but he was well up there, among the great ones.

Thommo stayed tall through the crease. Greg Chappell reckons he gained height:

> Thommo seemed to manufacture height. When he let the ball go, he seemed 6'9".[10]

Whereas Thommo seemed to gain height through his action at delivery, Brett Lee loses a lot of height, so too Shaun Tait. In Lee's case his action is very open because of the direction of his front foot. Thommo says:

> *Put your front foot straight down the track at delivery and you will collapse. That is why Lee collapses; his front foot points straight down the track. I reckon Australia needs to really encourage Shaun Tait. He keeps things simple, just runs in and lets 'em have it. I like his style; he's the most exciting fast man about.*

One wonders how much better Lee could be if he released the ball at his full height. According to Thommo:

> *Lee has improved a lot and will probably go past Dennis Lillee's wickets [355] and top 400. I don't think he'll ever be as good as Lillee or [Glenn] McGrath, but he will have some very good numbers before his career finishes.*

The Thommo catapult action was not unlike the Queensland Aboriginal fast bowler of the 1930s, Eddie Gilbert. There is a bronze statue of Gilbert in Brisbane. The sculptor shaped the statue from old photographs of Eddie's action and has captured the bowler driving over a braced front leg, just as Thommo did years later. As with Thommo, Gilbert loped into the wicket from just a few paces and he let them go at breakneck speed. Gilbert was the man Don Bradman labelled 'the fastest bowler I ever faced'. However, Bradman also had doubts about Gilbert's action:

> From the pavilion his bowling looked fair, but in the middle his action was suspect. He jerked the ball and only delivered it from a

very short approach. It's very hard that way to generate such speed with a legitimate delivery.[11]

Slow motion film of Eddie Gilbert bowling was inconclusive as to whether he chucked the ball or not. However, he had a short approach it is true, but so too did Thommo and he sent the ball down faster than anyone—and had a correct action.

In Gilbert's case a cloud over his career due to what the authorities called a 'suspect action' suited many at the time, including the Commonweath Government. In the 1930s Aboriginals did not have a vote (the right to vote came in the 1967 referendum) and the Government pursued what was called the White Australia Policy; an insidious racist policy designed to keep the European and Indigenous races of the nation apart. In effect it was Australia's brand of Apartheid.

Any Sydney grade batsmen who had to face the terror of a Saturday afternoon at Bankstown against a rampaging Thommo and Lennie Pascoe might relate to a short story by David Forrest, entitled 'The Barambah Mob', a humorous trip down memory lane, depicting ficticious characters expanding the Gilbert legend in the very area that Gilbert lived, worked and bowled. The last paragraph sums up Gilbert's deadly pace, but could well have been written bout Thommo:

> There was a time when Gilbert, in one of his most fiery spells, sent down a ball which rocketed past the batsman and the wicket-keeper, beat the long-stop who tried to gather it, crashed through a paling fence 50 yards from the wicket—and killed a dog![12]

For five years in the early 1990s Thommo coached the Queensland Sheffield Shield team, bringing on young players such as Matthew Hayden, Jimmy Maher, Andy Bichel, Dirk Tazlaar, Michael Kasprowitz and Ian Healy.

I did it for a reason. The players were doing a lot of stupid shit. I won't mention names. I believed we had the home-grown talent in Queensland. We didn't need to buy in players from interstate or overseas. But you'd be surprised what I had to do to convince the selectors about a number of these blokes who went on to play some great cricket for their State and for Australia. The selectors told me these kids couldn't play and I told them, 'No, you guys are the ones who couldn't play'. I bloody well know a good player when I see one and I know the likes of Hayden, Kasprowitz, Bichel and Maher can play. I sat in one selection meeting and while I didn't have a vote, I influenced team selections.

Thommo says coaching throughout the world was becoming too stereotyped. Natural flair is being stifled.

I think too many people run around and they think they're coaches—you'd have seen this Rowdy—and these blokes don't know shit from clay. They theorise. Theory is not a tried-and-true method to get the best out of your players. What they are saying about actions is all theory. When they start fooling about with someone's action, that's when it is bad. Nobody knows the right action. There are too many bowlers about today with the same action. We are producing a bunch of clones. What does that do? Shane Watson is a perfect example. Selectors and captains are trying to make this bloke Watson into an all-rounder. Let's face it, while the kid can bat, he bowls gun-barrel straight. He's a robot and he doesn't move the ball at all. Watson's not a bad bat, but he is no all-rounder because he can't fucking bowl.

I reckon the coaching staff in Australia have a lot to answer for, as there's a lot of young fast bowlers coming through and they all have the same-looking action. Queensland Cricket tried to change my son, Matthew's action. Thankfully he's now bowling with his old style. It really annoys me when the coaches try and change a bloke's action. There is no one perfect action. We don't want to see a bunch of 'cloned' bowlers walking about.

If everyone has the same action there is a sameness about the attack. Sri Lanka's Malinga and Shaun Tait are similar in that they each have very different actions, but they try and bowl as fast as they can and attack at every opportunity. Thankfully they continue to do it their way. Batsmen don't like it when they face a Malinga or a Tait. They'd be saying, 'Hey, hang on, you can't bowl like that—I'm not used to that bowling'. Everyone is different and that's the beauty of allowing bowlers to operate with their own particular action.

Thommo isn't impressed with the modern term 'reverse swing' or the people who pretend to have 'invented' it.

It's all bullshit. The ball has always gone 'Irish'. When FOT [Dennis Lillee] and I were bowling, there were plenty of times when the out-swinger kept going the other way and vice-versa with the in-swinger. We'd just change the shiny side by turning it around. And the ball would swing the opposite way to what it was supposed to swing, or it would 'reverse'. The same bloody thing happens today. You'd think they had invented the fucking wheel.

Thommo enjoyed his years as coach of the Queensland Bulls, but he wasn't a regimented type of coach. He was a mate and a mentor to his men. They loved his style and enjoyed the way he allowed them to play with flair.

I didn't drive 'em mad with batting, bowling and fielding. It was more about what you had to do—the mental side, between the ears—and I wanted the young blokes to feel a part of the set-up straightaway. I got the young blokes in and we enjoyed our cricket. The youngsters developed quickly.

Physiotherapist Lindsay Trigar was with the Queensland Bulls for twelve years—two years with John Bell and Ritchie Robinson; five years with Thommo and five years with John Buchanan. He rates Thommo as far and away the most impressive coach and communicator in that quartet:

Thommo coached in the era of Dirk Tazlaar, Craig McDermott, who you know considered himself a bit of a superstar, Allan Border, who was a really hard worker, and Thommo was the benchmark. He could bowl at the nets longer than any of the fast men. Athletically and aerobically he was easily the best. These were the days when we started to assess players more—stretching, flexibility, strength and endurance. Thommo won hands down.

Thommo not only bowled better and longer than anyone else in the nets, he had the ability to do it after a big night and none of the others could do that.[13]

In 1991, Queensland was short of fast bowlers and the side was stretched for quick men. There were rumours circulating that Thommo was about the make a comeback to the big stage. Trigar recalls:

So Thommo started getting himself fit, extra running and flexibility. I remember one day in Perth, our English import Graeme Hick [Worcester and England batsman] batted against Thommo in a net which had the side nets taken right back so the training was like a middle wicket practice. Thommo had worked himself up over the past couple of weeks and this day he just cut loose.

He bowled to Hick for 20 to 25 minutes and Hick said 'That was the fastest bowling I've ever faced'.[14]

Thommo was then 41 years old. Trigar adds:

He couldn't understand why the players could not go out, have a big drink and turn up and be as good as ever next day. He was an elite athlete and he knew he could do those sorts of things.[15]

In that year, 1991, tragedy struck the Thomson family. In the middle of a Sheffield Shield match in Melbourne, Thommo was called back to Brisbane. Trigar can never forget what happened next:

I was rooming with Thommo and he came to me and handed me a hand-written note. 'I have to get back to Brisbane now', he said. 'My daughter, Victoria, is going to die. I want you to read this letter out to the players before play tomorrow.'

I read the letter and began to cry. At breakfast on the morning of the game, I handed the letter to Trevor 'Cracker' Hohns. I told him I couldn't read this to the players and he said the same. Cracker also shed some tears. So we handed the letter about to the players one by one. It was the saddest of dressing-rooms.

We had to beat Victoria in Melbourne to make the Sheffield Shield final. Thommo wrote 'Don't let me down as I've put so much into this year. It would give me so much satisfaction to win here and play the final . . .' We only had 190 runs to win, but our batsmen struggled and we didn't make it.[16]

Victoria Thomson was only a couple of weeks old when she passed away. It was a highly emotional, tragic time for Cheryl and Jeffrey.

You always say, 'Why me?' but it's not a matter of 'Why me?' it's a matter of getting through it. You know there's a lot of people who have a lot worse things. But it's always hard and it was a terrible time for all of us. It really hit Cheryl hard.

As for Queensland's players, those who had come to love and respect Thommo, the tragedy in the Thomson family exposed a very human side of their coach.

I guess they learnt a bit of what lay beneath that tough exterior.

In fact, Thommo is very devoted to Cheryl and his boys, Matthew, Ben and Alex. Matthew is 24, Ben 21, and Alex 14. A quality control officer, Matthew plays A-grade cricket for Toombul. Ben is a personal trainer and Alex still goes to school. Both Matthew and Ben bowl with the same style of action as their dad, the one Thommo 'inherited' from his father, Don Thomson.

Jeffrey and Cheryl Thomson have a huge backyard in their Brisbane backyard. There is room for Jeff's gardening pursuits, a cricket pitch and a golfer's delight, an area to pitch and putt. Walk the area on any given day and you'll find the ground littered with discus, shot-put, baseballs, cricket balls, golf balls, even the odd javelin.

'Jeffrey's been marvellous with the boys', Cheryl says. 'He's a dad for them and a mate to them. Whenever he can he watches them play their sport and is always supportive. At times he takes them fishing or catching wild pigs in the Outback. There is always something. When Matthew and I were in England with Jeffrey in 1985. Before the tour Jeffrey spoke about retirement from cricket, he thought his touring days were over, so being selected for this one meant so much to him', Cheryl says.

There was a farewell flavour to the 1985 tour because Thommo's parents and Cheryl's mother also travelled to England stayed with Cheryl and Matthew at the London flat Thommo had arranged for them.

Leaving the game at the end of the 1985–86 season wasn't a tough decision at all for Thommo.

I'd played all the test cricket I was going to play. Not winning the Shield was a disappointment, but I had had a pretty good run. I missed Cheryl and Matthew and I was looking forward to more time with my family and enjoying Queensland's weather. I also want to establish my own business. I've always been keen on gardening and a landscape buisness had plenty of appeal.

Lindsay Trigar said Thommo was loved and respected by all he played with and those he coached with the Bulls:

He is still a legend in Brisbane. Craig McDermott took 291 Test wickets, but hardly anyone who comes into my practice has heard of him. But when Thommo is there, even the young kids are in awe of him.'[17]

Apart from his 12 years with the Bulls, Trigar has worked with Australian cricket team coach Bobby Simpson, Reds rugby coach John Connelly and Alan McConnell at the AIS. He has also spent a number of years with the Brisbane Broncos and had the chance to look at Wayne Bennett's coaching style. He says:

Wayne was very good coach, but Thommo is right up there with him and any other coach I've had the good fortune to work alongside. Thommo started off very green as a coach, but he developed coaching and communication skills that I thought were as good as the Bennetts of this world.[18]

After five years Thommo was replaced by John Buchanan and Queensland won the Shield in 1996, but according to Trigar, it was, in many respects, Thommo's team, the one he developed, that won the Shield:

> Buchanan was green as a coach first up. He can't claim too much for that victory. I can remember when Buchanan began. He left a note for each player, a print-out of feedback on their performance from the coach. I recall Allan Border screwing it up and throwing it away.[19]

Thommo was always a great team man. He led the sing-alongs in the team bus where he blew team-mates away by knowing every word to such old-time favourites as *Knees Up Mother Brown*, *If You Wore a Tulip* and *I Belong to Glasgow*. He also proved to his Queensland team-mates that success had not changed him. Wicket-keeper John MacLean says:

> Success never changed him. When he was running hot in the Test team he was always there for the next State game, ready to put in. It was always good when the boys were playing a Test and then having them back for the next State match.[20]

Thommo's larrikin nature undoubtedly appealed to his team-mates. MacLean recalls an incident in England in 1980.

> Thommo would always make a point of meeting the plane when you came in and having a few beers when we got back together again. I never saw him shirk his responsibility on the field. If you wanted another over out of him, he gave you one. I never saw him throw the ball back. And he put in with the bat too.
>
> At Lord's I was lucky enough to sit on Bob Cowper's table at the Centenary Test dinner. They had photographs of all the living Test players and Trevor Bailey [the former England Test all-rounder] was first up on stage as the players were presented in alphabetical order to the audience. Anyway, Bailey tripped up on the stage. Next morning at Lord's, Thommo in his inimitable fashion said, 'Who's that cunt Bailey?' He said all he does is sit in the commentary box and drink gin all day. Typical Thommo![21]

These days, Thommo's ability to speak his mind is put to good use as a public speaker, a gig he really enjoys.

I started doing a bit of public speaking when I began working for Radio 4IP. It was then against my wishes, but it was part of my contract and I had to make appearances at corporate shows, speak at other places and do a bit of coaching.

Nowadays I enjoy speaking more than anything else I've done in the workplace. Otherwise I wouldn't do it.

Cheryl says she hasn't really heard Thommo speak:

Jeffrey tells me he's good, funny, but I really don't know. I do know that he isn't embarrassed about getting up and telling a story.[22]

Thommo must like the speaking caper for in one calander year he manages to do more han 250 shows. Most were with Mouse Productions, and Thommo is a much sought-after speaker with a number of promoters.

I enjoy having to perform and I tailor each talk to the audience. That's important. There are some things you can say to one audience, and not to another. You need to 'work' the crowd, knowing what you can and what you can't get away with speaking about. It is interesting. You simply have to perform and in that regard it's a bit like cricket; perform well and you stick around. Every day is different. That's what I like about it. Unlike doing commentary, when you speak to an audience you can pretty much speak your mind. And I like to speak my mind.

Thommo, however, doesn't have the same passion for cricket commentary.

I don't enjoy TV commentary because you can't speak your mind. I'm not a good cricket watcher. I just hate sitting there and watching someone else play. I want to be playing. Playing in an era like I did, we loved it. We had so much fun. As a commentator you can't speak your own mind. It's all about trying to sell a program. I've always been a person who says what I think. It gets me into trouble sometimes, but you'll never die wondering with me.

I've been to some interesting places through working on television. And the company puts us up at top-quality hotels, not like touring with the Australian cricket team under the ACB. They sure weren't too good when I played.

There is a big contrast in the manner in which the current players and those of Thommo's era (and before) go about their work.

I think cricket is pretty boring these days. I know Australia gets out there and whacks 'em around and the reason they whack them around is because the opposition is pretty fucking shit. You know the bowling is poor.

Trouble is cricketers are getting so much money these days complacency sets in. They are going to get a truckload of money whether they perform or not.

India is a classic example of a country where its cricketers are pampered and yet they are underachievers.

In India the Test players strut around like Hollywood superstars, but outside of India they are shit.

The England players are also pampered. A few years back the ECB Cricket Academy spent two successive summers in Adelaide, while their huge facility at Loughborough, England, was being built. Each of the selected Academy players was given £15,000, plus a laptop computer. At Christmas all the people connected with the Academy were flown back to England for a two-week holiday.

Meantime the youngsters at the Australian Cricket Academy, the institution that helped develop the likes of Shane Warne, Ricky Ponting, Justin Langer, Jason Gillespie and Glenn McGrath, were paid nothing by the Australian Cricket Board. Menial jobs were found for them, and they collected something in the order of $10 an hour.

As a result though, Australia produced lean, mean and committed cricketers, hungry for success.

* * *

Thommo believes that the best team of the 1970s would give the best Australian team of the modern era a real test.

The Australian team is a good side. But they can only perform against the mob they are up against and the opposition is fairly ordinary. And that makes it tough to access just how good the Australian team is right now. Ricky Ponting's team do not play against anyone who's any good and when they have they've been found wanting. When they play the odd good fast bowler such as Shane Bond [New Zealand] *and Shoab Akthar* [Pakistan], *when he pulls his finger out, our batsmen have struggled.*

If we matched these two sides . . .

1970s AUSTRALIA	NEW AUSTRALIA
Ian Redpath	Mark Taylor (capt)
Rick McCosker	Matthew Hayden
Ian Chappell (capt)	Ricky Ponting
Greg Chappell	Michael Clarke
Ross Edwards	Andrew Symonds
Doug Walters	Steve Waugh
Rod Marsh	Adam Gilchrist
Max Walker	Shane Warne
Dennis Lillee	Brett Lee
Jeff Thomson	Glenn McGrath
Ashley Mallett	Shaun Tait

Thommo says:

There's no doubt we'd give Mark Taylor's team a good contest. Overall the general fielding would be better with Taylor's men. We had a few blokes like Tangles [Max Walker] *and FOT* [Dennis Lillee] *who weren't great in the outfield. But we could bat and bowl and we could catch.*

With fellas like Shane Warne and Glenn McGrath, who together have taken more than 1000 Test wickets, you'd expect them to be a good unit.

Ricky Ponting is a shaky starter, but he's done all that is required of him. He just keeps churning out the runs. He is a terrific puller of the ball and a magnificent fieldsman. I always had time for Damien Martyn. He should have been picked for all the tours of the Sub-Continent because he played swing and cut and spin so well. Marto always played late and gave himself time to adjust to the movement. Matthew Hayden is a bit of a flat-track bully, but he's got the runs on the board and he keeps getting runs like they are going out of fashion. Justin Langer might have struggled in our time. I think he would have been hit in the head so many times he would have been wandering about punch-drunk.

Mind you, batsmen such as Matthew Hayden wouldn't be wandering down the wicket to blast the likes of Dennis Lillee and Jeff Thomson down the ground.

We've seen how the Australian team struggles against a good attack. And we had a very good and balanced attack which could take on anyone. No-one messed with our actions. They were all different. We were led by a great captain, Ian Chappell, who never told you where to bowl. He just expected you to give 100 per cent and do your job. The Poms of 2005 made our blokes struggle. I think our side of 1975 would do the same and give it to 'em.

Thommo believes Greg Chappell to be the best batsman of his era.

I was batting with Greg in a Test match in New Zealand. Richard Hadleee was bowling and Greg came down the wicket. He had gleam in his eye and he wore a wide grin. 'Hey, Thommo, watch this—I'm going to get stuck into the bowling, now. Get a load of Richard Hadlee when I start to smash him. I'm gonna hit the ball high to leg. See those blokes', he pointed at the man at deep backward square and the man deep in front, 'they'll probably run into each other'.

I laughed. Thought it was GC just being a smart-arse. But he was right. He belted the shit out of them.

I watched in amazement at Bradman's batting that day on Doc Beard's backyard pitch, but having played with and against Greg

Chappell over many years and see him master good bowling under different conditions, I can't believe that Bradman was twice as good as Greg Chappell.

Thommo regards himself indeed fortunate to have played with and against some of the best cricketers of any era.

Viv Richards was another fabulous player. You always thought you had a chance with Viv and that's why I rated Greg just above him, but Viv was devastating on his day. In fact, if Viv had a day on, you might as well have gone home.

I only saw a bit of [West Indian] Rohan Kanhai and Colin Cowdrey [England], but you could tell from their footwork and poise that they were brilliant players at their peak.

The Groover [Clive Lloyd] was a good player. He hit hard and took you on. Javed Miandad was a player I admired. He was a bit like Freddie [Doug Walters], unorthodox but effective. Sunil Gavasker was a compact little opener with a good array of shots and plenty of courage, which he showed when he got four centuries against the West Indies in the Caribbean. Roy Fredericks [West Indies] was one of the better openers. He used the depth of the crease and was very much a back-foot player.

I don't rate many, if any, of the Poms, although I thought [David] Gower was a pretty good player. And Boycott avoided Dennis [Lillee] and I like the plague.

Ian Redpath was a terrific player of fast bowling. He wouldn't hook and he frustrated quick bowlers by playing as few shots as possible and swaying out the way of the short-pitched stuff. WA's Bruce Laird was a tough little player who never flinched against the fastest bowlers. He gained quite a reputation for his courage under fire against the WSC West Indies in 1979.

In our team of the 70s there were Ian and Greg Chappell, both were good, although I reckon Greg was better than Ian and Doug Walters, among the batsmen. Ian was good and gritty and Doug was, at times, sensational.

Among the moderns, Thommo has West Indian left-hander Brian Lara at the top of the tree.

> *Lara was the best Test batsman I have seen over the past fifteen years. I saw him cut Warne and McGrath to pieces in the Caribbean. They didn't know how to bowl to him. Lara played in a shit side, a star among a bunch of mug batsmen. He was a fantastic player. He had all the shots and plenty of time against the fast bowlers: always a sign of class.*

Surprisingly, he doesn't rate the Indian Sachin Tendulkhar.

> *Sachin Tendulkhar is supposed to get something like US$10 million a year. Mate, I wouldn't give you two-bob for him. I've never rated him as a great player. Tendulkhar is a good player and he thrives on the low, slow, flat shit-heaps in the Sub-Continent. If he had to play against genuinely quick bowlers on fast wickets, he wouldn't get a fucking run.*

I suggest that there would be a minimum of 800 million people in India who would totally disagree with Thommo's assessment of the diminutive Indian cricketer they call 'The Little Master'. But Thommo won't budge.

Thommo is outspoken and sometimes he shoots from hip, but he doesn't hold back—on or off the field—and that's why he'll always be remembered as one of the most-feared bowlers in cricket history. It was the sheer speed and hostility of Thommo that put the wind up his opponents. He never held back, not in Tests, Sheffield Shield matches or club games. Doug Walters loves to have the last say on any matter and here Doug talks about facing Thommo for the first time:

> I first played against Thommo in grade cricket. I was with Cumberland and we played Bankstown at Merryland Oval. I scored 56, but I always wondered whether it was worth it. Thommo and his mate Lennie Pascoe were bowling flat out and I was hit at least 50 times.

I saw Thommo bowl at amazing speed against England and the West Indies in the mid-1970s Hock youe was the fastest bowler of them all, but as fast as Thommo bowled against those Test teams, he reserved his fastest spells for Queensland against NSW. He felt aggrieved by his treatment by the NSW selectors and boy did he take it out on us. In terms of sheer speed I never faced anyone who came anywhere near Thommo's pace.[23]

16 'SOMEONE IS LOOKING AFTER ME...'

> ...among a string of disasters or near disasters in my life... There
> was the armed hold-up at the Commonwealth Bank; three emergency
> landings in planes; five riots in the West Indies; and an IRA bomb blast in
> London in 1977. After the Potters Bar train crash, I... wondered
> why I had been spared.

By 8 a.m. on Wednesday, May 9, 2002, the relentless sun was beating
down on the ancient city. The wailing call for prayers had been
answered by the faithful and a surreal quiet descended upon the hotel,
a seeming oasis and yet close to the centre of downtown Karachi,
which was teeming with people and cars and bicycles. Thommo had
finished breakfast and was heading for the lobby. Another day behind
a microphone, commentating for television on the Pakistan–New
Zealand Test match.

*Just as I was about to walk from the lift to the lobby, I thought, 'Ah,
shit, I've no tie. Must have left it in my room.'*

Thommo pushed the closed button on the lift and headed for the fifth floor. Seconds later there was a loud explosion, followed by an extraordinary shockwave which made the building shake uncontrollably. A massive explosion had ripped through a bus parked opposite the hotel, killing eleven French workers and three Pakistanis. A further 23 others, including twelve French nationals, were seriously injured in the blast.

Shit, think of it. I forgot my tie and that definitely saved my life. I would have been right in the thick of it. Windows were shattered and a number of the New Zealand team were worried that some of their mates might have been caught in the blast. The Test was called off and the New Zealanders went home.

US President George W. Bush labelled the suicide bombing as 'terrorist murders'. Meantime the New Zealand team decided to get out of the city straightaway. Some of the players had been breakfasting by the hotel pool, others in their rooms and none, thankfully, were caught in the blast. However, the squad was visibly shaken and captain Stephen Fleming was almost beside himself with grief until every member of his tour party were accounted for and found to be okay. In the past New Zealand teams have seen first-hand great tragedies which have left a lasting impression on their lives. During their tour of Sri Lanka in 1987 the Tests were called off after a massive truck bomb exploded killing hundreds of people. And in 1992 a number of players opted to go home after a bomb blast, but the tour continued with replacement players. The New Zealanders were unanimous: get out of Karachi.

Thommo didn't hestitate, flying out of Karachi that night for London. Dear old London. Safe as a church. Or maybe not . . .

Thommo had been at a London nightspot during the ill-fated tour of England in 1977 when it was definitely not safe.

Bacchus [Rod Marsh] *was there, so too Bookshelf* [Ritchie Robinson]. *The IRA detonated a bomb pretty close to where we had come down the stairs. It caused a helluva lot of damage to the club. We didn't hang around.*

Twenty-five years later, at 12.44 p.m. on Friday, May 10, 2002, Jeff Thomson jumped from his London cab. He hurriedly thrust a £10 note into the hand of the taxi driver, rushed away and was swallowed up by the madding crowd inside King's Cross Station. Thousands of eyes watched the flapping boards for information—train, departure time, destination, and what bloody platform. The platform number is always the last piece of vital information the English train-watching public are given. It comes late. Then there is a rush for the platform. But the 12.45 p.m. train heading for King's Lynn, Norfolk, was just starting to ease its way out of the station when Thommo burst on to the platform.

Bugger it. I missed the bloody thing. Only by a few seconds.

Less than 15 minutes later the train, hurtling towards Potters Bar at 160 kilometres per hour, leapt the platform and slewed across the track on the approach to the station. The train was not scheduled to stop at Potters Bar: it was destined to crash. Its rear carriage flipped across two platforms and became wedged under the canopy of the station roof. Amid the wreckage, the smoke and the dust, there were screams and cries for help. Seven people died in the Potters Bar train tragedy. Five people died at the crash scene and a further two in hospital later that night. It was the nearest Thommo had been to jumping from the frying pan into the fire.

Here I am, my life saved by fate, and I am so close to another disaster. These tragedies happened so close together. These were two among a string of disasters or near disasters in my life. There was the armed hold-up at the Commonwealth Bank; three emergency landings in planes; five riots in the West Indies; and an IRA bomb blast in London in 1977. After the Potters Bar train crash I thought about it and wondered why I had been spared. Maybe someone's looking after me . . .

There is a gentleness and a caring about the fast bowler who scared the hell out of just about every batsman who faced him in his prime. And we have seen how the Queensland cricketers saw the sentimental side of Thommo when tragedy struck with the death of his daughter, Victoria. There's also a quiet side.

I love getting away from it all. In the bush. I can be totally alone, yet I am at one with nature. It is fabulous driving through the bush, the wind in your hair. I don't like being in crowds of people, but I like mixing with friends and family. Yet at other times I can be content by myself, away from everyone, in the bush, surrounded by the sounds and sights of the countryside. It's great.

Greg Chappell reckons Thommo 'is one of the great guys' and one of the most 'entertaining and creative' men he knows:

He is a naturally funny bloke and comes up with lots of good one-liners. I used to go camping with him. Fishing and hunting, chasing down the razorback pigs. There, his sense of humour shone through; it did on the cricket field as well. One day Thommo turned up at the nets in Perth and he wasn't going all that well. He had had a big one. Graham Whyte, our off-spinner, was balding and had the tendency to sweat a lot. He was always looking red and the sweat poured off him this morning. Seemed he was on fire. Thommo was leaning against the rope which strained one of the nets. His eyes were closed and his head slightly bowed. Whyte, or Grimace as we called him, wandered past Thommo and asked about his health that morning, which had already registered a century of the Fahrenheit scale. Thommo opened one eye and said, 'Grimace, not everyone has an inbuilt solar hearth'.[1]

As I write, Thommo is either playing beach cricket against the Poms, speaking at a show, chasing down a razorback boar, or working on his house in Morningside. The house is actually three old 'Queenslanders' put together and Thommo has put his talented hand to transforming those three buildings into one elegant home.

I recall one day we sat on the verandah and looked out at his enormous backyard. Thommo's two dogs, both as big as Shetland ponies, lounged nearby. I asked would they bite?

Well, Rowd, they're pretty gentle during the day and here right now, but don't try coming in during the night. They'd knock you to the ground then ...

There is a lump of dirt away from the house which resembles a bunker at Gallipoli. To its right and closer to the house is a cricket pitch, a racy vehicle used to hunt pigs and a speed boat; while lying on the ground are two baseballs, three red cricket balls and a white one, a javelin, discus and shot put. Thommo looked out at his yard.

> *There was nothing here when we first came. I've planted everything here. That's a weeping fig, there's the mulberry tree, that's a mango and that's a mandarin tree. The thing you think is a bunker is a golf green. I'm building that so we can chip from near the house on to the green. We will have a couple of golf bunkers, complete with sand, to make it a little tougher to get there in one shot.*

At the top level of the house, off the landing, Thommo has rigged a large bowl full of seed for the birds. He has a pulley system, a rope can be easily pulled in so the long arm holding the bird seed is hauled back against the side of the house overnight. His keen eyes spotted a feathered favourite, a Kookaburra.

Thommo has an enthusiasm for nature and for animals. The kookaburra was tough to see, camouflaged against a background of bushes as it stood motionless on the handle of an old roller. Thommo's seed bowl attracts a host of birds, from rainbow lorikeets, to wattle birds, king parrots and, of course, kookaburras.

When Thommo finally hung up his cricket boots, he ran a pleasure cruise yacht for awhile. People could charter his boat for a day's fishing and Captain Jeff Thomson was the host. Then he ran a landscape gardening business. It was always outdoors. Thommo was never one to stay inside for any great length of time. Cheryl says:

> Jeffrey has always been terrific with the boys. He takes Matt and Ben and Alex fishing and hunting and they play golf together. I don't go with them on the hunting trips. That's boys' stuff.[2]

The landscaping business suited Thommo. He was outdoors and he could turn his creative hand to fashioning a veritable 'God's Little Acre' for a host of people in the Brisbane area.

I've been a green-thumber since the time I was an ankle-biter. They nicknamed me 'gardener' once.

I've always loved working with plants. Ever since I was a kid when Mum used to buy packets of seeds, I loved to see things grow. It was something to do and I always found time to grow my plants.

To boost my credibility in this area, I studied at TAFE Redhill to get my Diploma of Horticulture. I knew more than the bloody lecturer, but I decided to complete the course so there were no problems with my credentials.

Greg Chappell was astounded by Thommo's knowledge of plants:

Thommo knows all the botanical names for all the plants you can think of—he's amazing. And he's very creative. When Judy and I were living in Brisbane we asked Thommo to design and build an outdoor entertaining area at our place. What he created was stunning, quite magnificent.[3]

Thommo did well as a landscaper. But events have taken over. He speaks regularly and he speaks so well that he is in demand.

Before the Thomson family moved to Morningside, Thommo's garden produced an aroma of common jasmine, mock orange, balsam and gardenia. He grew orchids, mango, pawpaw, bananas and breadfruit. When the house is finally finished, Thommo will once again have a flourishing garden.

And his bar will have all 'the petrol-head stuff' you can imagine, but 'no cricket shit in there', and right next to the Thomson bar is the old pianola. No doubt tunes will continue to emanate from that ancient machine for years to come. And what fun they'll have with it.

The boys are good. They don't watch TV much. I bought one of those big plasmas tellies and no-one turns it on. That's good. We all prefer to be outside. The lads will bring their mates around and they'll have a few beers and have a chat. Much better than sitting around the television.

* * *

When Jeffrey Robert Thomson came into the world on August 16, 1950, at Greenacre, NSW, renowned astrologer Linda Goodman foretold:

> You might see this man basking in the bright sunlight and you might find him making flowery speeches.
>
>   But it won't be in the middle of a desert. Most likely, it will be on a stage in front of a circle of adoring friends and relatives. He may waste money—but he's not about to waste his sweetness on the empty air. There will always be an audience.[4]

Linda Goodman's prophecy came true.

Thommo scorched across the Test arena in a blaze of glory. He became the fastest bowler to draw breath and his often peerless fast bowling heroics were always played out before a circle of adoring friends and family, but also before hundreds of thousands of passionate Thommo fans. Yes, he wasted money, but as Lennie Pascoe says 'Thommo would give you his last dollar' and Thommo has a gentle, loving side which his family and close friends know so well. And he still commands an audience at his after-dinner talks.

Talk with Thommo and he revels in the stories. He can be a bit irreverent, but if nothing he is passionate about what he does, his family, his cricket, his golf, his mates.

In a way the music teacher who made it tough for Thommo gave him the determination to go the whole distance.

> *Yeah, when they said I couldn't do something, I always promised myself that I'd show them. I guess I showed him, but the music teacher didn't have a clue about cricket.*

Thommo didn't only show his doubting music teacher, Thommo's lightning speed shook the cricket world.

NOTES

Chapter 1 In the fast lane

1. Phil Wilkins, 'At the Crease', *Sydney Morning Herald*, 11 January 1974
2. John MacLean to author, Brisbane, May 2007
3. Phil Wilkins, 'At the Crease', *Sydney Morning Herald*, 11 January 1974
4. David Lord to author, Sydney, June 2007
5. Phil Wilkins, 'At the Crease', *Sydney Morning Herald*, 11 January 1974
6. Len Pascoe to author, Oyster Bay, Sydney, June 2007
7. *ibid.*
8. *ibid.*
9. *ibid.*
10. *The Torch*, Bankstown, 14 October 1970
11. David Lord to author, Sydney, June 2007
12. *ibid.*
13. Mike Denness to author, 1975
14. Greg Chappell to author, July 2007
15. Ian Chappell to author, 1975
16. Keith Miller, *The Sunday Mail*, Brisbane, 1 December 1974, page 60
17. Brian Luckhurst to author, Perth, December 1974
18. David Lloyd to author, Perth, 1974

19. Clive Taylor, *London Sun*, December 1974
20. Crawford White, *London Daily Express*, January 1975
21. Bill O'Reilly, *Sydney Morning Herald*, 10 January 1975
22. Ian Chappell to author, Gabba, 1975
23. Paul Rigby, *News Ltd*, 1975
24. Mike Brearley, *The Star*, London, 1980

Chapter 2 The Bankstown boy
1. Len Pascoe to author, Oyster Bay, Sydney, June 2007
2. *ibid.*
3. *ibid.*
4. *ibid.*
5. *ibid.*
6. Bankstown Cricket Club Yearbook 1966–67
7. Len Pascoe to author, Oyster Bay, Sydney, June 2007
8. Bankstown Cricket Club Yearbook 1968–69
9. Len Pascoe to author, Oyster Bay, Sydney, June 2007
10. Bankstown Cricket Club Yearbook 1969–70
11. Len Pascoe to author, Oyster Bay, Sydney, June 2007
12. *ibid.*
13. *ibid.*
14. *ibid.*
15. Bankstown Cricket Club Yearbook 1970–71
16. Len Pascoe to author, Oyster Bay, June 2007
17. Bankstown Cricket Club Yearbook 1971–72
18. Len Pascoe to author, Oyster Bay, Sydney, June 2007
19. *ibid.*

Chapter 3 Goodbye quavers and crotchets
1. Len Pascoe to author Oyster Bay, Sydney, June 2007
2. *ibid.*
3. *ibid.*
4. *Torch*, October 1972
5. David Lord, *Sydney Sun*, 11 October 1972

Chapter 4 A test of mettle
 1. Phil Wilkins, *Sydney Morning Herald*, 12 December 1972
 2. Bruce Matthews, *Melbourne Sun*, 22 December 1972
 3. Ross Duncan to author, Brisbane, 2004
 4. *Sydney Morning Herald*, 17 January 1973
 5. Phil Wilkins, 'At the Crease', *Sydney Morning Herald*, January 1973
 6. David Lord to author, Sydney, June 2007
 7. *ibid.*
 8. David Colley to author, March 2007
 9. Howard Rich, *Sunday Mirror*, 20 January 1974
10. Norman Tasker, *The Sun*, January 1974
11. Phil Wilkins, *Sydney Morning Herald*, February 1974
12. Phil Tresidder, *Sunday Telegraph*, 10 February 1974
13. Bill O'Reilly, *Sun-Herald*, Sydney, 10 February 1974
14. Greg Chappell to author, December 2007

Chapter 5 Cyclone Jeffrey
 1. Phil Tresidder, *Daily Telegraph*, 16 February 1974
 2. *ibid.*
 3. Lew Cooper to author, Brisbane, June 2007
 4. David Falkenmire, *The Telegraph* (Brisbane), June 1974
 5. Errold La Frantz to author, October 2007
 6. *ibid.*
 7. Sir Donald Bradman to author, Adelaide, July 1974
 8. Errold La Frantz to author, October 2007
 9. Jack Reardon, *Courier Mail*, October 1974
10. Tom Vievers, *Sunday Sun* (Brisbane), 20 October 1974
11. Norman Tasker, *Sun-Herald*, November 1974
12. Greg Chappell to author, October 2007
13. Howard Rich, *Daily Mirror*, Friday, 25 October 1974
14. Martin Kent to author, June 2007
15. Jim Woodward, *Daily Telegraph*, Monday, 28 October 1974
16. Phil Wilkins, *The Australian*, 21 November 1974

Chapter 6 Amazing pace
1. Ian Chappell, *The News*, Adelaide, August 1974
2. Dennis Lillee, *Back to the Mark*, 1974
3. Phil Wilkins, *The Australian*, 29 November 1974
4. Ian Chappell, conversation with author, October 2007
5. Dennis Lillee, conversation with author, October 2007
6. Ian Chappell, conversation with author, October 2007
7. *ibid.*
8. Keith Miller, *London Daily Express*, November 1974
9. Henry Blofeld, *Daily Telegraph*, Monday, 2 December 1974
10. Phil Wilkins, *The Australian*, 4 December 1974
11. Dennis Lillee, conversation with author, October 2007
12. *Sydney Morning Herald*, 5 December 1974
13. Keith Miller, *London Daily Express*, 8 December 1974
14. Phil Tresidder, *Sunday Telegraph*, 8 December 1974

Chapter 7 New Test hero
1. Mike Denness to author, Perth, 1974
2. Keith Miller, *London Daily Express*, December 1974
3. Phil Wilkins, *The Australian*, 16 December 1974
4. David Lloyd to author, Perth, 1974
5. Ian Chappell to author, Sydney, 2005
6. Colin Cowdrey to author, SCG, 9 January 1975
7. Murray Hedgecock, *Adelaide News*, January 1975
8. Ian Chappell, conversation with author, October 2007
9. Alan Barnes, *The Australian*, 1975

Chapter 8 Elephant riders down on their luck
1. *The Melbourne Truth*, Saturday, 15 February 1975
2. Greg Chappell, *The Australian*, 1 March 1975
3. Keith Miller, *The ABC Cricket Book*, edited by Alan McGilvray, 1975, page 8
4. Fred Trueman, conversation with author, The Oval, London, 1975
5. *London Sun*, June 1975
6. Sunil Wettimuny, conversation with author, Colombo, March 2007
7. *ibid.*

8. Anura Tennekoon, conversation with author, Colombo, March 2007
9. *ibid.*
10. Sunil Wettimuny, conversation with author, Colombo, March 2007
11. *ibid.*
12. *ibid.*
13. Duleep Mendis, conversation with author, Colombo, March 2007
14. *ibid.*
15. *ibid.*
16. Norman Preston, 'Australians in England 1975', *Wisden Cricketers' Almanack 1976*, page 320
17. *ibid.*, page 60
18. *ibid.*, page 63
19. Ian Wooldridge, London *Daily Mail*, 1975

Chapter 9 Thommo is a knock-out
1. Len Pascoe to author, Oyster Bay, Sydney, June 2007
2. *ibid.*
3. *ibid.*
4. Ian Davis to author, September 2007
5. *ibid.*
6. Phil Tresidder, *Sunday Telegraph*, 4 January 1976
7. Clive Lloyd 'Thommo's a Knock-Out', *Sunday Telegraph*, 4 January 1976
8. Phil Wilkins, 'Thommo hits 'em for Six', *The Australian*, 8 January 1976
9. Peter Simunovich, *The Sun*, Melbourne, 21 January 1976
10. David Lord to author, Sydney, June 2007
11. *ibid.*
12. Ian Davis to author, September 2007
13. David Lord to author, Sydney, June 2007
14. *The Australian*, January 1976
15. Don Bradman within earshot of Doug Walters, Adelaide, 1987
16. Cheryl Thomson to author, Brisbane, May 2007
17. *ibid.*

Chapter 10 Jonah Adelaide
1. Phil Tresidder, *Sunday Telegraph*, 28 November 1976
2. *ibid.*

3. Jeff Thomson, 'Thommo on Sunday, Did I enjoy ripping the hell out of NSW', *Sunday Telegraph*, 28 November 1976

4. Paul Wicks, *Daily Telegraph*, 18 November 1976

5. Dick Tucker, Sydney *Daily Mirror*, 23 December 1976

6. Ray Lindwall, *Sun*, December 1976

7. Editorial, *Sydney Morning Herald*, 28 December 1976

Chapter 11 1977: England tour in tatters

1. Sir Donald Bradman to author, Adelaide 1974

2. Len Pascoe to author, Oyster Bay, Sydney, June 2007

3. *ibid.*

4. David Lord to author, Sydney, June 2007

5. Lennie Pascoe to author, Sydney, 2007

6. David Lord to author, Sydney, 2007.

7. Peter McFarlane, *The Age*, June 1977

8. David Hookes to author, Adelaide, 1981

9. Ray Steele, quoted in *The Age*, August 1977

10. Phil Ridings to author, 1980

Chapter 12 Miracle on Beulah Road

1. Bill Brown to author, 1998

2. W.H. 'Fergie' Ferguson, *Mr Cricket*, Nicholas Kaye, London, 1957, page 154

3. Bob Willis quoted in all Australian national newspapers, August 1976

4. *The Cricket War*, Gideon Haigh, Text Publishing, Melbourne, 1993, page 185

5. Alan McGilvray to author, London, 1980

6. Tony Cozier, *Wisden*, 1979

Chapter 13 Back with mates

1. Greg Chappell to author, December 2007

2. Ian Chappell to author, Sydney, October 2004

3. *ibid.*

4. *ibid.*

5. *ibid.*

6. *ibid.*

7. Martin Kent to author, August 2007
8. Ian Chappell to author, Sydney, October 2004
9. Len Pascoe to author, Oyster Bay, Sydney, June 2007

Chapter 14 'I was the scapegoat'
1. Len Pascoe to author, Oyster Bay, Sydney, June 2007
2. Mike Selvey, *The Guardian*, UK, 12 July 2007
3. Allan Border to author, 1992
4. *ibid.*
5. *ibid.*

Chapter 15 Thommo's many talents
1. Greg Chappell to author, December 2007
2. *ibid.*
3. Neil Harvey, quoting Warren Saunders, to author 2007
4. John Benaud, 'My Favorite Cricketer', *Crickinfo Magazine*, 3 August 2007
5. John Maclean to author, Brisbane, May 2007
6. Ian Chappell to author, December 2007
7. *ibid.*
8. *ibid.*
9. Frank Tyson, 'The Twins of Terror', *Cricketer Annual*, 1975, page 60
10. Greg Chappell to author, December 2007
11. Excerpt from a widely circulated newspaper report (circa 1959) which has been used in stories and images and books about the Aboriginal fast bowler, Eddie Gilbert.
12. David Forrest, 'The Barambah Mob', reproduced in *SIX and OUT, the legend of Australian and New Zealand cricket* by Jack Pollard, Pollard Publishing Company, Sydney, 1975, page 199
13. Lindsay Trigar to author, Brisbane, May 2007
14. *ibid.*
15. *ibid.*
16. *ibid.*
17. *ibid.*
18. *ibid.*
19. *ibid.*

20. John Maclean to author, May 2007

21. *ibid.*

22. Cheryl Thomson to author, May 2007

23. Doug Walters to author, January 2008

Chapter 16 'Someone is looking after me . . .'

1. Greg Chappell to author, December 2007

2. Cheryl Thomson to author, May 2007

3. Greg Chappell to author, December 2007

4. John Byrell, *Thommo Declares*, Horwitz Grahame, Cammeray, 1986, pages 29–30

ACKNOWLEDGEMENTS

Thanks to Jeff and Cheryl Thomson for giving generously of their time to enable me to draw this book together. Thommo draws on the strength of his loving family and that love shines through when he talks of his mum and dad, Don and Doreen, his brothers and his wife, Cheryl. While on the field Thommo was a veritable Rambo-cricketer: a man of non-stop action and he loves getting away from it all, he is a devoted family man as his wife and children, Matthew, Ben and Alex, will attest.

My thanks also to a host of people including Dennis Amiss, Robin Bailhache, Alan Barnes*, Dr Donald Beard, Sir Alec Bedser, Daphne Benaud, John Benaud, Richie Benaud, Fred Bennett*, Steve Bernard, Henry Blofeld, Allan Border, Dion Bourne, Mike Brearley, Sir Donald Bradman*, Tom Brooks*, Peter Burge*, Ian Chappell, Greg Chappell, David Colley, Lew Cooper, Gary Cosier, Colin Cowdrey*, Barry Crocker, Alan Davidson, Ian Davis, Mike Denness, Dr Tom Dooley, Ross Duncan, Geoff Dymock, Ross Edwards, Ian Fisher, Roy Fredericks*, David Falkenmire, David Forrest*, Harry Frei, David Frith, Frank Gardiner, Gary Gilmour, Tony Greig, Gordon Greenidge, Lindsay Hassett*, David Hookes*, Barry Humphries, Bob Madden, Martin Kent, Barry Knight, Alan Knott, Errold La Frantz, Bruce Laird, Ray Lindwall*, David Lloyd, Clive Lloyd, David

ACKNOWLEDGEMENTS263

Lord, Dennis Lillee, Brian Luckhurst*, John MacLean, Ken Mackay*, Rick McCosker, Dave 'the Doc' McErlane*, Alan McGilvray*, Rodney Marsh, Duleep Mendis, Keith Miller*, Sandy Morgan, Mouse, Ken Mulcahy, Deryck Murray, Max O'Connell, Bill O'Reilly*, Kerry Packer*, Norman Preston*, Tony Radanovic, Barry Richards, Sir Vivian Richards, Austin Robertson, Warren Saunders, Mike Selvey, Bob Simpson, Sir Garfield Sobers, David Steele, Ray Steele*, Jim Swanton*, Brian Taber, Norman Tasker, Anura Tennekoon, Lindsay Trigar, Phil Tresidder*, Sam Trimble, Fred Trueman*, Alan Tyson, Frank Tyson, Derek Underwood, Tom Vievers, Doug Walters, Sunil Wettimuny, Crawford White, Phil Wilkins, Bob Willis, and Ian Wooldridge*.

Special thanks to Paul Rigby* for his wonderful cartoon of Thommo and Lillee in the wake of their demolition of England in the 1974–75 Ashes series Down Under. To Thommo's life-long mate, Lennie Pascoe, for his tireless efforts in telling of their exploits as youngsters—armed with five hours of recording tape I visited Len's place in Oyster Bay, Sydney, and, after the tape ran out, Lennie continued for two more hours. Thank you to my wife Christine for her first edits of the manuscript and to my publisher, Ian Bowring at Allen & Unwin, and Joanne Holliman, for her patience and skills as the company's senior editor.

Ashley Mallett

*deceased